Joe & Marge

Enjoy the journey

Alberto Sequeira

4/19

Please, God, Not Two

This Killer Called Alcoholism

By Alberta H. Sequeira

INFINITY
PUBLISHING

Copyright © 2010 by Alberta H. Sequeira
Book Cover Design by Susan Louise Tennent of Malaysia

Editors:
Adele Brinkley of Georgia
Co-editor: Al Sequeira

ISBN 0-7414-6029-7

Printed in the United States of America

Published August 2010

INFINITY PUBLISHING
1094 New DeHaven Street, Suite 100
West Conshohocken, PA 19428-2713
Toll-free (877) BUY BOOK
Local Phone (610) 941-9999
Fax (610) 941-9959
Info@buybooksontheweb.com
www.buybooksontheweb.com

"Forever in Our Hearts"

In Loving Memory of Lori Cahill
July 29, 1967 - November 22, 2006

Acknowledgments

My heartfelt appreciation goes to
Lori's children; Joey and Meagan Cahill
Lori's sister's family; Debbie, Brian,
Kerri, Michael Dutra
My husband, Al Sequeira
Richie's brother's family: Sonny, Anita, Paula,
Gilly and Gary Lopes
To the aunts, uncles,
and all who knew and loved Lori

My love and deep affection goes to my family for their support in helping me tell my story after the loss of my husband, Richie Lopes, in my memoir *Someone Stop This Merry-Go-Round:* An Alcoholic Family in Crisis, and now in this sequel, *Please, God, Not Two*; This Killer Called Alcoholism. These books would not have been possible without everyone's input.

This memoir is the continuation of our lives after Richie's death and the heartbreak of watching Lori follow the same path as her father. She fought her drinking addiction by entering alcoholic rehabilitation centers three times, only to lose her battle.

Lori's children, Joey and Meagan Cahill, had the desire to share their mother's life with other families of alcoholics.

My daughter, Debbie Dutra, and her husband, Brian, stood by Lori's side through her struggle, trying to understand her past. They opened their hearts to Joey and Meagan by taking them into their family and giving them the same love and support they give to their children, Kerri and Michael. I'm sure Lori is looking down with a smile knowing that her children are secure, safe, and loved.

My husband, Al, had tremendous patience and devotion in helping me put all the events in place, along with months of editing, while I was in a fog after losing Lori. He spent many months alone, while I typed my heart out through oceans of tears.

My respect, admiration and love goes to the whole Lopes family for being a part of the first book and now with this sequel about their niece and cousin, Lori.

To Adele Brinkley, my editor, for her many long hours of hard work and professionalism to help prepare the sequel for publication.

I'm grateful to the photographer, Susan Louise Tennet of Malaysia, for having developed a wonderful picture for my book cover.

Introduction

Please, God, Not Two: This Killer Called Alcoholism is the sequel to *Someone Stop This Merry-Go-Round:* An Alcoholic Family in Crisis. The first memoir goes behind closed doors into my private life and personal hardships of living with an alcoholic husband. I wanted the readers to share in the reality of our fears and frustration in trying to deal with his drinking. The birth of our two daughters, Debbie and Lori, were followed by confusion, broken promises, abuse, our divorce, and his death.

This sequel is the continuation of our lives after my husband, Richie, died and our subsequent realization that our daughter, Lori, had been taking the same path as her father with alcohol abuse. The family wasn't aware that she had become addicted to alcohol until her last two years of fighting this disease.

Our families wanted to unite and hopefully reach not only the drug and alcohol abusers, but also the parents, children, siblings, and friends who are trying to understand the disease of substance abuse.

We are far from being alone in this fight, but we know that family members need to come together to learn how to help the abusers overcome their addiction by showing support and love. It's so important for the abusers to know that it's not them we hate, but the disease itself. That alone, will help a great deal in their recovery.

When we lose a loved one, our lives are overwhelmed by all the questions: if I had done something different, could I have, should I have, and what might have been if I had. If there was a possibility of my going back and making changes, would they have saved Richie and Lori? I'll never know, but some changes in my actions might have helped me live with less guilt about how I handled certain circumstances.

I'm not a professional counselor or trained speaker; my writing and talks come from the heart of a wife and mother who has lost two people I loved to alcoholism.

Please, God, Not Two is based on my years of loving and raising Lori, only to lose her to alcoholism. Slowly, our happy lives as a secure family started to fall to pieces at different stages. It was completely incomprehensible to me that I ignored the signs of Lori's serious drinking problems after seeing her father die from this uncontrollable demon.

I wanted to talk about the powerful and emotional feelings of my physical and mental pain, being blind to the signs of Lori's drinking, even after being knowledgeable about the illness when trying to cope with Richie's addiction. This book was written for families who are living in this same dark hole and who need to come out of hiding and seek help without fear or embarrassment

We can't force our loved ones to get help. All our begging, crying, and pleading won't always work. They have to want it themselves; we can only try to support them.

Writing this book has made me see that there were missed opportunities that could have turned Lori's life around and helped her to let go of the demons that kept her from being able to move toward recovery. I'm ashamed to say that there were many.

If our family's experience can help others recognize the warning signs of alcohol abuse and save one abuser, then this story will have been worth telling. Every family member and close friend of the alcoholic suffers along with them. As sick as we become from this disease ourselves, we have to keep focused on the possibility of losing the abuser. Because of the high percentage rate of deaths from alcoholism, we need to keep fighting for our loved ones, no matter how hard the task, to help them take the steps to recovery.

There's no reason to remain silent about this illness. There are many diseases that kill, and this is one of them.

Families need to open up about substance abuse and seek counseling. This fight can't be fought alone; the dependency is too powerful. Once the disorder seizes a person, the demon holds them with more strength than we can imagine. Alcoholism is something abusers have to fight the rest of their lives; there is no cure. We should try to help them attain the desire to go into rehabilitation and recovery, and more importantly, with our love and support, the willpower to stay sober. We are far from being alone in this battle; it's a worldwide problem.

THE DEMONS

Life was full of hope as my husband and I said our marriage vows.
We didn't realize that our years would soon come for us to part.
You answered our prayers, Lord, and gave us two loving daughters,
Four years separated, but close in heart.

Our children grew up and made us proud of your creation.
As time passed, the demons fell upon our family formation.
The once happy, stay at home dad lost his way
He walked from his family and kept us at bay.

The bottle was his friend that broke our unity,
No love or begging brought him back to reality.
My loving husband became a stranger,
As I watched the terrible disease put his life in danger.

There were bitter years when he walked out of our lives
And he struggled to survive but lost his fight.
The demons had reached for this loving man
And they made him blind to the telltale signs.

I gave him back to you God with tears and heartbreak,
Knowing that I had lost him from the very start
I struggled through the years with a painful, empty heart
And I kept my daughters close so that we'd never part.

Life is unfair for the demons returned.
They were not happy with just my man.

They grabbed my daughter and tore her in two
Separation from her children and family was something new.
She thought the bottle became her friend,
The same thinking her father had way back then.

Family and friends pleaded with prayer
For her to see that the demons were there.
She entered three rehabs with hope and belief,
Thinking with each visit she'd be back on her feet.

The demons weakened her confidence and made her think
That there was no real harm in just another drink.
The years of counseling were pushed aside,
And her dreams were washed away like a receding tide.

There were too many shared moments with friends to drink
And her traveling had her back on the road only to sink.
I gave her back to you God with tears and heartbreak,
Knowing I had lost her from the very start.

I pray Lord that she is at peace with her dad
And I can go on sleeping and stop being so sad.

Crush these demons and put them in hell,
So the alcoholics are released, free to get well.
Open their eyes to God's presence and Our Lady's
So they won't feel alone when their strength is fading.

By Alberta H. Sequeira

Getting On with Our Lives

The blinding sun came shining through my bedroom window as I lay quietly in bed trying to wake up from a hard night of no peace. Tossing and turning restlessly was something that I had been doing for quite some time. I couldn't remember the last night that I passed out from exhaustion and slept deeply and rose with the feeling of being refreshed and energized.

Each morning, I'd open my eyes and had reality hit me as I'd think back to that freezing, February, 10, 1985, morning when my ex-husband, Richie Lopes, died after more than thirty years of drinking. His life was cut short at the age of forty-five. Three months had passed, and my world had stopped since his death. Instead of stretching each morning with zest to get up, I'd be swallowed up by despair.

My mind couldn't rest long enough to dispel the memory of all the grief I suffered by not being able to see Richie in the hospital. That horrible event played back repeatedly, like a programmed recorder. All my married years were controlled by his drinking, and I continued being obsessed after his death by thoughts of what I could have changed back then.

Coping with not being allowed to see him at the VA Hospital in Providence, Rhode Island, had been bad enough, but having his girlfriend, Sara Thompson, enforcing this rule with Richie's whole family to bar me from his hospital room had been beyond my expectation. I would never have anticipated a stranger shutting me out and separating me from my daughters who stood by their dad's bedside as he drew his last breaths. Debbie was twenty-one years old at the time, and Lori was so young at seventeen. They stood alone through this tragedy without me by their side.

The nightmarish actions at the hospital didn't end after his death. I was forced to abide by my niece, Paula Lopes', statement that I wasn't allowed to attend the wake or funeral. She claimed it was her Uncle Richie's last request. I didn't want to believe her.

Upset, I asked, "What will you do if I just show up?"

"We'll have you removed," she replied.

"You mean to tell me that you can't find some dark corner for me to sit at in case my daughters need my support?"

"No, we can't."

I didn't think another blow would hit me so soon after Richie's death.

The night of the wake, I watched my ex-sister-in-law, Anita Lopes, as she picked up Debbie and Lori and took them to the funeral home. I wasn't allowed to give my daughters any support or love through this stressful time. I was so hurt that I couldn't bring myself to hug them before they left for the memorial service.

The thought of Debbie and Lori going to the wake and seeing their father lying in a casket without me by their side tore my heart out. I leaned against the kitchen sink and cried uncontrollably. I couldn't understand the reasoning behind these horrible, cruel decisions that were being made against me.

I worked at the Dighton Police Department as a dispatcher and went to my jobsite the morning of the funeral. I needed to keep my mind busy so I'd forget being unfairly omitted from saying goodbye to Richie. It would have given me closure with him in this chapter of my life.

The police officer, Gary Sanson, who had worked the same shift that I did, led the funeral procession and had agreed to stop the motorcade by the front door of the police station. I waited with my heart pounding, hoping that the sight of the funeral would make me come to terms with the fact that Richie was gone.

Gary radioed ahead to make me aware that he was coming down the hill on Route 138 and was about to approach the building. Janet Simmons, Chief Karl Spratt's secretary, took over the phones so that I could stand in front of the long, glass door.

The black hearse had extended rectangular side windows. It stopped in front of me. A beautiful bouquet of bright, colorful flowers rested on top of the casket. My eyes and mind tried absorbing the sight to finalize my goodbye within those few seconds.

The two family cars followed behind, and I noticed people waving at me. I looked back at them in shock. I had witnessed Richie's funeral as a *drive-through*. I stepped back from the door so that no one would be entertained by my emotions.

I went to the side window of my office and watched the line of cars in the procession travel down the highway toward St. Patrick's Cemetery in Somerset, which abutted North Dighton, where the girls and I lived.

It was a small funeral, and I wondered where all his drinking buddies were. They didn't attend the funeral; maybe they didn't find Richie's passing that important. They had no problem finding the time night after night to sit with him at a bar or the Dighton Golf Course and drink until they were smashed.

When the procession disappeared around the bend, I tried to clear my head of the tragedy in the privacy of my own heart. There were times in our marriage when I tried talking to Richie about his uncontrollable and destructive drinking, the confusion in our lives, the broken promises, and the physical and mental abuse. It had reached a point where he began coming home frequently in a drunken stupor, and often have no knowledge the next day of what had transpired the night before. It would have been impossible to discuss the situation that night, or I'd be too drained the next morning to bring it up. We slowly drifted apart, and our relationship crumbled.

Our daughters had years of feeling the loneliness and fright when he turned from being happy with them to going into fits of rage and blackouts. He had gone from a gentle, loving man to having moments with wild, violent rages during his drinking that almost cost me my life from his abuse. We all rode a daily rollercoaster waiting to see his mood when he came home. It was a subject that wasn't discussed and erased once it was over.

I hid my emotions from my daughters and tucked my feelings away into the deep recesses of my mind. We moved on without sharing our feelings and hurt from their father's death. Their years growing up were filled with frightening memories caused by Richie's drinking, but we needed to hang on to the happy times in-between bouts in order to survive this heartbreak that devastated us.

As a couple, we held back from sharing the most important aspect of our marriage, intimacy. We loved one another in our own way, but we hadn't shown or expressed those feelings when we needed to share them. Because of this lack of intimacy, we became more friends than husband and wife. Our daughters were left to witness scenes that they never should have been exposed to in their young lives.

Without realizing it, we took away our children's security and confidence, when they should have been learning about love and enjoying life to the fullest. Most importantly, we took their youth and stole their happiness. They grew up in fear and lost belief in themselves.

I forced myself to pull the light-weight, summer bedspread back to start my day. My head felt like it was in a fog. The girls slept late Saturday mornings so there was no need to rush, since they were old enough to care for themselves.

It was May of 1985, and the raw, snowy winter had passed with my having no regrets at seeing it end. The winter boots, along with our gloves and heavy coats, had already been taken out of our closets and placed in boxes in the attic. Putting them out of sight always seemed to make the house look cleaner and less cluttered.

I opened the bedroom window to let the warm, fresh, clean air fill the room. I loved this time of year, with the crocuses, tulips, daisies, and roses pushing their way out of the once-hard winter ground. With spring in the air, I looked forward to going outside without having to wear heavy clothing.

I hoped this would be a year of new beginnings, filled with healing for me and the girls. Debbie had set a date of September 14 to marry her fiancé, Brian Dutra. They had dated for five years, and it was an event that everyone in both families looked forward to. The Dutras were outgoing people, and we were all comfortable together.

Lori had one more month before graduating from Dighton-Rehoboth High School. She had been dating Jimmy Westgate off and on for the last two years. He was a very shy and private boy whom I found hard to get to know.

I was now faced with the responsibility of being both a mother and father. Decisions, wrong or right, were going to be mine, with no one else to blame. Because I had done most of the disciplining with the girls during my marriage, there was no reason for me to be concerned about this duty.

Mystery Solved

Richie didn't own anything of value to leave to his girls, except one $1,800 life insurance policy. Debbie and Lori felt strongly about putting the money toward their father's gravestone at the cemetery. I was proud of them for not being selfish about the inheritance. Because he loved the sea, they wanted a stone with a boat on it, but cemetery rules wouldn't allow it. After the bill was paid, there wasn't much money for them to share.

To my surprise, Richie left his beat-up, Ford Pinto station wagon to Lori. Debbie already owned a 1978, brown Ford Mustang, which she had paid for with her wages from her part-time job at Almac's grocery store.

Richie's girlfriend, Sara Thompson, had someone drive the car to Sonny and Anita's home since he was Richie's brother. I surmised that Sara couldn't find a way of getting money for the vehicle; otherwise, I'm sure she would have kept it.

When the car arrived in our driveway, I was shocked by its condition. The Pinto looked like it had been involved in numerous accidents. There were rusted dents on the right side door and a twisted front bumper. I became upset when I opened the back door to examine the inside. Sara had not even taken the time to clean it out.

There were empty liquor bottles that filled the back floor and rose as high as the seat. I opened the tailgate only to discover that it was stacked the same way with empty bottles still smelling of stale liquor. How could she have kept them in there? Didn't she think it would upset Lori? I was glad that the girls weren't home.

I got a large, black trash bag and dumped the sour-smelling bottles into it before Lori came home from school. The car was in such poor condition; even the seat covers were torn and stained. The dashboard was covered with dried up food and thickly-coated dust; I assumed he had never cleaned it. It broke my heart to see how the pride he used to have in his possessions had diminished.

I kept the car in the garage for a few weeks, and Lori decided to take a small amount of money for it from a junkyard. I watched the car being towed out of the driveway; it was Richie's last possession, and I felt his death again. Even though there had been some horrible times when he was drinking, his death still tore at my heart. Before the drinking got out of hand, he had so much ambition to start his own business, and he was so proud of his family.

A week after his funeral, Anita called me with some surprising news. She was looking through a bag that Sara had given her and Sonny. The bag contained Richie's personal belongings. It was full of loose pictures, personal finance papers, and clothing. Anita started to separate the items and came across two envelopes from a life insurance company. It wasn't sealed so she opened it, thinking it belonged to Richie. She saw two life insurance policies taken out on Richie, showing Sara as beneficiary. They were filled out three months before he had been admitted into the VA Hospital. Combined, they totaled $60,000!

A day after the discovery, Sara, in a state of panic, called Anita to request the insurance envelopes. She claimed to have left them in the bags by mistake. Sara swore to pay Sonny and Anita something toward the cost of Richie's funeral expenses and promised to give Debbie and Lori some money; however, once she had received the legal papers, none of them ever saw a penny or heard from her again.

The insurance company tried to investigate the claim. They interviewed Sonny, since he was the next of kin and only brother, but they never questioned Anita. They wanted to know if Sara knew Richie had been sick when she took out the policies. Sonny didn't know a thing about what Sara had done, so she walked away with the full amount. The agents would have had the information they needed if they had interviewed Anita; she knew all the facts about Richie's illness.

How sad that Sara looked at Richie as an investment. She not only *acted* cold at the VA hospital during his illness, she *was* cold. She had been a sly, conniving woman who had controlled Richie's whole family, my daughters and me from the time he had been admitted into the hospital until his burial. Instead of being pulled apart by her, we should have all united as a family. Her actions almost tore us apart.

I had to deal with closing all ties with Richie's television business, which had been operated from our basement. I put a notice in a few local newspapers in the area stating that the television sets that were left for repair needed to be picked up. I made calls to other television shops and asked if they wanted to buy the testing equipment and the extra electronic parts that were still in their original packaging. Little by little, nothing of Richie's life was left in the house, except our memories of him.

Lori's senior prom took place in June, and she looked stunning in her powder-blue gown, set against her jet-black hair. She went with Joe Perry, a boy who was a close friend. He wasn't dating anyone special, but I think he had a secret crush on her; he was at the house a lot. She made no mention of why Jimmy wasn't taking her, and I didn't ask.

It was another event that her father wouldn't be sharing with her. He had never attended the school plays or other programs in the past. I could only sense the sadness Lori must have been feeling. Girls like to see the glow of pride in their father's eyes.

After Richie's death, I started to get calls from Lori's teachers informing me that she hadn't shown up for class, or that she had left school with friends. I was hoping after her graduation, she would stop this behavior. I was blind to the seriousness of her drinking during this time, and I prayed that it was just a phase she was going through while trying to expand her horizons.

Senior Prom: Diane Ferreira and Lori Lopes

Because Jimmy rarely came over to the house, I assumed Lori had broken up with him. I couldn't say I was disappointed, trying to converse with him was exhausting. When I tried to get close to him or make him feel welcome in our home, he had put a wall up and kept his distance. I remembered Richie being that way with my parents when we were dating.

Lori became interested in a nursing career, and she signed up to become a candy striper at Morton Hospital in Taunton. She also became an aid at the Marian Nursing Home in the same city. I was happy she chose the medical field and gave her support, explaining that she would always have a job no matter where she lived or even if she married, had children, or divorced. I wanted her to be independent. She was a compassionate and witty girl, and I knew patients would be happy being in her care. Her ambitions, however, changed frequently; she didn't follow her dream of nursing and dropped out after a year.

As time passed, I found out that Lori was still crazy about Jimmy, though he avoided coming to the house. They'd meet at a friend's home, and he'd pick her up there, avoiding contact with me.

One afternoon, Lori confronted me and said that she and Jimmy planned to move in together. Unbeknownst to me, they had been searching the newspaper for an apartment. In a month, she would turn eighteen, and she was serious about making the move after her birthday on July 29th.

"When I turn eighteen, Mom, I can do what I want. I love Jimmy," she told me.

"I'd rather you stayed here. It's not right living with a boy without being married." Back then, girls weren't considered respectable if they were single and lived with a man.

"We've found an apartment already," she said firmly.

My heart broke, but I couldn't talk her out of her plans. Legally she was old enough to leave with or without my consent. She moved out in August, knowing that I strongly disapproved. I didn't know a thing about Jimmy's parents or if he had siblings. Neither of them had ever offered any information about his family.

I didn't want to lose touch with my daughter, so I went to visit them a few times. They had rented a third floor apartment in Taunton. By the time I reached their flat, I was out-of-breath. When Jimmy knew I was going to arrive, he'd avoid me by staying in another room, or he claimed to have an errand to run. I wasn't comfortable with Lori being in this relationship.

I knew that not having a father in her life must have been hard for her. With fourteen years of Richie and me battling about his drinking and all the problems that stemmed from it, he never truly got involved with his daughters' activities.

Debbie and Lori

Debbie, Alberta, Lori

Changes in Everyone's Life

In 1979, Richie and I had divorced. His excessive drinking and abusive actions were the primary cause of our breakup. Those past, too frequent, nightmarish moments caused an empty gap in our marriage. Too many bad days smothered the good ones that could have molded us into a happy family.

In 1983, I met a wonderful man while searching for a car at a dealership in Taunton; his name was Al Sequeira. He was the manager and his crisp and clean attire along with his polite and out-going manner sparked my interest. From the first hello, he warmed my heart with his smile. Al was a very handsome man with a hint of gray fighting to mix in with his black hair. He kept his mustache and beard trimmed close.

A few days later, I began to get telephone calls from him. At first, our conversations were about cars he thought might fit my needs. Later, after I had bought a car at another location, his calls continued, and we began building a friendship. In a few months, I broke down and accepted a date. Something seemed to click with us that first day, but trusting and getting close had taken months before I relaxed and let go of my fear of reaching out to another man again. Slowly, I opened up with my feelings and emotions when I was with him.

I wanted my freedom after being smothered, stressed, and abused for years. I think Al felt the same about a commitment. In 1970, his first wife, Jean, had died in a head-on automobile accident with a tractor trailer truck. They lived in Worcester, Massachusetts, and he had been managing a dealership in Wareham, commuting weekly between home and office.

He had been at work when he received a phone call from his brother about the accident. It had happened in Auburn, MA, outside Worcester, and had devastated him and his four children, affecting them still. At the time, his youngest son, John, was only two years old, Carol was four, Lynne was thirteen, and Alan was sixteen. Al now lived in Rochester, Massachusetts, and his kids were around my daughters' ages, ranging from sixteen to their late twenties. We all grew close through the years, and our kids accepted us dating.

I took my time about getting close to him. I didn't need a marriage at this time, I was now independent.

Al and Alberta

The summer of 1985, went by fast, and before we knew it, September 14 arrived, and Debbie and Brian were married at St. Joseph's Church in North Dighton. She looked radiant; why not, she had caught the boy of her dreams. He was a hard catch, being the quarterback of the Dighton-Rehoboth High School football team, but patience and sweetness from Debbie had won him over.

Al accompanied me, and it felt good to share this special day with him. My eyes filled with tears as Sonny proudly walked his niece down the aisle to Brian. She couldn't have chosen a better man to give her away in place of her father, but his presence didn't take the painful ache away from me not seeing Richie lift her veil and kiss her. I'm sure Debbie was thinking the same.

Sonny and Debbie

Debbie and Brian
Back: Lori and Larry Dutra

Debbie and Brian had invited close to two-hundred people. The atmosphere at the Elk's reception hall in Taunton became relaxed when the band played the soft dinner music. Al and I sat with my parents and siblings. Once we ate, like all bands, the songs changed to louder, livelier dance music. Everyone filled the floor with excitement to let loose and celebrate.

During intermission the music continued with Brian, his brother, Larry, and sister, Cheryl, entertaining the guests with their own family band. Larry played the drums, and Cheryl played guitar. Brian was the lead singer. My parents were so proud that they were now part of our family, and my father was completely surprised by their musical talent.

Brian and Debbie left on their honeymoon, and I felt secure that my daughter was about to have a great future with Brian. His parents adored her, and we all felt the same about him.

Our friends, Jeanne and Richard Noons, were renting out their second floor apartment two streets away from me. Debbie and Brian had given them a security deposit before they got married and had bought their new furniture. The apartment was set to move into before they left on their honeymoon. The Noons were a wonderful couple, and I felt the kids would be safe living above them.

Meanwhile, after Lori had stayed with Jimmy for five months, she asked to come home. They were breaking up, and selfishly, I was relieved. A few months later, another surprise awaited me. One night, Debbie came for a visit and walked with Lori into the kitchen while I was doing the dishes.

Lori looked nervous, but finally blurted out, "Mom, I'm pregnant!"

I stood at the sink in shock. Those were words that I never expected to hear. I had been juggling three jobs so that I could meet the daily bills and hold onto the house. I worked eight hours as a dispatcher for the Dighton Police station, and when it was quiet, I did proofreading for a telephone company in the area. I was a waitress at Friendly's Ice Cream in Raynham three to four times a week at night or on weekends. Within seconds, my mind filled with questions of how we were going to handle a baby. Panic set in.

"You're pregnant! You can't have this baby, Lori. I can't give up any of my jobs to baby-sit." I couldn't see a way out. "You're going to have to have an abortion." It just came out of me.

"I don't want one."

"Tell me how you're going to take care of a baby?"

"I don't know."

"That's not an answer. I gather Jimmy's the father?"

"…Of course, Mom!"

"Does he want to get married?"

"No."

"Where does that leave us? I can't stay home so you can work."

I had made up my mind that an abortion was the only answer. Looking back, I don't know how I had made such a horrifying decision.

I made the arrangements with a clinic in Providence, Rhode Island. Lori said that Jimmy was going to come with us and would meet us at the house on the day of the appointment. He never showed up, so Debbie and I took Lori.

There were protesters outside the clinic door, and some of them stood in our way as we tried to enter, getting right in our faces and shouting, "Save your baby. Jesus doesn't want this. Turn away from this!"

The guilt choked me, but we continued through the door. When the nurse took Lori down the hall, my stomach had a knot in it.

Guilt overwhelmed me more, but I couldn't see any other answer to the problem. I hadn't been to church for years and didn't have God in my life. I didn't put my faith in His hands to help us. I should have sat down with Lori and listened to how she felt about becoming a mother. She was carrying a child. How would I have felt with either of my own pregnancies if someone had not only demanded, but *forced* me to give her or Debbie up? I was so wrapped up in how this new baby would affect *my* life and worrying about Lori not being married and possibly getting a bad name in town.

In the eighties, unmarried, pregnant girls were still ostracized. I couldn't tolerate knowing that she would be talked about or degraded. What boy would want to marry her? Yet a new life was being given to us, and I never entertained a thought that the baby could be a blessing, and not an inconvenience.

Today, I realize that God has a reason for every child who comes into this world, whether it's from love or from a mistake. We should think hard and long before ending a child's life. I didn't consider any of this reasoning in my decision.

When we got home, Lori ran to her bedroom. Without looking at me, she yelled, "I hate you!" as she slammed her bedroom door.

There was every reason for her to feel this way toward me. I tried to convince myself that I had done the right thing and that she would realize it years later. We never talked about it again; just as we had avoided talking about Lori's feelings and the baby's future.

Today, I believe that there never was, is, or will ever be a time when it's right to take a child's life because he or she may disrupt ours. Giving a baby up for adoption is giving them life. That child could have given something to society, become a leader for a fight in some cause or just given love to each member of our family. In retrospect, I forced my daughter into a decision against her will. It was her choice to have the baby, and I should have respected that, regardless of any hardship, real or imagined.

Lori Reaching Out

Months later, I was ironing one evening, when the phone rang. An unfamiliar boy's voice on the other end asked, "Mrs. Lopes, do you know where Lori is?"

"She's over at Wendy's house."

"No, she isn't. She's actually next door at Jeff's house, smoking pot."

I chuckled thinking it was a joke. He hung up. A few minutes passed before I realized that maybe this warning should be checked out. No matter how much I loved Lori, it didn't mean she was incapable of doing something wrong.

I called Wendy's house and spoke to her mother. "Can I speak to Lori?"

"The girls went out, Alberta."

"Do you know where?"

"They went for a walk."

I went next door to Jeff's house and saw flashing, psychedelic lights coming from an upstairs window. I knocked on the door and braced myself for a battle because the woman, who owned the house, had argued with me in the past because one of my huge weeping willow branches hit her garage during a storm. She had taken me to court to get money for the damage and had lost the case. Since then she had considered me her enemy.

Her daughter, who was about eight years old, opened the door. She was an adorable little girl with long, blonde hair.

"Is your mother home?"

"No, she's out."

I felt my body relax.

"Is your brother, Jeff, home?"

"He's upstairs."

"Is it all right if I talk to him?"

She opened the door. "He's up there," she said turning to point to the winding stairs that went up to the second floor apartment.

I climbed the narrow flight of steps and stood quietly by the door for awhile. I could hear laughter and loud music coming from inside. I knocked.

A commotion started in the room before Jeff opened the door.

"Hi, Mrs. Lopes."

"I'd like to talk to Lori."

"She's not here."

"I think she is."

"I haven't seen her."

I acted calm and said goodbye and went down the stairs. I went outside and leaned against the house under the upstairs apartment window.

"Wait a minute, I think she's gone." Jeff yelled loudly.

I heard his remark and became a raging maniac. I ran up the stairs, pounding my fists on the door. "Open this door, or I'll break it in!" I screamed, wildly.

When Jeff opened it, I burst into the apartment. Another boy stood in the living room, scared to death.

"Lori, come out here, or I'll drag you out," I said through my teeth while I stood in the middle of the living room. I couldn't see her, but I knew she could hear me.

Within seconds, she and Wendy came from a back room. They looked petrified.

"How dare you lie to me," I said, looking back at Jeff. I grabbed Lori's arm. "Get home!" I ordered.

She ran down the stairs, flung open the bottom door, and ran through the shrubs that divided our property. By the time I got through our front door, she was in her bedroom with her door closed. I opened it and walked to where she was standing.

Alberta H. Sequeira

For the first time in my life, I pushed her against the wall, "What's wrong with you? Are you involved with drugs?"

I had never acted physically toward my daughters or gotten out of control; this jolted her.

"What do you expect, Mom? I have no father." She started to cry.

My heart broke for her, but I didn't want to show compassion or I'd lose control of the situation. "That's a cop out. A lot of kids don't have parents, but you don't throw your life away over it. You're grounded for two weeks."

"You can't be serious?"

"Oh, yes I am." I walked out of her room, closing her door gently.

Looking back to that day, I could have handled the situation so differently. I should have held my daughter in my arms and listened to her hurt and pain from missing her father. Maybe she would have opened up to me about the road that she was traveling on with alcohol or drug abuse.

I might have gained some knowledge of her secret life if I had listened to her talk about the empty gap in her heart, or she might have talked about feeling neglected by her father through her years growing up. At the time, I thought I had handled the situation correctly.

It's a stage, I thought. With no father in her life, I tried to be strong; I needed control.

Sympathy would have gone so much further. Instead, I closed her door and left her alone to handle her hurt and loss. She was trying to reach out to me, and I didn't give her a chance to talk; I didn't listen. I believed that I had to be hard to keep her in line. That moment, way back then, might have been the time for us to connect. Lori needed a mother, but I didn't react to her cries.

Lori's Marriage/Birth of the Grandchildren

Lori took the rough road after her father died. Instead of talking to me about her pain from his death, I found out years later that she had constantly talked about him to her friends. I never witnessed her being depressed, so I came to the conclusion that she had no issues eating away at her. Debbie was moving on with her life. Brian was a great guy, and they were happy and so compatible together.

One day, while I was preparing supper, Lori sat at the kitchen table watching me. "Mom, you may not believe what I'm about to tell you."

"What's the matter?" I asked.

"I was driving to the store yesterday and this chill came over me that went right through my bones. I felt the presence of Dad so strong, like he was actually sitting in the passenger seat next to me."

"I believe in those things, Lori."

"Well, I normally don't, but it scared me. The incident was freaky!"

"It shouldn't frighten you. Don't be afraid of the presence of a loved one. If anything, he came to comfort you."

We both discussed the event, but passed the episode off. I believe that we all experience something mystical at one time or another; we don't have answers for everything that happens to us.

Lori was employed at Lopes Construction with her sister. Debbie was the Office Manager, and Lori became the Payroll Manager. The responsibility seemed to keep Lori's life intact; she stopped drinking with her friends.

In 1987, Lori began seeing a young man named Joe Cahill. She brought him home for me to meet. He was very handsome with black, curly hair and the brightest blue eyes I had ever seen. I could see how Lori was attracted to him. He was very outgoing and friendly. I enjoyed being in his company since he was a joker and conversation flowed easily with him.

I couldn't help but notice how crazy Lori was about Joe and hoped he felt the same about her. They seemed to have a solid relationship, and they dated every weekend.

Within six months, they made plans to marry. She had finally found someone who loved her.

She was to be married at St. Joseph's Church in North Dighton, the same place as her sister. Panic spread before the ceremony when the best man lost Lori's wedding ring. Everyone searched every inch of the church grounds. Finally, they decided to use another ring that Lori had on her finger so that the people in church wouldn't be aware that the ring was missing.

A miracle happened when my friend, Joan, found the ring hidden in the grass by the church walkway. Not realizing that it was Lori's wedding ring, Joan mentioned the discovery to someone standing with the wedding party, and one of the bridesmaids overheard Joan talking about it. The group was overjoyed; Lori got married with her new ring and the best man breathed a deep sigh of relief.

I had been smart, putting money in the bank during the years I worked while being on my own, but the wedding cleaned out my savings. My father gave me five-hundred dollars to pay for the band. Even with three jobs, money flowed out faster than it came in, leaving the funds in my nest egg low.

Lori looked beautiful that day. We all say that about our daughters, but she was stunning, just as Debbie had been on her wedding day. Sonny again walked another one of his brother's daughters down the aisle. I cried, feeling the emptiness of Richie's absence as his second daughter was being given away by his brother. He had missed out on so much with his girls.

The hall at the Columbia Cultural Center in the Myles Standish Industrial Park in Taunton was packed with family and friends. Anita and Sonny paid for an open bar in Richie's memory; they had done the same for Debbie.

The band had everyone up on their feet and the floor filled with music lovers, including Al and me. The time came for cutting the cake; Joe had been talking with his buddies about his plan to put the cake in Lori's face. I held my breath hoping he was only joking. Much to my disappointment and everyone else's surprise, he wasn't and mashed it into her face.

She had it all over her veil, hair, eyes and face; her makeup was smeared. She tried to smile about it, but I could see she wasn't happy at all, and neither was I.

I had witnessed the same ritual at other weddings. I guess it was supposed to be the big event for a bride and groom to shove cake in each other's faces. I couldn't imagine that being done to me.

The gesture made me think back to the time my cousin, Delores, experienced the same thing from her husband. He thought it was funny, but she had to go into the girl's restroom because she was choking on the cake which he had stuffed down her throat. I never could understand how that trend started or continued.

I watched, in tears as Lori and Joe had their last dance before leaving the hall for their honeymoon. I felt fortunate to have had both my girls find happiness with good men. I prayed that Debbie and Lori would never live the life I did with their father.

Alberta H. Sequeira

Sonny and Lori

Lori and Joe

Getting ready for their honeymoon

Joe was hired at Lopes Construction; now he and Lori had stable employment and could plan for their future together. They had rented an apartment in Raynham, about a twenty minute ride from my house. Lori became pregnant, and four months later, Debbie announced the same wonderful news.

In Lori's seventh month, she developed toxemia after gaining sixty pounds. She had always been slim, and I was shocked at the weight gain. I worried about her health, and how it would affect her ability to have a normal delivery.

On January 16, 1988 at Morton Hospital in Taunton, Joseph Cahill IV was born. Lori had to have a Caesarean Section. There are no words to describe the proud moment for a grandparent when they hold their first grandchild.

When I held my precious grandson, his tiny hand grabbed onto my index finger with a tight hold. At that moment, the realization hit me about what I had done by forcing Lori to abort her first child, my grandchild.

I couldn't push aside the questions running through my mind about the other baby that I didn't bring into our family.

What would the child have looked like? Would it have had blonde hair like Jimmy, or would it have had Lori's tight, curly, black hair? Would it have been a girl or boy? If I thought about the lost grandchild too long, I would have been racked with blame.

God had presented Lori with a healthy son. Holding him in my arms and smelling that newborn, powdered body brought back thoughts of my own children's births.

After I left the nursery, Lori's doctor took me aside in the corridor. "Mrs. Lopes, Lori's condition is very serious. Her blood pressure is sky-high. We've tried all kinds of medicine to bring it down, nothing is working. I'm going to have to place her in a dark room with no visitors, except immediate family. We can't allow anything to upset her."

I looked at her with absolute fright. "What happened?"

"Her tremendous weight gain brought this on. Toxemia can create liver and kidney damage or failure. The problem can affect the eyesight if left untreated, and can cause her to go into convulsions, slip into a coma, or possibly, even die."

My knees gave out. The news jolted me.

"Are you okay, Mrs. Lopes?" she asked, grabbing my arms.

"I can't believe this is happening. Oh, my God, I can't lose her!"

The doctor continued, "We're going to try a new medicine in a few minutes. We haven't used this new drug with anyone before, but we'll know in 24 hours if she'll be okay. You can go in to see her. Please, stay no longer than a few minutes and let her rest."

I walked into a dark room that contained no windows. I felt like I had entered a closet.

"Hi, Honey. You have a son, congratulations!" I tried to act as though nothing was wrong.

"Have you seen him?"

"Yes, and he's beautiful. I can't stay long. The doctor wants you to rest."

"How come I'm in a dark room? There's not even a window? They're not letting me see Joey. Are you sure he's all right?"

"Joey's fine. Your blood pressure is very high, and they want you to rest for a day. Take advantage of it because after this, you'll be taking care of a crying baby," I said laughing. I tried to hide the fact that her situation was life threatening. A few moments later, I hugged and kissed her.

"I'll see you tomorrow. Get plenty of rest, okay?"

I walked out into the hall and put my head against the wall in the corridor, and cried my heart out.

Jackie Cahill, Lori's mother-in-law, came over to me and put her arms around me. "She'll be okay, Alberta."

Her words didn't make me feel any better, I was bitter.

"If Lori dies, you'll have your son and grandchild, but I'll lose a daughter."

I couldn't fathom the possibility of losing Lori. Jackie couldn't say or do anything to comfort me.

Within two days, Lori made it through the critical time and was moved to a maternity ward. She came home in a week, but a few weeks later, Joey had developed a cold and was hospitalized. They placed a tent over his bed. I looked at his tiny body in the enclosure, filled with vapor containing medicine. He looked so helpless.

After a week, he was released and came home. Lori's husband, Joe, took a week out of work to be with Lori. Because of her having had a C-section; he wanted to help care for his son. I tried not to visit too often so they'd have precious time together.

Lori took three months maternity leave. She wanted to give Joey all her attention. She didn't feel it was worth paying someone to come in and baby-sit.

Four months later, May 10, 1988, Debbie gave birth to a daughter, Kerri. She was beautiful with light, blonde hair, and her eyes were bright blue. It was like having twins in the family with the two babies so close in age.

Debbie took maternity leave, and Lori returned to work. Al and I babysat when the girls needed time to themselves. One night both grandchildren were in my care, and Al saved me from an anxious moment. Both babies were hungry at the same time and cried non-stop. Al walked in during my "grandmother crisis" and took Kerri to feed her while I comforted Joey. I can't explain the relief I felt when both babies calmed down so fast.

In April of 1989, Lori gave birth to her daughter, Meagan. She was a peanut with tiny features. She was the picture of Lori, with dark, brown hair and brown eyes. This time, Lori took time off from work to stay home with both children. She didn't give any indication of how long she would be out, but when she didn't return after four months, Debbie was forced to hire a replacement.

Lori holding Kerri with Joe; she was the Godmother

Joey and Meagan

Michael and Kerri

Marriage Problems

Joe and Lori moved several times during this period. Joe left his job at Lopes Construction, and with the loss of income, they were struggling to keep up with their bills and the rent for their apartment. He took a job working nights as a bartender. Lori told me that, when they were both working at Lopes, there was a time they had so much money that she carried numerous paychecks in her pocketbook without depositing or cashing them. Now they were wondering how to pay the smallest bill.

One afternoon, Lori came to visit me. She asked if her family could live with me until they got on their feet. I took the four of them in so they could save some money to get ahead. Lori stayed home with the two babies while I continued to work. Joey was about two and a half and Meagan was a year old. I actually enjoyed the two grandchildren around me. I found myself excited to come home and see all of them.

On Saturdays, I offered to take Kerri so she could spend time with her cousins. I used every excuse to watch them. If Debbie or Lori needed to go grocery shopping, I took the kids so that they'd have time without the added burden of children to watch.

I thought Lori and Joe were extremely happy. I knew it had to be difficult living with a parent, especially after they'd been on their own.

Joe started coming home late. I could see Lori getting nervous every time he went to work. It was impossible to hide our private lives while living together. I prayed they weren't having marital problems. I related to Lori's emotions each time I saw her look up at the clock. I had spent many years in my own marriage doing the same with her father. I was heartbroken seeing her going through the same stress.

One night, Lori opened up to me while we sat on the couch watching television. "Mom, I think Joe's seeing someone."

My heart sank. I could see the pain in her eyes as she broke down in tears.

"I love him so much." She was crushed.

All I could do was put my arms around her. When Joe came in at night, I tried to separate myself from their problem, thinking they could work it out. I was afraid that if I confronted him, he wouldn't be comfortable facing me or living in the same house.

After a few months, they moved to an apartment in Taunton. Al and I visited often, and things seemed to be going well. Lori never said anything more about having a crisis with Joe. She was so proud of her kids, and she took pride in dressing them; her children were her world.

In 1989, I took Lori's family in once again. I could see that Joe didn't like the living arrangements. Maybe he felt confined or didn't feel like the "Man of the House", but I could feel the tension. After four months, they came to me and said they were moving out. I was so close to the grandkids, I selfishly hated to see them leave.

"You came here because you needed to save money. Why are you moving out?"

"We want to be on our own."

"So do I, this living arrangement isn't any easier for me. We're all giving something up, but the sacrifice will be worth more than having the independence right now. I bet you two haven't saved a dime. How are you going to manage? If you insist on leaving, I can't stop you, but I won't take you in again. Do you understand that? I don't have a revolving door to this house. I think it's time you both grew up. You can't keep bouncing like this, especially with two kids."

Joe still didn't have a steady job. To me, bartending was a part-time job. I figured if he had a full-time position, they would be able to meet their monthly bills. There would be no need to go from one place to another.

"We'll be all right, Mom," Lori stated, trying to ease my concern.

I wasn't convinced.

They left, taking another rented apartment in Taunton. It wasn't long before they finally separated and divorced. Meagan was only a year and a half old. Lori told me that Joe said he didn't want to be married. *A nice time to realize it, after the birth of two children,* I thought. Lori had lived with hurt in the past with her father, and now another man walked out of her life. I couldn't spare her the agony she was going through, being on her own again. Debbie was happy, while Lori's world had fallen apart.

I never said anything to Joe about his coming home so late after work; my silence helped him cover his actions. He never had to explain his outside activities. Instead, I remained silent and watched my daughter suffer without trying to help her through another rough, emotional time.

Lori found a first floor apartment on Wellington Street in North Dighton. Joe didn't keep up with his court ordered child support payment, and she struggled trying to pay her bills. She finally broke down, swallowed her pride, and applied for Welfare.

She never told me anything about her trials. I found out later through Debbie.

One evening Debbie called. "Ma, last night Lori called saying she had no diapers for the kids."

"I didn't realize she was having any problems. Lori never said anything to me. I thought she was making ends meet."

"She said Joe was behind in child support, and she couldn't keep up with the rent."

The next morning before going to work, I went to Shaw's Market and bought over a hundred dollars worth of groceries and items that her food stamps didn't cover. She was thankful and relieved, but she never talked about her financial struggles or asked to come home.

When things became that serious, I should have just followed my heart and brought her and the babies' home. Welfare wasn't even helping her meet the everyday bills.

She was too proud to ask for help. After all, I had told her she was on her own after leaving twice. If she had asked, I wouldn't have been able to say no. I was feeling responsible for not being able to fix *their* mistakes. Joe could have helped his family more by just keeping up with his child support payments. Having money from him could have made a big difference to Lori.

I knew it would be hard for her to lose her privacy by moving back; she didn't like rules either. Each of us did things our own way, and living under the same roof wouldn't be easy. I analyzed the situation over and over and still wasn't sure what to do.

I felt it was Joe's responsibility to be supporting his children. If Lori could have depended on a weekly paycheck from him, the money would have helped her meet the bills and buy food for Joey and Meagan. She wouldn't have been worried about being able to give her family a place to live.

As a father, he was not only hurting his kids, but causing Lori to go without the necessities for them. I knew Debbie was helping her sister without saying anything. I got angry and blamed the court system. They made it easy for deadbeat dads to avoid helping with their children's care. I had gone through the same pattern with Richie. Many men work under the table and claim they aren't employed; the system never investigates them. No one is holding them accountable to provide for their families. Not having a job was just an excuse as far as I was concerned. I worked three jobs to support my girls, pay a mortgage and the monthly bills, not to mention the unexpected expenses that always occurred. I felt that if any man took his responsibilities seriously, he could find a way to meet his obligations to his children.

Dad's Death

My parents lived in Hull, Massachusetts, but their beautiful property became too much for Dad to keep up with. He was in his late sixties and suffered from vertigo; climbing high ladders to paint the top sections of the two-story home was no longer feasible. After years of not being able to keep up with this stressful task, he had offered the gorgeous property to anyone in the family who wanted to purchase the place at a price well below market value.

The area had many attractions, including boating, Nantasket Amusement Park, and a long stretch of the beautiful shoreline of Nantasket Beach. Every one of my siblings had visited there with our children numerous times throughout the years. The most enjoyable and memorable moments were spent at the in-ground pool in the backyard. Dad had it installed when he first bought the home. He maintained the pool and kept the whole yard immaculate for any time we came to visit.

None of us opted to purchase the home. We all lived in other towns at least an hour away and were pretty well settled in our locations. My parents' home was put up for sale in 1977 for $100,000. It wasn't very many years later that the homes on the hill where theirs had been situated were selling for $600,000 and higher; today some are in the millions.

My parents found a one-level, ranch home in East Falmouth, Massachusetts, a town on Cape Cod. The dwelling was a house that Dad could take care of without needing help. Because he didn't have to spend so much time with maintenance, he and Mom could get away from the constant responsibilities of repairs by going to the beach, which was not far from their home. On their way dad would often stop at a grocery store to buy grinders, drinks, and snacks to have at the beach.

They'd spend a few hours sitting on a blanket, walking on the soft sand along the beach or wading in the salt water. Dad brought his binoculars to study the yachts that sailed by or tried to catch sight of the seals that occasionally surfaced off shore. Water skiers always used this stretch of shoreline, and they were interesting to watch, zooming along not far from shore. They had always enjoyed the sound of seagulls and the smell of salt air and never wanted to live too far from the ocean.

It didn't take long for our families to start visiting our parents' new home on weekends, kids and all. My parents kept their freezer full of food for such occasions, and there were many. Summertime was always a time for family gatherings, with days full of laughter and playing games with the children, the closeness of the family at those events was always treasured.

In 1988, when Dad was seventy-eight, he was diagnosed with prostate cancer. He had surgery, and the doctor was sure he had caught it in time. A year later, he began to suffer from pains he described as being in his stomach and right side, under his rib cage.

With a full medical examination, blood test, and an MRI, the doctor discovered that Dad's cancer had returned and had spread to his liver and stomach. During the next few months, much of his time was spent in doctor's visits and chemotherapy treatments. After six months, the doctor called with the results. It was worse than they thought. Dad insisted on knowing all the facts and told the doctor not to hold anything back. He was advised to put his things in order because he had only a few months to live. The news devastated him and the whole family.

My father wanted Mom to be secure after he died. In 1943, my mother had suffered a few breakdowns after my brother, Walter, died from polio at eight years of age. My brother, Joe, and his wife Marge wanted to care for our parents and find a place where they could all live together. They began a search for a new home. At the time, my brother had an upholstering business in Yarmouth, located further down on Cape Cod. After investigating the town's bylaws, he discovered they couldn't move his shop into our parents' home because the neighborhood wasn't zoned for business.

Within two months, Dad purchased a wonderful home in South Dennis. It was a good hour away from all of us. There were three bedrooms and two baths. The two car garage was easily converted to house Joe's upholstery shop. Above the garage was a full apartment for Joe and Marge, which gave them privacy. Dad had only four weeks to enjoy the new home.

Bill, Albert, Leona, and I took time out of work to help Mom care for Dad for the last two weeks of his life. Hospice became our support and taught us the correct way to make him comfortable and helped us to handle our final goodbyes to him. On October 19, 1990, Dad passed away peacefully, at home with his family around him.

During the time that I cared for him, I had a spiritual renewal. I had witnessed how strong Dad's faith had been as he fought to concentrate on praying his daily rosary. During his years fighting in Europe in WWII, he had promised the Blessed Mother that if he was allowed to come home to his family, he'd pray the rosary every day of his life; he kept that promise.

He lived to be eighty years old, but the foundation of our family was gone. Mom suffered a few minor strokes after he died; she was completely lost without him. It was painful when I'd visit and drive into the driveway knowing that he was no longer there. My father had made a ritual of going into the driveway when anyone left and waving until we were out of sight, even during a snowstorm. Leaving to go home and not seeing him there for my send-off, left an empty gap in my heart. I usually drove home in tears.

Pilgrimage to Medjugorje in Bosnia

In 1993, after dating for ten years, Al and I married at St. Rose of Lima Church in Rochester with a candlelight wedding. We both had been married before, so, neither of us wanted to make a huge affair of our special day. At first, the family was disappointed, but after the announcement, they understood our wishes. We were blessed and had no problems with stepfamily members.

Before our wedding, I had put my home up for sale. Within three months, a young couple purchased it. When the home was emptied of all our belongings, I took one more walk around the house to reminisce about my memories of the years spent there, both good and bad: it choked me up.

I roamed through the girls' empty bedrooms and thought back to the birth of each one. I remembered their teen years and could picture their friends sitting on their beds laughing with them. I thought they had been happy during those days.

All the dreams that Richie and I had shared were shattered. His workshop downstairs was an empty shell. Our faithful dog, Heidi, had died after thirteen years of being a devoted companion. I looked across the street and saw our wonderful neighbors, the Ferreiras, who were still busy in their yard raking leaves together, a family project for them.

Richie was gone, the girls had their own lives, and now I was leaving our beautiful home. We had some horrible years with Richie's drinking. The house was another chapter in my life that I had to let go and close the book on. It was sad losing the last tie to him; the sale finalized my loss.

In 1998, because of unexplained events, which I deemed miracle started to happen all around me. I went on a ten day pilgrimage to Medjugorje in Bosnia. Since 1981, six visionaries from this tiny, remote village had been claiming to have daily apparitions with the Blessed Mother. They were being given ten secrets that one day would be revealed to the world.

The first of what I considered a miracle happened in Medway, Massachusetts, when Leona and I took Mom to a shrine in the woods where people, who had been there, talked about seeing the sun spinning in the sky and turning a mixture of bright colors. Some claimed their illnesses were completely gone after praying at Our Lady's statue.

On our visit there, the three of us were praying in an open area sitting at a picnic table in a section surrounded by thickly wooded trees. I had walked my mother over to a small shed, when a woman stepped from the corner of the building and stood beside us. None of us knew how she could have gotten to the area without being noticed. There was a marsh on two sides and only the one open path.

She introduced herself as Marian and said, "I come here often to help people pray. I'd like to do the same with all of you."

She took Mom's arm and helped her to the picnic table. She sat with us, and we held hands, joining Marian in prayer. After a few moments of complete peace, I opened my eyes and saw all the leaves on the trees in bright gold.

Astonished, I said, "Look at all the gold leaves!"

I looked at Marian, and she had a radiant smile on her face as she stared at me. She didn't seem to find the occurrence important enough to turn and look. Instead, she seemed to take it as her cue to leave. She stood up, kissed Mom, and started to walk down the path.

Marian stopped at Mom's wheelchair that was stuck in the mud from a heavy rainstorm the day before, making the pathway impossible to push my mother to the picnic table area. The woman suddenly put her hands up in the air to the heavens as if she was praying to God. At that very moment, Leona's rosary fell, which took our eyes off Marian for a split second. We looked back, and she was gone, as mysteriously as she had appeared. There was no way humanly possible in our minds that Marian could have walked down the long pathway without being seen on the trail. She was nowhere in sight.

The other incident took place in 1993, when I had a scheduled hysterectomy and was in my bedroom packing the night before the procedure. I was extremely distraught thinking about the surgery.

Suddenly, I heard a voice inside my head say, "Don't be afraid, I'll be with you."

I felt a sensation from outside my body enter my head and a tingling feeling went to the tips of my fingers and toes within seconds. At that instant, I felt a calm come over me that I had never experienced in my life.

These unexplained events, along with the memory of Dad having had the desire to make the journey to Medjugorje in the hope that a miracle would cure his cancer, led me to take this pilgrimage. The visionaries who were seeing the Blessed Mother ranged from ten years old to sixteen when the apparitions began in 1981. Even today, after twenty-nine years, Our Lady is still appearing to them daily. When each receives the last of ten secrets that she is giving to them, a priest will reveal them to the world. There are only two visionaries remaining to receive one more secret each, the others having received all of theirs.

While I prayed in the famous, over-crowded St. James Church in Medjugorje, I received inner healing from my father's death. The next morning, our group took a two hour, very steep climb to reach the top of Mt. Krizevac, where a 15 ton cement cross faces the village of Medjugorje. After battling heart problems all morning with severe fibrillation, I offered my discomfort up for my father's soul during my climb. Once I reached the summit, my heart rate went back to normal, and I felt an overwhelming peace that my father was home with Jesus.

After my return home, I went back to the Church with a stronger faith. I also experienced a deep need to encourage my family to turn back to God. I joined a prayer line, became a Eucharistic Minister, and volunteered my time to help clean the church every week. Al became an usher at Mass and volunteered his time to help at the church during their summer chicken barbeque and other events. We even joined the St. John Neumann Couples Club.

I continued to pray for my children and family to go to Medjugorje someday. I slowly realized that I had to let the wish go and put the plan in Our Blessed Mother's hands.

A New Man

Over the following four years, Lori started to date off and on, but she didn't feel inclined to marry any of the men she saw.

On January 16, 1991, Debbie and Brian had a son, Michael. Now both of the girls had a son and a daughter.

After I married and moved to Rochester, I was less involved in the family's daily activities. It was our frequent phone calls to each other that gave me the updated news about what was happening to everyone. Lori wasn't one to just chat, so Debbie and I did most of the conversing.

Al and I made most of the trips to North Dighton to see the girls. Once the grandchildren reached their early teens, Lori and Debbie were too busy with the kid's sports activities to drive to Rochester, especially on a weekend when they had full schedules. There were the basketball, baseball, and football games. Meagan became a cheerleader and our grandkids on Al's side had the same busy agenda.

By now Lopes Construction had grown beyond any-one's imagination. My nephews, Gilly and Gary Lopes, had taken over the full responsibility of running their parents' business. Debbie needed to hire another person for the office, so she offered Lori her old job back. Lori took the position and became more secure with a steady paycheck to count on, and she earned a good salary.

With a dependable job, Lori left her apartment on Wellington Street and rented a house on Somerset Avenue, which was route 138 in Dighton. There was a gas station across the street, a local mini-mart down the road and Georgio's Restaurant next door. The eatery had good food, reasonable prices, and pizza. It was a central location for a small country town.

It was wonderful knowing that she and the children had a home to themselves. There was a screened in-porch in back, a large living room, bathroom, kitchen, three bedrooms, and a huge concealed backyard that gave them plenty of privacy. The thick, cluster of trees at the end of the property hid the railroad tracks and the river beyond. Lori seemed to be getting her life back.

She was a good mother, and her world revolved around her children. They came before anything else. Debbie and Lori became close, doing a lot of things together with their kids. Every time we went to visit Lori, she was upbeat and happy. Full of life, she repeatedly had friends at her house.

Joey was now thirteen years old and Meagan was twelve. Having teenagers gave Lori more freedom. The kids were old enough to be alone for short intervals. A run to the grocery store or meeting a girlfriend was easier than when she had to get a babysitter. No matter where Lori lived, her friends flocked to her place.

Summer came and Debbie had her usual family gatherings. At one cookout, my niece, Paula, was present. It had been years since she and I had our last contact before Richie's funeral.

I made up my mind to swallow the hurt I felt since Paula had refused to allow me to attend the wake or the funeral. I decided to push the episode aside; I had to forgive her or my life would be on hold.

When Paula walked into Debbie's living room, she avoided looking my way as I stood in the kitchen watching her. I decided to take the first step and went up to her. She embraced me with tears.

"I'm so sorry," she whispered.

"Paula lets not talk about it. We're family, and we can't change what happened years ago."

"I love you," she said, holding me tighter.

I kissed her and said, "I love you too."

That's how we closed the door to the resentment that had engulfed us for so long. I decided that letting the hurt go and having my niece's love was more important to me than holding a grudge and losing her completely. I had shared too much with Paula through the years. I knew Richie wouldn't want us separated as a family.

After being divorced for close to twelve years, Lori met a special man, Mark Nadeau. He was the Heavy Equipment Shop Supervisor at Lopes Construction Company. They had met years ago, but both had been married to someone else at the time.

Lori called me one night, excited. "Mom, I met my Al." She adored my husband, and wanted to meet someone just like him.

"That's wonderful, Lori, but I didn't know that there were any Al's left," I joked.

"I'm serious, Mom. I knew on my first date that he was the one. I'm going to marry him, you watch and see."

"We'll look forward to meeting him."

I prayed for him to be the one to love her and the kids. She had stayed single for so long after divorcing Joe and struggled with everything that came with being a single mom.

A few weeks later, we met Mark on our next visit to Lori's. When we walked in, he was standing in the kitchen, leaning against the counter with a beer in his hand. He was warm and friendly, offering Al his hand when Lori introduced us. I was comfortable with him right away.

He was close to six-two, slender and in his middle thirties. He kept a trimmed mustache, had dark, brown hair, and was always smiling. His personality was as outgoing as Lori's. I could see that Joey and Meagan were very relaxed with him. They seemed to enjoy being in his company. He was very attentive toward the kids and included each one in our conversation.

No other man had meant enough for Lori to talk about marriage. I could see that this one was different, I could feel it. All of them seemed so happy.

Lori's Wedding

In 2002, Mark and Lori were making plans to marry. Joey and Meagan were going to be in the wedding party. Their dream was to have the wedding at the Onset Point Inn in Onset, Massachusetts, where they were to take their vows on the beach. The inn was on Onset Bay, near the entrance to the Cape Cod Canal. They had taken the kids there often on weekends, and the location had become the family's favorite getaway. There was so much excitement about the upcoming wedding.

Lori called one evening, ecstatic. "Mom, we're going to have the whole wedding party stay at the Onset Point Inn the night before the wedding. I want you and Al to come, too."

"How much is it a night?" It was an elegant location, and I knew it wouldn't be cheap.

"It's $230."

"Lori, I hate to pay that when we live ten minutes away. We can go that night and return the next morning."

"No, Mom, I want you here, please! Share this with me."

"I'll have to talk to Al first."

"Okay, let me know."

Al smiled, "That's a lot for one night, but if it means that much to her, we'll stay over."

The wedding party and both families arrived at the inn the night before. The area was beautiful! Every bedroom on the second floor had a gorgeous view. The windows faced a small private island that sat in the middle of the bay on which a home was situated. Yachts and sailboats sat anchored offshore. An open porch wrapped around two sides of the inn, which faced the water. The main doorway opened onto a huge glassed-in porch. The place was spectacular!

We spent the evening across the street at the Harbor Watch Inn. Everyone had dinner there, and we sat around enjoying drinks and listening to stories about Mark and Lori. They decided to take my reading glasses and Al's and put them on and started to mimic us. A few of the men told some off colored jokes, and the room was filled with laughter. It was worth staying over and joining in the pre-wedding fun. There was no doubt Lori and Mark shared sociable personalities and mixed with friends easily.

Lori, Meagan and Mark

Mark and Lori wearing Al and Alberta's glasses

We stayed quite late at the restaurant and then walked a block back to the inn. No one wanted the night to end. Some in the group took advantage of the peaceful atmosphere and the warm temperature by walking along the beach.

I sat with Lori and Mark on the steps to the open porch watching the moonlight reflecting on the water. By now, the all day drinking had affected Lori's conversation, and her voice took on a more confrontational tone. I was shocked by how heavily everyone drank, especially Lori. I wasn't used to seeing her drink so much. I blamed it on the excitement of marrying the man of her dreams in the morning.

She looked at me with glassy eyes. "You know, Mom, you never call or come to see me."

"What are you talking about? Al and I always visit. You and Debbie only come to our place at Easter. Other than that, you never drop by." I replied.

I was trying to make a joke of our visiting habits, although what I said was the truth. I continued, "Besides, you have a phone. You can call me anytime. As for traveling to each others homes, it's the same distance for both of us."

I didn't understand where this remark came from since the topic wasn't being discussed.

"Furthermore," she continued ignoring my answer, "You don't know how much you hurt me when you didn't take me in when I lived on Wellington Street."

My jaw actually dropped open in shock; she was serious! Her drinking had her bringing out issues that I never knew bothered her, and she wasn't joking with me. She was upset.

Mark stood up from the step, the best he could after drinking quite a bit himself. "I'm going to leave you two alone," he said and left.

I had a feeling that he was aware how Lori felt toward me about this topic, though we had never discussed her moving back in.

"What are you talking about, Lori?" By now, I was aggravated. The incident had happened a good twelve years ago.

"You knew that I was struggling. I had no money to buy the kids food or clothing." Her tone became nasty.

"Lori, I'm not a mind reader. How could I know what you needed from me? You never told me. I gathered that everything was all right. Besides, I took you, Joe, and the two kids in twice. How can you make such a statement?"

"Yeah...but when Joe left me on my own, and I really needed you the most, you left me battling alone trying to make ends meet."

"I didn't leave you struggling—Joe did! It was *his* responsibility to support those kids, not mine. If it was that bad, why didn't you call me?"

"I didn't want to ask."

"Well, that was your fault. If I had realized you needed me that much, I would have taken you back. You're my daughter for God's sake. It wasn't that long ago you made the statement to me that you were glad I *didn't* take you in. You said it helped you stand on your own two feet. So, which is it?"

"I won't forgive you."

I felt all my excitement about the wedding leave me. I didn't want to sit with her any longer. I had stayed past my welcome. It was the first time in our lives that we argued or became upset with each other.

"I'm sorry you feel this way, but I think it's time to call it a night. If not, we won't be able to take back what we may say to each other."

I got up off the step, trying to hold back the tears that were surfacing. I didn't want to cry in front of her. I was deeply shocked and hurt that she resented me this much over a situation that had happened so long ago.

When I walked into our bedroom, Al could tell that I was upset. I told him the story while sitting on the edge of the bed crying.

"I'm absolutely stunned that she said those things to me. I've been there for her every time she's asked for help."

"She's been drinking all day, Alberta."

"Her words were cutting. She acted like I never did a thing for her."

"The problem with drinkers is that they won't know tomorrow what they said today," he replied, sitting next to me and putting an arm around me.

"You always told me, Al, 'A drunken man's words are a sober man's thoughts."

"Well, maybe she has had this bottled up, and it's just coming out. Sometimes, it takes drinking to say what you can't say sober."

"She may forget it, but I'm not going to. It hurt too much."

I took a shower and slipped into the bed with Al. I pulled the covers over me knowing that in the morning, I would remember every word that passed between my daughter and me. I fell asleep with the soft sound of the waves hitting the beach.

The sun rose and everyone was running around getting dressed. After I was fully awake and clothed, I walked into Lori's bedroom. She looked beautiful. She was glowing! Her girlfriend, Karin, was fixing the veil over her hair, which she wore pinned up. Lori's curls fell softly around her face. She looked stunning with her black hair framed against her white gown.

I still felt numb from our conversation the night before and went through the motions as if the incident didn't bother me. Lori smiled, hugged, and kissed me without mentioning the ordeal we had endured the night before. She was beaming with excitement.

Although I was a proud mother, I tried to ignore Lori's immature words that had cut me so deeply. I usually didn't let remarks bother me, but hers did. Al was right; she had to have been too drunk even to remember our conversation.

It was a special day seeing Joey and Meagan in the wedding party. Joey looked like a young man in his tux and Meagan, more like a young teenager than a twelve-year-old in her soft, blue gown.

The weather cooperated, giving way to a perfect hot summer day, with the temperature in the high eighties. Chairs were placed on the hot, beach sand where the couple would be saying their wedding vows. A huge, white tent had been put up beside the inn on the lawn area where the buffet would be served and the reception held. Sheets of tongue-and-groove plywood had been put down for dancing.

The wedding took place at 10 am and Mark walked toward the flowered arch on the beach and stood there waiting for Lori. He looked so handsome. His tuxedo was white, and he wore a white, collarless shirt, with no tie, buttoned to the neck. His oldest son, Terry was best man.

Karin Brady, the matron-of-honor, led the party. Debbie and Meagan were the bridesmaids, and Timmy, Mark's youngest son, and Joey, were ushers.

Lori walked slowly onto the sandy beach slipping her arm into Brian's as he gave her away. When Lori walked up to Mark, they looked like the perfect couple. I felt that she had finally found happiness.

I watched the glow on Lori's face and the pride in her sister's eyes as Mark and Lori said their wedding vows. Lori seemed to be in complete peace for the first time in years.

Once they were pronounced man and wife, Terry placed a fake, black ball and chain on Mark's right ankle. He walked through the sand, dragging it with him all the way. The joke had everyone laughing. The guests were in high spirits, and anxious to celebrate this event.

An hour after the ceremony was over the waitresses started serving stuffed mushrooms, scallops wrapped in bacon, cocktail shrimp, and clams casino. Family and friends mingled in and the loud laughter was echoing everywhere.

The decorations on the tables were in sync with the seaside atmosphere. Beach sand was placed in the center of each table with seashells scattered on the sand. A large seashell with wax melted inside with a wick formed a candle and was presented as a gift to each guest from the bride and groom as a remembrance of their happy day. I still have the candle on a table in my sunroom in front of their wedding picture.

Mark and Lori had hired a band, and our son-in-law, Ron, brought his equipment and worked the sound system for the band. They started off with soft music. The buffet was served at noontime, a delicious assortment of entrees, offering a variety of seafood, meat, and chicken.

The invited guests sat down to eat with family members and friends. Al and I were placed at a table with my siblings and my mother. Our plates overflowed with food, and we ate while listening to the serene music and watched a few couples dance. In such a relaxed atmosphere, some of the guests didn't bother to wait until the bride and groom had their first dance.

About an hour later, I began to feel sick. I asked my family, "Does anyone feel nauseous?"

They answered no and stated they all felt fine. I looked over at the buffet table and noticed a small area where the sun was shining directly on a section where the food had been placed.

Within fifteen minutes, pain was shooting through my stomach. "I don't know what's wrong with me, but I've got to lie down."

I didn't say anything to Lori or Debbie because I thought an hour's rest would take care of me. I headed up to my bedroom where I spent the rest of the day, leaning over the toilet, sick as a dog. Each time I tried to get up and go back to the reception, I'd become nauseous again. I was upset about being gone so long; I was missing out on Lori's special day. Whatever had hit me didn't pass until eight o'clock that evening. I had been gone for five full hours. In that time, I had only a few people check on me. I thought later that maybe some potato salad or seafood meal that sat in the sunny area of the buffet table had gone bad. I hadn't eaten much, so I didn't believe it was from overeating.

When I finally walked down to the tent, most of the guests had left, along with my siblings and mother. I had missed my daughter's whole reception celebration! I never saw Mark and Lori's first dance, the cutting of the cake, or the tossing of the flowers and garter. I was devastated.

Lori didn't seem to be upset that I was gone all day. In fact, she never mentioned anything about it. She never came up to my room. Al drove us home, and I became depressed about being up in the bedroom for so long. I tried to put the event behind me. I hoped that Lori didn't think I had avoided sharing her day on purpose; especially after our argument the night before, no one mentioned my absence.

Debbie, Lori, Mark and Brian

Lori and Mark

Anita and Sonny

Lori and Brian

i and Mark had good paying jobs, so money was not
for them. They bought the house that Lori had been
ˌ. For the first time since Joey and Meagan were
ˌes, they finally had a family life. The kids adored Mark,
ˌd he was so good to them. Joey was relaxed, talkative and
laughed more than he had in years.

Mark bought Joey a four-wheel drive, all-terrain
vehicle, and he and his buddies rode every chance they
could. At first Lori was afraid he wouldn't be able to handle
the vehicle. He was small at fourteen and looked lost on the
bike. Mark's gift seemed to take Joey out of his shell and put
life back into him.

In 2004, they sold a piece of their property and put the
money into fixing up the house; it had needed repairs and
changes for quite some time. They hired a remodeling
company to do the work. They changed the rooms to their
taste and added large bay windows to make it brighter. The
house was also re-shingled. Lori finally had a solid marriage
and a home to enjoy.

By a strange coincidence, Lori's ex-boyfriend, Jimmy,
was one of the carpenters. One morning, she told me that she
and Jimmy had sat on her front porch and talked about the
baby they had lost through the abortion. She felt so strongly
that it would have been a boy. She said she still had feelings
for Jimmy.

"Mom, Jimmy will always be the love of my life."

Jimmy was in his middle thirties then and had never
married, but he was living with a girlfriend. I understood
how she could still have feelings for him while being in love
with Mark. I had felt the same about my ex-boyfriend,
Danny, while being married to Richie. We always wonder
about the first, true love that had slipped through our fingers.
We hang onto what could have been without knowing if it
would have worked out.

My heart broke, knowing the abortion still affected her.
Why did I think it wouldn't? Lori was a good mother and
loved her kids. It was a subject we had ignored until now. I

still followed the same pattern as I had with her father by overlooking the importance of talking, and listening to each other's needs and wants.

Mark bought a forty-two foot cabin cruiser, something he had always wanted. The family went on fishing trips each weekend when the weather was good. I was thrilled when Al and I were invited one Sunday afternoon. It brought back memories of Richie's boating and the fun the girls had with him when they were so young. Lori reminisced about those days as we sailed out of the bay.

"Dad would have loved being on this boat, Mom."

"You're right, especially one this size...and one that could leave the dock!"

We laughed at the remembrance of staying in the bay all day because the boat broke down so often.

"I think of him every time we go out on the water." Lori's eyes filled with the hurt that was still buried deep within her after losing her father.

I put my arm around her. "I know you miss him a lot."

It had taken years, but Lori had finally gotten her life together. Al and I really liked Mark. I could now relax mentally, living an hour away and knowing that he was taking care of all of them. Being a mother, I felt much more peaceful knowing I no longer had to go to bed at night wondering if she had food or if she was able to pay bills.

Mark and Lori took vacations with friends, with Debbie and Brian, or they'd disappear for a weekend alone. Most of the time, Joey and Meagan were included. They were always on the go.

Paula and Lori started spending more time together. Either, Paula would visit or they'd go out for a few hours together. They had been close cousins since childhood.

Al and I were invited to a few summer parties at Lori's. I couldn't help notice how much everyone drank. I started to worry about Mark's drinking. He drank continuously the whole day and was tipsy much of the time, though he was always pleasant. He drank more than what I considered normal. Lori drank, but her personality never changed. Guests would leave unfinished drinks on the counter and take new ones. Beer flowed freely, and most of the guests brought packs of their own to add to the supply already on hand.

At one of the parties, I went to put trash into the wastebasket and found it full of liquor bottles. Paula attended a lot of their parties, and I noticed she drank steadily. I tried not to think about the drinking and told myself that these were social events and that people were relaxed and having fun. Being an occasional drinker, I suppose I was possibly more aware of how much alcohol was being consumed. My past with Richie couldn't be erased, and I was back to counting who drank and how much.

I've attended plenty of parties where drinking went on but not at the level of those at Lori's home. To me it was excessive. No one seemed to nurse their drinks. During the gatherings, I didn't notice the over consumption with just one person; there were many who drank what I considered to be too much.

One afternoon, I had a conversation with Mark's mother, and she told me that her husband had been an alcoholic. I knew then that there was a reason to be worried about Mark. When he came to our house at Easter or to Debbie's for a family function, he usually brought a case of beer, and before long, he'd be in his truck in the driveway, asleep, not eating with the family. I feared that Lori was going to have a marriage like I had. Mark was such a great guy; I prayed to be wrong.

Struggling to Find Her Faith

In 2005, Mark and Lori were excited to learn that his son, Timmy's girlfriend, Bethany, was pregnant with Mark's first grandchild. When the birth was near, Lori called and told us that the doctor was worried because the baby's lungs weren't developed. She said they were told the chances of the baby surviving were slim.

Lori and Mark left for the hospital to be with Timmy and Bethany during the delivery.

She called me once they arrived. "Mom, please put Bethany and the baby on your prayer line. I know that you pray and believe."

"I'll call everyone tonight, honey."

We had over thirty people on the list who prayed for anyone who needed help.

"Lori, you have to pray and believe yourself."

"Mom, I wish that I believed like you. I'm not even sure if I believe there's a God."

My heart fell. I was completely taken aback. How could she not believe after all the years of going to Mass and religious classes? I had no idea that Lori thought this way.

"Lori, if you didn't believe deep down, then you wouldn't be asking me to pray."

"I know how faithful you are at praying, Mom. I'll call you when the baby is born."

"I'll be waiting."

About five hours later, Lori called. "Mom, it's a boy. He survived the birth. His lungs are developed, but his kidneys are bad. He may need a transplant in three years."

"Can he live that long with both kidneys not functioning as they should?"

"He has to be on numerous medicines until the surgery. They aren't going to take the kidney out. They're going to put a third one in."

"I never heard of putting a third kidney in a body."

"It's odd, isn't it?" she replied.

"What did they name the baby, Lori?"

"Carl, and he's beautiful. Your prayers came through."

"God has a reason for him to be here. Give our congratulations to everyone."

"I will. Call you tomorrow."

On October 18, 2003, Carl blessed our family. Mark and Lori had a grandson. Lori called often. She worried about the baby's health because he had to be on certain medicines of different doses at different times, and the mother was confused keeping up with all of this, and she had problems paying for the high priced prescriptions. Neither Timmy nor Bethany had health coverage, nor did Bethany have a car to take the baby to his medical appointments.

Mark went every weekend to pick up Bethany and Carl and brought them home to stay at their house. Having them there was the only way they could monitor his daily medicine doses and his overall health.

Lori took over caring for the baby and taking him to the doctor's appointments in Boston. At first Bethany went, but soon, Lori found herself going alone. She was struggling, trying not to miss too many days at work.

Lori called me a few weeks later and stated that the doctor had told her that Carl couldn't miss *any* of his medicine because of his condition. It could be life-threatening.

Mark decided to take the baby into their home in order to watch Carl more closely. Lori was now burdened with caring for a baby around the clock. Her children were teenagers, and she had a full-time job.

Joey adored Carl. He would get up early to change and feed him when he could. When I talked to him about the baby, he would smile and say, "You know, Grammy, when I

get my license, I'm going to take Carl everywhere with me."
He called him his brother whenever he spoke of him.

"Mom, do you think God's replacing the baby that I
had lost with Carl and giving me another chance?" Lori
asked one day.

My heart broke. This was the second time that she had
mentioned the loss. Lori had kept the tragedy deep within her
all these years not wanting to talk about her hurt. My poor
daughter was still agonizing over a child that should have
been with her.

"I don't know, Lori," I answered, feeling accountable
that I had made that horrible, heartless decision.

"Lori, I'm so sorry for forcing you into that abortion.
I'd do anything to turn the clocks back."

"I'm not upset with you, Mom. It was long ago."

"I know it was, and I'm still carrying guilt over your
loss."

"I was young, and you did what you thought was best at
the time," she said.

Her remark didn't make me feel less remorseful.

Lori's Life Crumbling

After a year, Mark and Lori decided to go to court and become the guardians for Carl. Having no problem with the court giving them the responsibility, they moved him in permanently.

Taking care of Carl was the most stressful time of Lori's marriage. Every day was confusion. It was extremely difficult trying to schedule babysitters. The daycare locations wouldn't take him because of his medical needs. She had a girlfriend, who was willing to baby-sit for a few months, and everything was working out well, but the girl decided that she couldn't continue because she needed a fulltime job to meet her expenses.

Mark's mother volunteered to watch Carl. Lori and Mark took turns picking her up in the next town to take her to their house. Sometimes they took Carl to her place. She loved watching him, but she was in her seventies and in poor health, so that arrangement couldn't continue for very long. This left Lori in a tizzy every weekday wondering who could take care of the baby so she could get to work on time. It was a blessing that Joey and Meagan were both in high school and could fend for themselves.

Carl was a year and a half years old when I began to see the toll this was putting on Lori. Everyone around her was going along with their day by day routines and enjoying life, while Lori's had come to a halt.

She mentioned to me how Mark continued to go out on his boat, but Lori could no longer join him. She said packing all the things for the baby and watching him on board was too much stress. The trip wasn't enjoyable for her when the baby needed so much attention; it was better to stay home where she could easier tend to his needs.

The kids had their teenage friends and didn't notice that their mother was struggling with the changes in her life; responsibilities that shouldn't have been hers. She was scrambling for babysitters, food shopping, working, picking up Carl's medicine, and getting him to doctor's appointments in Boston, which was an hour's drive each way with bumper to bumper traffic, and all the other unexpected problems that arose.

Lori would call me and break down crying about how family and friends all too often were sitting in her kitchen when she got home from work. Then she had extra people to feed as well as caring for the baby.

I felt helpless living so far from her. My daughter was crying out for help, and no one was listening to her, including me. I didn't realize that there was much more going on that I wasn't aware of.

Parties continued at their house, Al and I attended many, I couldn't help but notice how so many people were continuously drinking one after another. They weren't just drinking beer; the hard liquor was flowing just as freely. It wasn't long before I had started to notice many were getting bombed. There were always volunteers to make runs to the package store, a short distance away to purchase more.

Lori had always been thin, but lately she had snow-balled from a size eight to size fourteen; she was obviously compensating for the stress by eating. She was the heaviest I had ever seen her. Her life was fast-paced, but I didn't live in North Dighton anymore, and couldn't see all the bad things that were happening to her.

She called one day, sounding very upset. "Mom, I'm exhausted. I don't know how I can keep up with this. I'm getting to work late and all this responsibility with Carl is getting to be too much. I can't afford to lose my job. Getting someone to baby-sit is my biggest problem. Mark's mother has been great, but the baby is getting too heavy for her."

"I'm more worried about you trying to do all this alone, Lori. You're taking on too much."

Mark was happy to have his grandson in the house so he could cuddle and love him or take him to his mother's, but the burden of caring for him was mostly on Lori. She would tell me about the weekends the boat trips were planned or when the gang grouped together at the dock just to sit on the boat to socialize and drink. Lori couldn't keep up with those fun times anymore.

Lori was in a whirlwind with no time to unwind. One moment she had kids who were grown up, and the next she had a baby. She couldn't make any weekend plans. Her life had stopped; someone else's responsibility had landed in her lap.

A few weeks later, she called and asked, "Mom, do you think that I drink too much?" The question caught me by surprise, coming so suddenly.

"If you're asking the question, Lori, you probably do. What do you think?"

"I'm not sure. Everyone around me drinks whether we're out or if they come here. I don't know."

"Lori, alcohol abuse becomes noticeable when it causes your life to be nothing but problems from the drinking, and it affects the people around you. If it is, you may be an alcoholic. Do you feel that way?"

"Please, Mom, I'm not an *alcoholic!*"

"Your father didn't think so either."

"I drink no more than anyone else in our group."

"Can you stop after a few drinks?"

"I don't count how many I have."

"If you're asking the question, Lori, you'd better think hard about the answer because this is a hereditary disease."

The conversation faded in my mind days after we talked. I should have talked to her about the drinking and kept in touch more often. Her questioning about drinking too much had been a chance to discuss her actions before it got out of hand. The question still didn't register in my mind that her drinking might be *serious*. Bells should have been going off in my head. Lori was trying to reach out again.

The Lopes Construction Company Christmas party came, and it had always been a big affair. It was held on a Saturday night two weeks before Christmas. The girls wore formal dresses to this event and always managed to look gorgeous. There were a lot of young employees who worked there, and I was pleased that Lori would be with people her age. She needed to have time away from Carl and be around her friends. She deserved to have a good time.

The day after the party, I received a call from Lori. She was sobbing. "Mom, I got laid off!"

"What do you mean?"

"I was with Gilly, joking with him, like I always do, and he wasn't acting like himself. I kept asking him what was wrong.

"He said that he'd talk to me about it Monday morning, but you know me; I kept pushing and told him, no, I want to know now, why wait?"

"He told me that he was going to lay me off. I couldn't believe what he said. I had no idea there had been a problem. I got angry and told him that I'd leave now and walked out of the room."

"You did what? Lori, you didn't quit?"

"Why wait till Monday. It's so embarrassing. He wanted to talk to me, but I guess I heard enough."

"Lori, you don't know what he would have offered you. Gilly is your cousin, but he's also an owner of the company. He wouldn't leave you hanging. You should call him Monday and ask to hear him out."

"I can't walk in the office knowing everyone knew about this."

"You'd better forget about pride. You can't afford to be without an income."

I knew that there had to be more to it. *My God how could things get any worse for her?* She didn't try to talk to Gilly and stayed away from the company.

I heard months later that Lori went into a state of complete depression, having crying spells and not wanting to see or talk to anyone.

It was winter, and everyone was busy with their own lives, so visiting was harder with the bad weather. Lori and I had some conversations on the phone, but most of the time Debbie kept me updated about Lori's situation.

There were small things going on that I brushed off as being petty, but they weren't to Lori. She seemed to be more down.

I can't comprehend how her condition didn't alert me to the fact that her confusion and despair might have been the result of drinking. I should have had more awareness after what I'd been through with Richie, or when she had asked my advice about her drinking. I honestly thought she was losing her job because of being late so often at work. I blamed the problem on the responsibility of Carl being forced on her. I grew angry at Carl's parents, feeling he should have been in their care, not hers.

A few days later, Debbie called me. "Did Lori tell you she was having trouble walking after falling feet first into an open section on the boat?"

"She did what? When did that happen?"

"It happened about a week ago. A cover was off a hatch, and she didn't notice the open hole. She fell into it."

"I've been talking to her, and she never mentioned this. Did she go and get checked?"

"No, you know how she feels about doctors."

"I'll call her right now. I'll talk to you later, honey."

I hung up and called Lori.

"I'll be okay in a few days. Stop worrying," she said.

"Lori, if you're having trouble walking, you could have broken bones in your feet."

"As long as I stay out of shoes and wear slippers, I'm fine."

"And you think that's normal?"

Nothing changed her mind. I couldn't stand the thought that she couldn't function on her own. Now making meals and cleaning would be impossible. I didn't know how she was managing to care for a baby.

About two months later, her situation worsened.

"Mom, Mark walked out." She was crying uncontrollably.

"What do you mean he walked out?"

"He wanted to go fishing for awhile and asked me to make a special meal that he liked before he left. I mentioned our anniversary was coming up, and he told me to make a reservation somewhere so we could stay overnight. We always go away for that day. He left to go back to the boat and said that he'd be home in an hour."

She stopped in between sobs. "When he arrived home and started to eat, he got furious and threw the plate in the sink and then took off again! I have no idea what happened or where he went."

I was beside myself, thinking that she was once again facing problems in a marriage. I had been so relieved thinking that they were happy. What was happening to my poor daughter? Everything was collapsing around her.

"Mark didn't come home. He stayed on his boat." Lori was absolutely torn apart.

The next morning she called, "Mom, I honestly don't know what's happening." She was in tears again. "I think I'm having a breakdown. Too much is happening to me all at once. My life is falling apart, and I can't get it to stop."

Now I feared she was going to have a breakdown.

"You have to call a doctor, Lori, to get help."

Warning signs faced me, but I became blind to them believing her despair was from her marriage falling apart.

The next thing I heard was that Carl's parents took him back. After two years of having him as part of the family and caring for him Lori and the kids were devastated, but I was relieved that the responsibility was finally taken off her. It shouldn't have been hers in the first place. Maybe Carl kept her going. She could barely walk; much less take care of a baby.

Signs of Failing Health

Lori phoned me and spoke about how Joe and Meagan told her how crushed they were when Mark walked out of the house without even saying goodbye to them. They thought the world of him. It's sad when children have to suffer because adults mess up their own lives.

I couldn't stand knowing that the three of them were alone again. Everyday I woke up thinking how her life had changed from security to uncertainty. I heard from Debbie that Lori was doing a lot of sleeping. Al and I took a ride a few times to see her, but she wouldn't answer the door. Her car would be in the yard, and the door to the house would be locked. When we called her about our visit later in the day, she said she was in the shower.

A shocking telephone call opened my eyes to her problems being more serious than she had admitted to me.

"Mom, I'm going into an alcoholic rehab tomorrow."

"You are…Where?"

"It's the Gosnold Rehabilitation Center in Falmouth."

"I'm glad you're reaching out for help, Lori. What can we do to help? Can Al and I take you?"

"No, Mark's taking me."

"Mark?"

"Yes, he just came back from a ten day stay and really recommends this place."

"We'll come and see you, honey."

"I'd rather you didn't. Let me do this on my own."

I was relieved that she was going into an alcoholic rehabilitation center, but we were all shocked in the family that she needed professional help with drinking. I asked

Debbie if she ever saw Lori drunk and she said that Lori was never intoxicated at any event.

I was glad that Mark was taking her. They were both facing their demons. I prayed he would work out his own feelings in the marriage and go back to Lori. Their life might have been messed up because of their drinking. Al and I wanted so badly for them to work their problems out. Lori loved Mark and so did we.

Lori spent a week at the rehabilitation center, and I tried to absorb the fact that she was an alcoholic. I started to piece together her teen years with her drinking and started to realize the dealings were not from her trying to fit into a group of friends. It had started way back then, and I didn't take serious notice to the wild parties at my house when I wasn't home. I thought she would stop once she had graduated from high school.

I couldn't understand how a week of rehab was enough time to overcome her addiction. She had been drinking for fifteen years or more. She still wouldn't talk to me about her life. I put all my trust and prayers into the hope that the treatment facility would give her the will to change her life and stop the alcohol abuse. I knew that giving up drinking was Lori's responsibility. She had two beautiful children who adored her; they alone were reasons enough to fight this demon.

She called when she arrived back home from Gosnold Rehabilitation Center. Not once did she mention her experience of being in detox or any other steps she had gone through with counselors. She omitted talking about the incident completely. If the subject came up, she changed it. We had no idea if the recovery program helped her or not.

About a month later, Debbie invited us to a family cookout. I was sitting on her back deck with family and friends enjoying the hot sun on my pale, white, freckled face. I'm of Polish descent and had never been fortunate enough to develop a golden tan or anything even close. I'd spend hours out in the sun only to retreat into the house with severe sunburn, followed by weeks of peeling, and looking as white as I did before the painful experience of trying to achieve a tan.

Lori entered the front door of Debbie's house and walked through the living room to the door facing the deck. I gasped as she pushed the screen door open to step onto the deck.

I felt faint from the shock. She was heavy the last time I had seen her, but now she was so thin, I could see her chest bones above the opening of her blouse she was wearing. The weight loss made her look sickly. In place of shoes, she had on big, fluffy, worn-out, blue slippers. From the looks of them, she must have been wearing them every day for quite a while. The pain showed on her face as she limped to a chair at the table, she looked stressed. She couldn't put pressure on her feet when she stepped down on them. Her condition showed the physical effects that her uncontrollable and confusing life was putting on her.

She had lost so much weight that her summer blue jeans and over-sized, white, button down blouse were hanging off her. She was so thin I felt that I could touch my thumb and index finger around her wrist.

My God how sick is she? I wondered as the blood went to my head, making me feel dizzy.

I fought back tears. All these months, I thought her feet had healed; she had never mentioned a thing about them during our conversations. How could she be this sick and not call for help or talk to us about how serious her health problems were becoming?

"Hi, honey," I said standing up to give her a hug. I could feel her ribs when my arms went around her. I choked up.

Twenty to thirty friends and family members were gathered on the deck and in the backyard enjoying the summer cookout; Debbie and Brian hosted these events quite often. Some of the teenagers were playing baseball while others were playing games in the pool with the younger children. With so many people around me, I couldn't talk to

Lori in private. She never did like me asking questions about her life.

I knew then that my daughter was dangerously ill, and I realized that her problem was more serious than just a fall into a hole on the boat. She had kept her life completely private from all of us and changed the subject anytime she was asked anything that had to do with her physical condition.

I learned later that foot problems can be related to alcohol abuse: Heavy drinking is a health risk for many reasons, including the effect on bones. I found an article by Primal Kaur, MD, an osteoporosis specialist at Temple University Health System in Philadelphia written on the WebMD website by Jeanie Lerche Davis.

Dr. Kaur stated, "Heavy drinkers are more likely to suffer frequent fractures due to brittle bones and nerve damage. The hormones are important to bone health. Some studies suggest that alcohol decreases estrogen and can lead to irregular periods. As estrogen declines, bone remodeling slows and leads to bone loss."

Years earlier, when Lori was in her late twenties, she had told me that her periods were sometimes three to five months apart. She never talked to me about her medical appointments or what conclusions the doctor came to about the problem.

Dr. Kaur wrote, "Excess alcohol kills osteoblasts, the bone-making cells. To compound the problem, nutritional deficiencies from heavy drinking can lead to peripheral neuropathy -- nerve damage to hands and feet. And chronic alcohol abuse can affect balance, which can lead to falls.

"Alcohol interferes with the pancreas and its absorption of calcium and vitamin D. Alcohol also affects the liver, which is important for activating vitamin D -- which is also important for calcium absorption."

Throughout that whole summer, Lori insisted she didn't need anyone's help. She refused to let Al and I take her to doctor's appointments. I kept insisting that the health problems she was going through weren't normal, especially her inability to walk or even wear a pair of shoes. She lied constantly, telling us that the doctor said she'd be okay, but that the healing would take time. She never mentioned what the damage was or if she had been put on any regimen to help with the process of healing or even what the condition was that she was healing from. She never provided us with any details.

In the fall, Paula began to see Lori more often. Since Mark was no longer living at home, the cousins bonded more tightly. Paula's visits gave me mixed feelings. I had no doubt that Paula loved her, but she too had been struggling with alcohol abuse.

Anita and Sonny had recently sent Paula to the Hanley Hazelton Rehabilitation Center in West Palm Beach, Florida to manage her drinking dependency. After a month at the rehabilitation center, Paula returned home. The counselors wanted her to stay longer, but she checked herself out. She continued drinking, but fortunately she turned herself around and began attending AA meetings. We were all elated when she went nine months without drinking.

I wanted her to give Lori hope and strength to fight this disease. The incidence of alcoholism was so high in Richie's family.

Lori's physical and mental strain was taking a toll on her. I was quite worried. She had lost her job, the responsibility of caring for Carl, whom she loved, and her dreams of getting back with Mark. Her skin and the white of her eyes started to get a yellow tint. I knew yellow skin could mean a serious sign of liver damage. Her father had looked the same way. She wouldn't face what was happening to her.

She called me one morning, in a state of confusion, "Mom, one minute Mark doesn't want to talk to me and then he's acting like he wants to come back and try again. I'm fighting to keep myself together. I asked the doctor for tranquilizers, but he wouldn't give them to me."

"Lori, you're an alcoholic, alcohol and tranquilizers are a dangerous combination."

"Mom, I'm not an alcoholic!"

After being admitted into the Gosnold Rehabilitation Center, she still wouldn't admit to having a drinking problem.

I had her on my mind constantly, knowing that she was falling into a deep black hole. I had stepped back when she said she was handling her drinking, though I knew she wasn't.

Request to Travel to Medjugorje

One morning, Lori shocked me with a call for a request I never expected. "Mom, I want to go to Medjugorje with you."

"That's wonderful," I replied, thrilled that she wanted to go. I had prayed for years for my girls to go with me. "We can ask Debbie, too."

"No, Mom. I want just you and me to go."

I could tell by her voice that she was drinking. "That's okay, we can go alone."

I knew Debbie would understand, and I could go with her another time. Maybe Our Lady would heal Lori's addiction.

It was February of 2005, and I thought about how cold it would be in Bosnia. "We should go in May when it's warm. I'll start looking around and see what pilgrimage is available leaving in our area."

I told Al about Lori's wish for making the trip to Bosnia.

"Alberta, she's been drinking, tomorrow she won't remember asking you. That's a lot of money to put out for her if she backs out."

"I'm going to look around," I said with a deep faith she would go.

I looked on the Internet to see what religious groups in our area were going. I wanted to pick a pilgrimage with a priest accompanying the tour. I had a lot going on at that time and decided to put off looking until spring; I thought we'd make a summer trip. We never did manage to go. I made a stupid decision by not acting on her request when she asked. I put unimportant things first until planning the trip started to fade into the background.

Maybe she wouldn't have gone when the time came, but I could have at least obtained the information and given her the option. I wanted her to meet Fr. Ed Sousa, who had accompanied me on my pilgrimage to Medjugorje back in 1998. He was in his mid-thirties and close to Lori's age. I had hoped she would relate to him.

"Lori, you would understand a younger priest. Will you meet with him if I can arrange it?"

"Yes, give me his telephone number, and I'll call him, too."

She and I tried a few times, but he was away. As with most things, Lori gave up. This was another time that I should have persevered in her introduction to this priest. A meeting with Father Sousa might have given her strength to overcome this disease.

I didn't follow-up when Fr. Sousa returned to his parish because Lori had requested his telephone number and I assumed she would contact him. Our plans to go on a pilgrimage to Medjugorje slipped through the cracks. I could make a list of reasons; family members got so caught up in Lori's problems within her life, I didn't search hard enough for a group going, Lori wouldn't be available to talk or she wouldn't be home for a visit. We both let an event go by that could have helped us become much closer as a mother and daughter, and the possibility of her developing a stronger faith in God.

Trying to Offer Support

A few days later, Debbie called saying that Lori had been admitted to Morton Hospital.

"What happened?"

"Remember when we noticed that Lori's eyes were yellow?"

"Yes."

"Well, I told her that I was worried about these signs and asked her to go to the doctor to find out what was happening to her."

Debbie always kept in direct contact with her sister. I depended on her to apprise me of Lori's actions, since she never wanted to talk to me about them.

"Lori told me the yellow was from drops that she was using for allergies, I told her that she didn't look good and should be checked."

Debbie took a deep breath and continued, "She went to the emergency room at Morton Hospital."

Lori had to be extremely concerned if she went to the emergency room; she was scared to death of hospitals.

"I couldn't reach her by phone so I called the emergency room, and they said she was still there. I went to see her, and she said that they were going to keep her. The doctor is giving her a blood transfusion."

Al and I drove to the hospital the next day. When we saw her, she looked like she had lost even more weight. She was holding a Kleenex to the side of her nose putting pressure on it. There was a sore she had scratched that wouldn't stop bleeding.

After a half hour watching her doing this, I asked, "Lori, how long has that been bleeding?"

"It started a few hours ago."

"And it's still bleeding! Don't you think you should tell the doctor?"

"They know, Mom. He has me on vitamin K because my blood is too thin.

"What's causing it?"

"I don't know. They're taking all kinds of blood tests. I'll be fine," she motioned with her other free hand in the air. She seemed upset that I was questioning her.

I hated the Patient Privacy Act. There was no way that we could talk to the doctor about Lori's health problems. Lori gave permission to Debbie, but she didn't want me or Al to have anything to do with her healthcare. If it weren't for Debbie, we wouldn't have known a thing about Lori being in the hospital.

An older woman, who looked to be in her sixties, shared the room with her, and I could hear her coughing continuously behind the closed curtain. It sounded like it was deep in her chest.

I whispered, "Lori, what does she have?"

"…pneumonia."

"And they have her in here with you!"

I was extremely upset that a patient in this condition would be put in the same room with Lori. The medical staff had to know the chances of her getting infected would be high. There was no screening and the precautions were lax.

Within two days, Lori developed pneumonia and had to stay in the hospital longer. When the hospital staff didn't find the situation important enough to separate Lori from the other patient with a contagious disease, it angered me. How did the doctor expect her to avoid contracting the sickness when the other woman had been coughing and sneezing in the next bed?

A few days later, Debbie called. "I offered to have Lori and the kids stay with us when she gets out of the hospital. She finally agreed, and said she felt so much better with the meds they had her on. They also gave her a lot of blood. She had no strength to take the kids anywhere. She told me that she never wanted to leave the house either. A few months ago, Brian and I took her to a party at a friend's house, she said it had been such a big step for her to actually go out and have fun. I was so encouraged by it."

"Why didn't you tell me she was afraid to leave the house?

"Mom, she never talked about her health problems or fears. Her moods and personality never changed with her drinking, either."

On Lori's release from the hospital, she and the kids stayed with Debbie and Brian for two weeks, after which she felt strong enough to return to her own home.

I called to see how she was doing. She sounded weak, so I drove down to see her. I made her some hot tea while she sat on the couch. She watched as I ran around gathering food to make a meal for supper and cleaned the house.

Lori was still unable to walk normally; instead, she hobbled. Debbie had taken her to the doctors a few days before for x-rays of her feet. Nothing was broken. I couldn't understand why she had so much pain walking.

"Lori, let Al and me go with you to the doctor. I want to talk directly to him to find out what's happening to you. Your inability to walk properly doesn't seem normal."

"He said that the healing was going to take time. There's no need for you to go with me."

I finally poured myself a cup of tea and sat on the couch next to her. "Lori, what's actually going on with you? We want to talk to your doctor, but you won't let us. Why?"

"The doctor wanted to put me on a liver transplant list. He said that if I didn't stop drinking, I'd be dead in two years. All I thought about was how Dad died. I have never forgotten his suffering."

I froze in shock. *This couldn't be happening again*! "Why in God's name didn't you tell us? Did you tell the doctor you'd sign to be on the list?"

"I have to be off drinking for a year before they'll put my name on the list." She hesitated and looked down. "I can stop. I'll be more aware of taking a drink."

"Lori, this is a life and death situation. It isn't something to play around with or ignore because you're scared. I don't want to lose you. If you keep this up, you'll die like your father. You have to keep all your appointments. Please, let Al and me get involved with helping you."

"It's only in Taunton. I can drive myself."

"I know you're capable of driving yourself, that's not the issue. It's about being a family and giving you support."

"I just don't like going weekly to get blood drawn."

"I don't enjoy going monthly to have my blood drawn for my coumadin readings, but I do it. You have to want to get better. I can't do it for you, I wish I could. You've also lost a lot of weight. Were you trying to do that on your own?"

"The doctor said I'm bulimic. I took laxatives and anything that would clean me out fast. I've been throwing up. I was getting heavy."

"That's not how you do it. I'd rather see you with extra weight than being like this. You're putting your body through hell."

I was traumatized that my daughter was this ill. I sat for a moment in silence, stunned by this horrifying news. I had no idea any of this was going on. I couldn't fathom the emotional and physical pressure that she had been under. I went along every day thinking she was getting better, when she was actually getting worse. She wasn't eating normally, and more than likely, very little.

I'd like to mention the dangers of a person being bulimic and an alcoholic. Starvation and restriction of food, calories, and/or fat grams sometimes accompanied by self-induced vomiting, taking laxatives and diuretics, deprives the body of all the vitamins and minerals it needs to survive. Eating disorders do kill.

Besides Lori's excess consumption of liquor over a prolonged period of time, she was causing damage to many of her body's organs. This is a time when family should try everything possible to get professional and medical help without delay.

Lori continued. "You know, Mom, I was partially to blame for losing my job."

"What happened?"

"It doesn't matter now." Again, she started to tell me and clammed up.

"Why don't you open up to me? What are you afraid of?"

"It's not important now. It's over."

"It *is* important, Lori. You're all bottled up, and I don't know how to reach you unless we talk about your problems. That's why you're so depressed. You should have gone back and talked to Gilly. He might have given you time to get yourself together and then let you return to work."

"What, to a lower position? Do you know how I'd feel seeing someone else running the payroll department?'

"I *do* know how you'd feel. I was replaced at my position four months ago, remember? I went through the hurt and depression. Pride is a killer, Lori. You have to go on and do the best you can with what's facing you. We all say and do things that we regret without realizing the consequences at the time. By then it's too late."

"I couldn't walk in there after being let go."

"Lori, you need a job in order to run this house. If not, you'll lose everything. Mark won't be supporting you forever. You need to stay independent."

I thought back to when she had started a direction in nursing. Now is when the education and job experience would have kicked in, and she wouldn't have been lacking a job. I didn't bring it up; she couldn't go back and change things.

I looked at her and put my arm around her. "You need to bring God into your life."

"I don't pray, and I told you that I don't even know if I believe in a God."

"He already knows you're weak in faith. You need to turn to Him. Praying is just talking to God, just like we're talking. You don't need to say a rosary or long prayers. Ask Him to help you make it through the day and thank Him at night when you go to bed."

"How can there be a God when He lets my life become a disaster?"

"He gives us the free will to make choices. You have to make a decision with your life about what path you want to take. God doesn't close doors on us. He's there waiting for us every day. We're the ones who close our heart to Him."

I looked at her. She looked so defeated, and my heart broke. "You're sick and need to get help by staying in the AA program. You have Al, Brian, Debbie, me and the kids to help you. You're pushing us all away."

"I've never prayed."

"At one time or another, you have. You turned to the prayer line when Carl was being born; that's faith. You probably have turned to God through your whole life and never thought about it as praying. I want you to do something. When you walk into the living room, pick out a chair, and picture Jesus sitting there. Look at it this way; if you physically saw Him, you'd never walk by and ignore Him. This is when faith comes into your heart. Know that He's there. Ask the Holy Spirit to help lead you to Him."

Within weeks, Lori had bought a few statues of the Blessed Mother. She called more often, and during our conversations, she'd say, "I prayed today, and I found that special chair."

My heart rejoiced knowing that she was turning to God. I continued with my daily rosaries, praying to help her get through this nightmare she was living. I regretted not taking her to Medjugorje. Now, her health was too bad for her to go. I thought of how my father wanted to make the same pilgrimage, but his health failed him. *Was Lori that sick?*

Even with prayer, this was the beginning of a series of heartbreaking events in Lori's life. Everything was going from bad to worse. It's hard to believe that she couldn't control the landslides. She refused to go to AA meetings, get a sponsor, or attend counseling.

Five months went by, and Lori began to walk without much pain. She gave up the slippers and wore shoes. I felt relieved that the bones in her feet had begun to heal.

A few weeks later she called. She sounded absolutely devastated and was crying uncontrollably.

"Mom, Jimmy died!" She was sobbing her heart out. I knew she held a lot of affection for her ex-boyfriend.

"Died? How?"

"He went to a party and when he came home he told his girlfriend he didn't feel good. He went upstairs to the bathroom and kept throwing up. When his girlfriend went up to check on him, he was dead. Jimmy was only 38 years old!"

"I'm so sorry, honey. I know how much he meant to you."

"I can't picture him gone and never being able to see him again," she said heartbroken about the loss.

We talked, but nothing I said could calm her down. Lori had told me years ago that he drank, took drugs, and beat her during the time they had lived together. I wondered if drugs had contributed to his death. I never did hear what the actual cause was. His death was an unexpected tragedy in her life. Another man was taken from her.

I don't think she ever got over Jimmy's death. The wake and funeral had to be extremely agonizing. If I hadn't forced her to have the abortion, she would have had his child and kept a part of him. He would have left something of himself behind. Maybe that's why God wanted her to have the baby. He had a reason for her to have had that child, and I took it away from her.

A few months later, Mark asked her to sign for a huge equity loan against the house. Friends and family warned her not to do it.

Al spoke to her. "Lori, you don't sign a mortgage loan when your husband is planning to leave you. If you sell the house, you'll have to pay that back. That's a large amount to come out of the profit. When you divorce, your share will be that much less."

"I'd have money to make my mortgage and car payment. I need food for us. Besides, he's talking about us maybe getting back together."

"That may be, but until you do, you don't sign anything," Al stated.

Lori didn't listen; she lived on hope of them getting back together. She called to say a check for fifty-two thousand dollars had been deposited in their bank account.

"I feel like a ton of weight came off me. Now I can meet my payments for the house and car," she said with relief in her voice.

The following day, she called me in a state-of-panic. "I went to take money out of the bank to make the payment for my car loan, and the account was empty! I told them there had to be a mistake. We just made a deposit last night."

My heart sank. Lori had made a decision based on emotion and was now going to suffer for it. She had signed the loan agreement, holding onto the possibility that the money would be for both of them. I couldn't fault her for thinking that or dreaming they'd become a couple again; I had gone back to her father four times. Our mates seem to use our remaining love for them to lull us and then shock us with another side of them that we didn't expect to see. I was disappointed that Mark would clean out their account and not leave Lori any money to keep up with her debts.

Lori called me some days later; she was upset that her hair was so matted that a comb couldn't get through it.

"I'm using all kinds of conditioners and nothing is working. I used the whole bottle," she remarked.

I went for a visit to see for myself what she was talking about. Her beautiful, long, curly, black hair was tangled tightly, like a birds nest. We couldn't understand how nothing she used could loosen the snarls.

Paula came over to help her. The only course left was to cut Lori's hair. The short hairstyle looked nice on her, but I knew she wasn't happy about losing her long hair; she had never worn it short, except when she was a child.

So many signs of alcohol abuse passed us by. We didn't have the knowledge to look for signs of when a body is breaking down because of it. I learned later that dry skin, brittle hair and nails, and hair loss, are caused by vitamin and mineral deficiencies, malnutrition and dehydration. Alcohol is a diuretic, so it causes accelerated dehydration. A lack of body fluid causes dry and brittle hair. Excessive alcohol consumption can deplete levels of iron in the body, leading to hair loss. Being bulimic added to her malnutrition.

Now I sit back and wonder if her drinking could have been why her hair became so matted. I had never seen hair with snarls that couldn't be straightened with a conditioner.

As the months went by, Lori was finding it more difficult to keep up with the payments on any of her bills, so she had no choice but to put the house up for sale. She was too sick to go out to look for a job, much less to work at one. She had rented this house when she was on her own, and it gave her pride and meant security for her and the kids. I knew that it would take her years to ever own a home again.

I wondered where she and the kids were going to go. She'd never come to live with us; we lived too far from her friends and the kids still had a few years left in high school, and she would never uproot them. I couldn't blame her because I had refused to move to my parent's home in Hull after my separation from Richie.

I felt her loss so deeply that I wished we could have afforded her mortgage payments so that they could have stayed in their home. Joe and Meagan were confused, wondering what was going on. They probably felt their mother was the only one at fault for losing everything.

My nerves felt like they were unraveling. Lori's uncontrollable life became my worry; her pain became my pain as I watched her being stripped of her life's accomplishments. She was on the brink of living on the street with nothing to her name. Just a few years ago, she had it all. I couldn't believe this was happening to her. What went wrong?

Butler Hospital

It didn't take long before Lori had another catastrophe hit her. The finance company called to repossess her van. When she told me this news, I couldn't believe that they hadn't paid off the car with the money they had received from the sale of a piece of their property. I wondered how she was going to be able to get to her appointments, shop, or even to take the kids anywhere they had to go. Lori's humility had to be at its lowest. Having a company come to take her car had to be demeaning.

In June of 2005, Lori was still living at home and playing with the idea of attending some AA meetings. She kept asking Paula to go with her. Paula had fallen off the wagon after nine months of sobriety and was back to drinking. They were in the clutches of this demon at the same time.

Instead of giving strength to each other, they became poisonous to one another. They found any excuse to start drinking, especially if anyone or anything upset them. I didn't know if Lori was buying the liquor or if Paula was purchasing it. Their justification ran the scope of reasons; family picking on them, no one understood, they had a bad day, their relationships were breaking up, or they couldn't handle going to meetings and listening to losers. The list went on and on.

In 1985, together they had witnessed Richie die at the VA Hospital in Providence, Rhode Island, yet they couldn't see that they were taking the same path. They were both in denial about their drinking which shows how strong the disease becomes. The frustration was that everyone else saw them heading toward disaster but couldn't do a thing to stop them.

Debbie kept in constant touch with Lori. The next thing Al and I heard was that Lori's telephone had been disconnected. We worried because she couldn't be reached.

Debbie phoned me from work. "Mom, I think Lori has to go into a rehab again. A few months ago, Paula went to Butler Hospital in Providence, Rhode Island and swears it's a good place. Maybe we can talk her into going. Brian and I went to see her, and she looks awful. She's so thin and shaky, and I don't think she's eating."

"Al and I will meet at your house, and we can all go together. Will you be calling her first to let her know that we'll be coming?"

"No, let's just go over."

Brian, Debbie, Al, and I met and went to Lori's house. When we knocked on the door, there was no answer. Brian tried the door. It was unlocked, so we went in.

We couldn't see her anywhere, and Lori didn't answer when we called out her name. Debbie walked into her bedroom, and we heard them talking softly. It was ten o'clock in the morning, and Lori was still in bed. The kids had taken the bus to Dighton-Rehoboth High School.

Lori came out of her bedroom; her condition was worse than I could ever have imagined. *This happens to other people, not my daughter*, I thought as she walked toward us. She was in her pajamas and sat at the kitchen table. There wasn't a part of her body that wasn't shaking. Her lips were quivering and her hands were trembling so much that she sat on them trying to control the shaking. I wanted to break down crying.

I remembered back to the time when Richie had knocked on my backdoor in the early morning hours in the same condition. He swore that he was having a breakdown. My daughter was in the same state.

Seeing her in this terrible condition made the reality of losing Lori hit me like a ton of bricks; she had been staying home, alone, and so sick.

I assumed that Lori would wait until Joe and Meagan went to school and then go back to bed. None of the family knew what she did. The kids never talked about the situation with their mother; not even a word about her drinking. We think Lori drank when they left the house.

Debbie started the conversation. "Lori, we think you should go into Butler Hospital. Paula went there and said it's the best place to go." Debbie's eyes filled with tears at seeing her sister in such awful physical shape.

I couldn't get my eyes off my precious daughter. It was the hardest thing in the world to sit there and watch Lori suffering. There wasn't anything that any of us could do, but try to give her support.

"I don't know," Lori answered weakly. The muscles in her face and eyes were actually jumping.

Al looked at her. "Honey, you can't stay like this. You need help."

Lori loved Al, and he felt the same toward her.

"I'd rather go back to Gosnold Rehab in Falmouth."

Al continued, "We can try to get you into Gosnold, but it's further away. Get your things together, and we'll take you to Debbie's. We'll make the call and see how soon they can take you. We don't even know if they'll take you today."

"I'll pick the kids up here when they get home from school," Brian volunteered.

Debbie went with Lori to her bedroom to collect some clothes. Lori could hardly keep her balance, she was shaking so badly. After seeing her, I knew that she hadn't eaten anything substantial for days or maybe months.

How were the kids eating with no paycheck coming in? I had thought that Mark was still giving her support money.

Gosnold had no beds available, and Butler Hospital couldn't get a bed for her until the next afternoon. There were so many people suffering from drug and alcohol abuse that the beds filled up as fast as they emptied. Lori and her kids stayed at Debbie's, and after a few hours, Al and I returned home.

The next afternoon Al, Debbie, and I took Lori to Butler Hospital. It was a forty-five minute ride, and I sat in the back seat with Lori. All the way there she continued to sit on her trembling hands while her lips quivered.

My God, this disease is killing her, I thought, as I watched my daughter falling apart.

We reached East Providence, Rhode Island and drove along the beautiful grounds of Butler Hospital. The long road in was winding and thickly landscaped with vibrant azalea bushes and different colored, budding trees and plants on the side of the road going up to the parking lot. The old, red, brick building looked cold to me. I felt myself becoming nauseous, thinking how frightened Lori had to be. This was a strange place to her.

"I don't want to go here."

"We know, Lori, but Gosnold doesn't have a bed, and you need help now," Al said when he took her overnight bag out of the car.

I think back and hate myself for not showing her the same affection and support that Al and Debbie were giving her. I wasn't strong and became an emotional mess. If I said one word, I knew that I'd lose the control and would not be able to hold back my tears. The sight of her in such bad health made the throbbing that was constricting my throat feel like it was choking me. Lori didn't need me coming apart, so I stayed silent. I didn't think at that moment that my holding back emotionally probably came across to her as being cold and uncaring.

What Lori needed was my arms around her and me not being afraid to show how much I loved her. I started to realize that I wasn't as open with my feelings as I had thought.

Getting her admitted was a nightmare. Even though we called ahead a few days ago with Lori's information, she had to fill out paperwork. We sat for over four hours waiting for her to be admitted. It was ludicrous! Couldn't they have a better system to get a sick person to their room? They gave us a time to arrive, but no room was ready, and no one showed any concern.

The staff had to see patients being admitted everyday in horrible states, the shakes or being completely intoxicated. They seemed to be separated from the patient's condition. Others, sitting with us in the room, could have been worse than Lori as they battled withdrawal, but it didn't lesson our anxiety. The substance abusers must have simply become numbers to the workforce.

After two hours, Al couldn't stand seeing Lori shake. He went up to the desk. "I'd like to have someone give our daughter something to calm her down."

"We have to have the doctor's approval before we can give her anything," the girl at the desk replied in a routine voice.

"Well—call him!" he shouted. "There's no need for her to shake this way for so long."

Al had never been intimidated by people in authority, and I loved him for it, especially at this time. He was disgusted with this unwarranted treatment. It took another hour before she was given something.

"I still can't stop shaking," Lori said trying to cross her arms when she wasn't sitting on her hands.

Al put his arm around her, "You'll be all right, honey, but you've got to quit drinking this time. You don't want to go through this again."

I had to get up from my chair twice and go into the women's restroom. I fell apart with hard, heartbreaking sobs. I wanted to deal with Lori's emotions and pain, but I was selfishly trying to control mine. Al and Debbie looked calm, and I became like jelly.

A nurse finally came to get Lori to take her upstairs. We were allowed to go as far as the ward on the second floor, and then they stopped us from passing through the locked doors.

"This is a private area, and we can't allow you to go any further with Lori," the girl stated with a smile.

We each hugged and kissed Lori, and the fear on her face was obvious when she passed through the doors. We watched through the door window as she was led down the long, empty hallway.

There was a sense of relief knowing that we left her in the care of professionals, but letting her go had been just as hard as taking her. She was at the best place she could be, but my heart overrode logic.

We went to see her during the week. Paula and Debbie helped us alternate opposite days so Lori wouldn't have a day without visitors. There was no private room in which family could talk. The hallway, which had the patient's private bedrooms off it, had windows at the far end with chairs in a straight row for visitors to sit and have conversations with their loved one. The atmosphere felt cold. Everyone could hear whatever we discussed.

I looked into the bedrooms; twin beds were against the tiny walls, almost on top of each other, divided only by a nightstand. I thought how hard it must have been to be placed in a room with a stranger who might have been loud or foul-mouthed or sat in a daze. I noticed both men and woman were on the same floor. I wasn't comfortable with that arrangement.

"I don't like this place," Lori said to Al and me. "Gosnold is much better."

"Why is that?" I asked.

"At Gosnold they have meetings every hour all day long from 8 am until 8 pm. Here we sit around all day reading or talking. They had one speaker yesterday around ten in the morning, and the man looked to be in his seventies. I couldn't relate to a thing he was saying about his life. Then the rest of the day, we just sat around. It's boring!"

Now, I felt guilty about not having waited a few more days to take her to Gosnold Rehabilitation Center in Falmouth, though I knew her condition required immediate attention. It didn't take much for me to burden myself with guilt. I wanted *someplace, someone* to open her eyes and cure her.

"Honey, listen to everything they're saying to you. You need to get well."

"I know!" she said, losing patience and looking away from me. When I tried to communicate with Lori, I truly believe she didn't know how badly I wanted to help her. I feared losing her, as I had Richie, and the fright overwhelmed me.

Al, Debbie, and I had the opportunity to talk to Lori's doctor during one of our visits. It was the first time a doctor included us with updates on her condition. He spoke of the seriousness of her disease. We weren't told anything about her counseling or her attitude about wanting help. Each time we went to see her, she seemed to be her old self again and enthusiastic about getting counseling and going into a recovery program.

She avoided my questions about going to classes for her bulimia. "Did your doctor schedule you for a meeting?"

"It's in the next building, but I've been busy and haven't signed in for the class."

"I think it's important, honey."

"Don't worry, Mom, I'm planning on going," she said.

We received a call from her one afternoon. "They're having a family day here, and we can invite our families so that we can see what you're going through because of our drinking. Could you and Al come?"

"We'd be happy to attend." We wanted to give her all the support she needed. It didn't matter what it took. "When is it?"

"Tomorrow at two o'clock. Let them know downstairs at the desk what you're here for, and they'll tell you how to get to the meeting."

"Okay, we'll see you then."

The following day, we headed for Butler Hospital right after lunch. It always seemed forever to get to any location to see her, but I lived for those moments; she was allowing me into her recovery program. I was thrilled.

The counselor took Al and me into a private meeting room with twelve patients sitting against the walls, most of them were men. Most ranged in age from their early twenties to mid forties, two looked to be in their early sixties. Lori sat with us, and we could see that she was proud to have us there.

The meeting was delayed as we waited for other patients' family members to arrive, but not another person showed up. Al and I felt sorry for the other patients who looked toward the door now and then with disappointment showing on their faces. Maybe some families didn't care anymore, one way or another. It showed how a family unit can reach the point of not being compassionate with the alcoholic or ceased to hope for their loved one's recovery. Maybe the drinker disrupted their lives too much.

Family members suffer as much pain and heartache as the substance abuser, sometimes more, because we remember the things that were said or done to us in the alcoholic's blackout or rage. The episode is blank to the drinker.

The counselor gave Al and me a chance to introduce ourselves. We talked about our lives with Lori. Once we answered a few questions, the counselor turned on a twenty minute film about alcoholic families and the trial they were in because of the over indulgence of a relative. A short discussion went on at the end of the film.

A girl spoke about carrying a tiny bottle of vodka in her purse because it was colorless and didn't cause her breath to smell of liquor.

Lori remarked, "I've done that."

So much about Lori's episodes was shocking because I never witnessed her daily abusive life. I depended on her telling me what was happening to her. All we heard was, "I'm fine."

There was a time to socialize later with pastry and coffee. Again, Lori introduced us to the ones who hadn't met us. One pretty, blonde girl in her earlier twenties looked bitter and upset at being there. She said that she didn't care, one way or the other, if her parents came. Her remark seemed to be a way of protecting her emotions and hurt.

I looked coldly around the room at the poor, mentally and emotionally messed-up, patients from substance abuse. I never thought I'd see Lori enclosed in a facility for alcoholics. I wondered how I had missed knowing my own happy daughter had been suffering silently.

We took time and talked to the men and women who wanted to hear from us. I wanted to wrap my arms around all of them, they looked lost like Lori. It was an action I should have done more often with my daughter.

"Mom, everyone thinks you and Al are so nice." Lori was enormously proud that we showed up, especially being the only family to come.

"We're glad you invited us," I said hugging her.

I was delighted that she had asked us to be involved with her meeting. We wanted Lori to see the love and support she had from all of us to help her fight this demon.

"I'm supposed to start going to meetings at the other building for bulimic patients," Lori said to me, acting enthusiastic about it.

"Oh, I'm glad to hear that," I replied.

She never did attend. Each time I brought the topic up she avoided the question or said that she missed the meeting because she was in counseling at another location. I knew it was an issue that she didn't want to face. Each time she hesitated to get more involved in the program, the more I feared she wouldn't get better. She was battling more problems than just alcohol abuse.

AA Meetings

While Lori was in Butler Hospital, Al and I went to her house and gave it a thorough cleaning. The house hadn't sold yet, and I felt the neglected housework might have been the reason. I scrubbed the kitchen floor, and Al fixed a kitchen cabinet door that was off the hinge. We vacuumed all the rooms and even moved the washer and dryer to get under it. I washed multiple loads of clothes, put up window curtains, placed flowers in the kitchen and living room, scrubbed the bathroom area spotless, cleaned the clutter off the kitchen counters, and tried to make the house presentable for sale. No one had made an offer on the house for the past four months.

I looked around her home that we had visited for so many years. I couldn't picture another family living in her residence. I felt that Lori, Joey, and Meagan had been happy for the first time in years living here. Now the house echoed emptiness. I felt the ache, knowing that Lori had to be thinking the same thing. It had been tough when I had walked away from my home after my divorce even when the decision was my choice. Losing her home had to be depressing and must have made her feel like a failure. Her dignity was taken from her.

Our hard once-over cleaning paid off. Within the week, while Lori was still at Butler Hospital, a couple made an offer on her house. I knew that she and the kids were going to be heartbroken. I don't think that Joey and Meagan understood why their home was being sold. We didn't know at the time that Lori had never sat them down and discussed her illness. She refused ever to tell them of their grandfather's drinking. Debbie, on the other hand, was open with Kerri and Michael about the history of drinking in our family.

Lori came home and was thrilled to see the repairs and changes to the house. I could sense the sadness she felt losing the ownership. If she had kept her job, she would have been able to keep the house. I'm sure her nerves would have been on edge being locked into an 8:00 am to 5:00 pm job while she was drinking, but, then again, if she were working, she may not have been drinking so heavily.

I continued to think about what could have been while time passed. Many moments I wished that I had never left North Dighton, I could have been on top of what was happening to her; although, no one knew at this time that Lori was having any problems in her life. As parents, we feel we should nurture a child and fix their problems.

Debbie and Brian offered to take Lori, Joey and Meagan into their home.

"Staying here will give you a chance to look for a job and get an apartment," Debbie said, trying to give Lori encouragement.

The kids were uprooted again. It was devastating and embarrassing to them losing their home. They had been so content living there.

After Lori's house was sold, Brian and Debbie opened their door and hearts and so did their children, Kerri and Michael. Kerri shared her bedroom with her cousin, Meagan. Joey slept on a couch in the den; and Lori used the sofa in the living room.

Debbie took on the responsibility of getting Lori's furniture, appliances, clothes, and houseware items into a storage center in Taunton. They offered to pay the rental fee until Lori got a job.

It was months after Lori had been discharged from Butler Hospital that she admitted to me that the administrator had set up an arrangement with her insurance company for her to go directly from there to a long-term rehabilitation center in Florida. She refused, and it was too late to make plans to arrange the admittance once she had left the facility. Lori claimed she didn't want to be away from her kids. She was running from all sources that offered help. I felt frustrated knowing she had a chance to go into a long-term recovery program, and she didn't talk to the family about the opportunity so we could have discussed the opening for her to recover. We knew she needed more than week of rehabilitation to fully recover.

Lori's family lived in harmony at Debbie's for eight months. While Debbie worked, Lori had offered to do all the housecleaning and prepared the meals. Debbie actually enjoyed coming home knowing that she and her sister had a chance to share time together. At night, the family rented movies or played games on the rug in the living room. The kids were all teenagers, ranging from Michael, being the youngest at fourteen, to Meagan, who was sixteen, to Joe and Kerri who were seventeen.

Lori started going to a few AA meetings. The past programs that Paula had attended helped her realize that she could change her life; she was now taking a real estate class but didn't want to go to the meetings.

A few weeks later, Lori called to inform us that she was going to attend an AA meeting at the St. John Neumann Church grounds. It was the church that Al and I belonged to in East Freetown.

"Lori, if you want, Al and I would be happy to go with you."

"You would? I'd like that."

"How are you getting there?"

"Debbie's letting me use her car."

"Good, we'll meet you tonight at seven in the parking lot."

Lori was a half hour late after taking a wrong turn, but we had plenty of time before the meeting.

"What beautiful grounds here," she said as we walked toward the building.

The Fall River Diocese owned the land. A lake bordered the property with boaters racing across the water. Benches faced the lake with beautiful, big homes that surrounded the far shoreline.

"You should come down here sometime just to sit," I said as she watched the activities on the lake. Like most people, she loved the water scene because of the calmness. I'm sure she missed going out with Mark on their boat.

"I was just thinking that," she said softly.

I hoped that the tranquility surrounding the building would make her want to keep coming back every Thursday night to the meetings at this location. I'd be more than willing to come with her.

We walked through the door of the old, tiny structure hidden within the wooded area, and a few people said hello. There were no greeters at the entrance. The room was packed with people running back and forth trying to get settled in their seats after helping themselves to coffee and snacks at two side tables against the back wall before the meeting started. Al and I chose chairs against the side wall that faced the center of the room that was filled with other seats facing the podium. Lori spotted a few friends she had met at Butler Hospital and joined them.

We listened to members talk about how they became alcoholics and the obstacles they had to overcome to try to recover. A man got up to talk about himself and his wife who had both become alcoholics. He decided to join the Alcoholic Anonymous program and was proud to say that he had been sober for twenty-one months. He tried to get his wife into the AA program, but she refused.

He stood at the podium, fighting to control his emotions. "I buried my wife four months ago."

Al leaned toward me, "His story reminds me of the movie, Days of Wine and Roses."

It had been a 1962 movie with Jack Lemmon who had overcome his battle with alcohol, and his wife, played by Lee Remick, couldn't stop. It was so sad.

Stories flowed from each person as they stood up to talk about their life, losing family, children, jobs, homes and friends. The memories rolled back to losing Richie twenty years earlier.

Where had the years gone? I would never have believed back then, while I sat with Richie at that AA meeting, that I'd be attending one with my dear daughter.

"I'm surprised there's no one to greet people at the door," Al said. "It would have been nice for someone to welcome Lori to make her feel comfortable."

With each speaker, I hung onto hope that Lori might identify with someone's experience in fighting her addiction. I wanted her to connect with another person so a bell would go off and have her realize how bad a path she was traveling; the same familiar desire I had wanted for Richie.

That night was the only time she attended a meeting in East Freetown. She called Paula a few times, but Paula still said she didn't need to go. She insisted that she could do it alone. I prayed so hard for the two cousins to support one another and face their drinking addiction. Our daughter went to a few more meetings in the Taunton area and then stopped.

She went to an AA meeting in Berkley which was a short distance from where Debbie lived. It took Lori about three minutes to get there from her sister's house.

Lori phoned me. "Mom, I met four wonderful women at a meeting in Berkley, they have offered to take me to other locations they travel to during the week. Since I'm at Debbie's, and it's only a few minutes away, they'll pick me up."

"That's wonderful, honey. Now you don't have to be concerned about how to get there. It'll be more fun than going alone."

I hung up thinking my prayers were being answered. She was mixing in with other women who had the same problem.

A month later, I asked her, "How are the girls in your AA group? Been to any meetings with them?"

"I'm not comfortable with them," Lori said.

"Why?" I asked as my heart sank in hopelessness.

"They're a lot older than me, and I can't relate to them."

"Lori, you just met them, and their experiences can help you."

I was afraid she wouldn't attend any more meetings. What was it going to take for her to realize she needed these meetings and staying connected to other people who were fighting their drinking addictions too? She had lost everything. Why wasn't she fighting to get her life back?

She always had excuses as to why she couldn't attend. She didn't want to face the fear that drinking could mean her life. Lori ignored the necessity of going to meetings and keeping in touch with counselors and other recovering alcoholics. I pleaded with her to find a sponsor. I felt that a sponsor would call her, and relate to what she was going through. Maybe he or she would be Lori's strength.

I couldn't shake the doctor's warnings about her liver failing if she didn't give up drinking. "*In two years she'd die.*" A year had already passed!

Lori's Divorce

When Lori's divorce date finally arrived, she called Al and me. "The case is going to be held in the New Bedford Probate Court tomorrow. Do you know where it is?"

"New Bedford is only fifteen minutes from us. Al knows the location. We'll be happy to take you. That way you won't have to get stressed searching for the court."

"Do you mind? I'll be a wreck that day. Debbie's giving me her car to use."

"Meet us at the house, and we'll drive you."

The next morning, Al drove the three of us to the courthouse. Lori looked very professional in a brown and white plaid blazer and a brown skirt. Her hair was pinned up, and the makeup she had applied emphasized her deep, brown eyes. I stared at her, knowing that she didn't realize how beautiful she was.

We stayed in the hallway with the other people waiting for their cases to be heard. Mark arrived and walked into the lobby. Once he spotted us, he disappeared outside to have a cigarette. He looked sharp, dressed in a casual blue button down shirt and black dress pants. He was a handsome man. I couldn't help noticing how Lori's eyes lit up when he came through the courthouse door. My heart broke for her.

"What ever happened to these two?" I whispered to Al as my eyes filled. I don't even think Mark knew how much we had hoped they'd get back together.

Lori leaned against the wall, as I had done so many years ago when I had divorced her father. She had been madly in love and had big dreams; now they stood looking at each other as enemies. The sad part was that Lori had told me she still loved Mark. I prayed that they weren't breaking up because of pride. We never did find out if drinking played into their breakup or if it had been from something else. Lori never talked about the reason.

Al couldn't accept this happening to the two of them and remarked, "I'm going out to talk to Mark. Maybe I can stop this crazy divorce."

Lori overheard him. "Please, Al, don't!" she yelled and grabbed his arm.

"Are you sure you want this, Lori."

"No, I don't, but he does. Talking to him won't stop this from going through. You'll embarrass me if you talk to him."

Al went over and hugged her. I wondered how many couples could have worked out their problems and saved their marriages if they really tried. What a shame that divorces are looked at as a normal occurrence today. No one stops to think that it might be a major cause as to why so many young kids from broken homes are into drugs and crime.

In an hour, Lori's short years of being a wife to Mark ended. She was completely lost without him. It's a shame when one wants the marriage, and the other doesn't. What do we do with those feelings that are still alive inside us? How do you ignore them? How do you forget about that special person you had slept with, went on vacations with, laughed with, had children with, socialized together, and had been a couple for years? Her pain was bad enough with her first divorce, but now she had lost another husband; one she had waited twelve years to come into her life. She didn't deserve all this heartache.

After the hearing, Al and I waited for Lori to go to her lawyer's office across the street. There was a check for her from the sale of the house. Because of the loan they had taken out and having had to reduce the price of the house, she received only about five thousand dollars.

Lori needed a car, and mine, though ten years old, was still in good condition. Al and I talked it over and decided to sell it to her at a price she could afford and get another one for me. Lori was thrilled to have wheels again. She had *something* that was hers. Her next step was to get a job and get back on her feet.

I can't explain how her divorce affected me personally. I missed Mark's smile, his laughter, and the kids joking with him. I had believed Mark was going to love Lori forever. Their personalities seemed so alike, and they blended together. Joey and Meagan had a chance to have a steady father figure in their lives. Their father wasn't around much for them. Instead of security, the kids were back to the ups and downs in their lives. When our children divorce, it's hard to ignore the feelings we had for their mates after years of having them in our family.

Slowly and timidly, Lori started to believe in herself and began the process of reading the newspapers daily to search for job opportunities. She called companies and sent copies of her updated resume to them. If she didn't receive a call back, she'd call them.

I felt each disappointment when Lori didn't get the positions she applied for, especially those with which she had the experience because of her former job. Having been a payroll manager for such a big construction company should have been impressive to any firm in the same field. She had a great resume with years of skills listed. She'd return from an interview all excited, believing she got the job, only to be disappointed to receive the news that it had been filled. She needed *something* to get her confidence back.

Interviewers kept telling her that she was overqualified. Suddenly, her skills were too good. After having all her material goods taken from her, her personal experiences were considered worthless. It only added to her struggles in trying to keep her life calm while fighting her alcoholism.

Not being able to find employment caused her to lose her confidence and completely give up looking for work. No matter what she tried to do to get back on her feet, something would happen to discourage her.

The calm atmosphere in Debbie's home started to change. Lori's desire to help around the house faded. Brian and Debbie began finding liquor missing from the bottles in their liquor cabinet.

"Lori, I had a full bottle of Bacardi here, and there's none in it," Debbie stated one night.

"Oh, I had a girlfriend over, and we had a drink."

"...you drank the whole bottle?"

"Gee, Debbie, I'll buy you another bottle if it bothers you," she snapped.

The only money that Lori collected weekly was from Joe's child support, which she couldn't depend on, and whatever she had left from the sale of the house.

To avoid an argument, Debbie dropped the discussion, knowing that it would only escalate, especially if Lori had been drinking. Debbie always gave her the benefit of the doubt. She really didn't believe that anyone came over to see Lori, but even if her story were true, Lori didn't have the right to pass out their liquor. Debbie started to mark the level of liquor in the bottles; she was concerned at how much was disappearing. These are the crazy things we do, questioning ourselves, when we know we're being lied to. She wasn't sure how to handle the situation. If she confronted her, Lori would always deny taking any. Debbie was at her wits end.

"Mom, I can't concentrate at work. All I do is worry about Lori. She's not looking for a job. She's lost interest in helping around the house. When I come home, she's sleeping in the den with the shades drawn.

"She must be drinking, Debbie."

"I don't know what to do. Trying to talk to her is almost impossible. She gets defensive and denies that drinking is playing a part in this. The kids are beginning to notice her odd behavior. I get calls at work from them saying that they can't wake her up."

Al and I were never able to visit Lori. If we called to tell her we were coming, she'd say that she wasn't going to be home or that she had somewhere to go. Debbie felt that

115

Lori checked their telephone's caller ID and didn't answer certain phone calls.

Debbie had to work late one evening and called home to inform everyone. Lori answered, "I'm going out with friends and won't be home tonight myself."

"What do you mean you won't be home?" Debbie asked.

"I have a chance to stay over somewhere. God, Debbie, I haven't been out in so long, I feel like a caged lion. I need a night out."

"Yes, but you don't have to stay out all night!"

"I'll be home tomorrow morning."

Debbie called me, and my first reaction was to question where she went and with whom.

"I'm going to be up all night worried about her," Debbie said. I could hear the stress in her voice. I knew exactly what she was going through. It was a repeat of my past with their father.

"Debbie, go home and relax. There's nothing you can do. You have no control over her decision at this moment. Try to enjoy your family, lock the doors, and go to bed."

Telling Debbie what to do was easy. Memories of the same situation made me realize that Debbie was going to worry all evening. It's like our world stops, and we wait to see what the alcoholic is going to do. Their drinking problems become ours.

Knowing she'd be staying over *somewhere* was better than knowing she would be driving home after drinking. She could get in an accident and kill herself, or God forbid, someone else. I couldn't stand the thought of her being arrested or knowing that she could end up taking an innocent life. I couldn't bear the consequences of her spending years behind bars.

Al belonged to a health club at the Holiday Inn in Taunton, and it was only fifteen minutes from Debbie's. He went regularly three mornings a week. I decided to go with him the next day so that we could go to see Lori when he got out of the gym.

Our plans changed when Al woke up feeling sick and wasn't able to go to the club. Maybe it was for the best because Lori would have probably been hung over. She wouldn't have been up to discussing her reasons for staying out. How could I demand that she stay home? She was thirty-eight and old enough to make her own decisions.

I began to regret selling her my car. Going out to drink wouldn't have been so easy for her if she didn't have a vehicle at her disposal. This was another guilt trip for me. There were too many times that she would go out without letting Debbie know her plans.

Joey and Meagan were now feeling the emptiness of her not coming home. Their life was in turmoil. They lost their home, their father hardly ever saw or called them, and now their mother wasn't there.

"I'm so frustrated with Lori," Debbie said when she called me. "She's not coming home and thinks nothing of it. She has no cell phone so I can't reach her."

"Al and I wanted to come down to talk to her, but she's never home. Has she gone back to looking for a job?"

"Not to my knowledge. I can't watch her all day long. If she says she has been looking, I have to believe her. She's not going to any AA meetings either. I've told her that it's been a year and she has to do something with her life. I honestly wouldn't mind all this, Mom, if she was trying to get better. She seems to be getting worse. I don't want this to affect my job. When I'm at work, I'm constantly calling home to see if she's there. If she isn't, my mind starts to race trying to figure out where she is, and I'm spending hours calling people. It's like checking up on your child. I'm running out of excuses to give Joey and Meagan about where their mother is."

"I never thought she'd stay away from her kids, especially at night. She has always been a good mother. This isn't the Lori we know," I said.

I was upset over Lori's condition, but at the same time, felt bad for Debbie. She was becoming emotionally and physically drained. All Debbie wanted was to help her sister, but Lori was blind to all the support from her family; she felt we were interfering in her life.

Debbie sighed deeply, "My heart breaks every night for Joey. He confronts me with, 'Auntie, do you know if my mother is coming home?' What do I say to him? I don't even know myself."

"Do the kids *know* she has a drinking problem?"

"I'm not sure."

"Maybe Al and I should come down tomorrow to talk to them."

"I'd appreciate that," she said sounding relieved that someone else was going to take some pressure off her.

We arrived the next day, a Saturday, and the four kids were watching television in the family room.

"Joey and Meagan can you join us in the sun room so we can talk?" I asked after we had greeted and hugged everyone.

Looking nervous about what we may say, they walked into the room and sat next to Debbie on the couch. They had to know the truth.

"We want to tell you why your mother has been staying out and acting like she doesn't care. She has a drinking problem; your mother is an alcoholic. Do you know this? Did she ever talk to you about her illness?" I asked.

They looked at us and shook their heads no.

I continued, "The reason she's been lying around in the den with the shades drawn, and sleeping all day is because of her sickness. Right now, drinking means more to her than anything else in her life. We don't want you to think that she's doing this because of something you've done. What's more important is that you know she loves you. I know it doesn't seem like it right now."

I looked at blank faces staring back at me. It was the same conversation I had with Debbie years ago about her father's behavior. At the time, Lori was only four and too young to be told. She wouldn't understand about alcoholism.

"Do you have any questions?" Debbie asked.

They just looked at her and offered no reply.

"I want you to come to me and Uncle Brian anytime to talk about this," Debbie continued.

"Is she coming home tonight?" Meagan asked.

"We don't know," Al replied.

It was hard to continue the discussion when there was no feedback from Joey and Meagan. We hugged them, and they went to rejoin Michael and Kerri watching television. I knew that they had to feel hurt that their cousins had parents who were with them every day. Kerri and Michael never knew what it was like not to have their parents there for them. They had the secure family life of no worries except what teenagers consider problems with their friends or school.

After we talked, Lori called to speak to the kids. When she was finished, I took the phone.

"Lori, where are you? Maybe you don't realize it, but your kids are asking every day where you are. They need you to be with them."

I was angry about her absence and had witnessed the kid's gloominess and confusion through the last few months. They'd walk around going from one thing to another or sit in silence staring at a television set at night. Joey isolated himself in his bedroom, and it was rare that he mixed in with the family.

"I call them every single day, Mom."

"Well, why don't you move to California? I guess you feel that it doesn't matter where you are, as long as you call them!"

By now I was furious. *What's wrong with her? This isn't my daughter!*

She had always been a good mother, and now she was acting as though she had lost her love for them by not seeming to care about her responsibilities to them. I wanted to take a hold of her and shake some sense into her.

She hung up, giving me absolutely no answer, though she did swear to be home soon.

High School Problems

Debbie received Lori's mail and saw a notice from the school that Joey was flunking English. It was his last year of high school. He seemed to have no interest in school. Their lives were in so much mayhem that he didn't seem to care whether he passed or not.

Brian and Debbie took Joey to the school and met with the principal and his teachers. They talked with his guidance counselor and explained that he was living with them because Lori was battling alcohol abuse and was trying to straighten her life out.

"All he has to do is pass this one course. There are only three months left before graduation. It's mandatory that he pass English, or he won't graduate," the teacher stated.

"We'll help him," Brian assured them. "He's an intelligent kid. I know he can complete this class."

They asked the counselor to send a report on his grades to them every two weeks and to call if he didn't show up for school. They received his grades only once, and the school never called to say that he wasn't attending, though he missed many days.

Deep down I could understand why he lost all his ambition. If I were he, I'd feel the same, but I didn't tell him that. Both kids were suffering emotionally from abandonment and not understanding why.

With the time Joey had missed and his low grades, it was now too late for him to graduate. Counseling had been offered, but he refused it. At this stage, he had more than enough stress in his life. In spite of everyone's effort, Joey showed no interest in trying to pass. It reached the point where he didn't go to school at all and took a part-time job with Lopes Construction.

Gilly and Gary Lopes helped by giving Lori's kids vehicles. Joey received a used company pickup truck, and they purchased a used Mazda for Meagan.

When Meagan was in her senior year, the school found out that she was living in Berkley with her aunt and uncle. It was mandatory that her residence be in Dighton or Rehoboth in order to attend the Dighton-Rehoboth High School. Meagan told her mother about the school's concern when she called.

Instead of coming home to handle the problem, Lori made a phone call from wherever she was to her girlfriend, who was the mother of one of Meagan's friends in Dighton. Lori asked if she could use her address for her daughter as a residence. Meagan spent some nights at their house, but it was only temporary.

The school informed Debbie that they had to start getting strict about allowing kids from out-of-town to attend the school. Debbie informed the vice principle that Meagan had been going to Dighton schools all her life. Somehow, all this commotion passed over, and they never heard another thing about the problem.

These were trying times for Joey and Meagan. Brian and Debbie supported them and cared about what was happening in their lives. Lori had always shown them love and had been in their lives continuously. Now, she disappeared for weeks at a time, and they couldn't understand why, and neither could the family.

As much as the two of them loved living with their aunt and uncle, I'm sure they didn't really feel that it was their home. Visiting in the past was one thing, but staying there permanently without their mother had to feel uncomfortable.

After two months, Lori came back home. It was a relief, and not much was said about her absence. We hoped she'd get back to one of the rehabilitation centers. Debbie decided to give her Michael's cell phone to use so she could be reached when she was out. He had the phone only for emergencies or when he needed a ride after sports practice. The service had minimal minutes allotted to it, after which, there was a per minute charge; he never exceeded the time allowed on the phone.

A month later, Debbie called. "You won't believe this, Mom. I got Michael's cell phone bill. Are you sitting down?"

"How bad is it?"

"It was $1,800 for last month!"

"Oh my Lord, I never knew someone could run a cell phone bill that high! How could she talk that long?"

"Lori calls her friends when she's drinking and talks for hours. I had to take the cell phone from her. When I showed her the bill, she acted shocked. Now we're faced with this payment. This doesn't include the monthly storage unit fee that Brian and I have been paying for since she sold her home a year ago. She's not doing anything to get better and doesn't show any interest in looking for a job, and she still stays out overnight, nothing is changing."

Debbie put up with the continuing chaos as long as she could. She wanted to keep Lori at her house, but the situation was getting worse. The kids were still coming home from school and finding Lori passed out on the couch in the den, and shaking her wouldn't arouse her. The room was always in total darkness. I can imagine the fear this caused them.

Finally, Debbie and Brian had to make a painful decision; she called to run it by me.

"Mom, I can't do this any longer. I think we have to put Lori out of the house, and I feel sick over it," Debbie's voice broke with emotion.

She was frustrated, worried and angry about not being able to reason with Lori. No amount of pleading, consoling, threatening, or bargaining could get her to stop drinking and seek counseling or go to an AA meeting.

Lori kept lying, saying that she'd go to meetings or look for jobs, but she promised and she never followed through. There was always an excuse as to why she couldn't go to a doctor's appointment and refused anyone to take her. We had no way to force her to do anything.

"It's not an easy decision to make, Debbie."

My heart sank. Where was Lori going to stay? We had no idea how much money she had left from her divorce settlement, the cash couldn't be much. She wanted her privacy in the dark world of drinking with no one watching her every move or asking questions. I knew deep within my heart that she didn't want to live that way. She was drinking herself to death and couldn't stop.

"Brian and I will let the kids stay here. Do you think that Lori might get her life together if we force her out on her own? Do you think that action will wake her up?"

Debbie wanted someone to tell her that she was making the right decision; it was a decision that was tearing her apart with guilt.

What's the right thing to tell her? I questioned.

I remembered back when I was trying to make the same decision with Richie. If I had allowed him to stay, I would have had a breakdown. Debbie was now feeling what I felt back then. I thought the action would make Richie feel the loss of his family. Instead, the desire to drink became stronger than the wish to return home. He finally drank himself to death.

Selfishly, I didn't want to tell her to make the move. Sleeping nights would be impossible, and I'd be a mental wreck wondering where Lori was while I lay in bed. We knew she wasn't eating right. Where would she go? Where would she stay?

I knew that living under all this stress was unfair for Debbie and the kids. I remembered how my mind and health started to fail me when I lived in an alcoholic atmosphere. Debbie was now at that point. Maybe Lori needed to reach that "rock bottom" that AA talks about. *How far down could she go without killing herself*? I thought about the situation for a few moments.

"Maybe she'll see a choice has to be made about her direction in life. I can't believe she'd be able to handle the separation from Joey and Meagan."

"I'll talk to her tonight and call you tomorrow, Mom."

"I wish I could do this for you, honey."

The next morning, I worked around the house, staying busy and waiting for Debbie's call. Her responsibilities as a manager at Lopes Construction didn't leave her much time to make personal calls. I didn't know when she'd be free to talk to me, so I didn't want to bother her by calling.

In the early afternoon, the phone rang. "Hi, Mom."

"Hi, how did you make out?"

"I didn't. She never came home."

"Now you have to wait to confront her?"

"I won't be seeing her."

"Why, what do you mean?"

"Last night I put her belongings into trash bags and put them on the front porch. I wrote a letter this morning and put the envelope with her items."

I pictured Lori coming home discovering her things sitting next to the door. I tried imagining how she would feel. Following through with this step had to be a heartbreaking decision for Debbie.

Why did I sell Lori our car? I truly felt she wouldn't be staying out overnight, if she didn't have a vehicle to travel around with so freely. Without the car, she would have had to stay at home.

"Let's pray that the shock of finding out that you aren't going to put up with her behavior anymore will make her see where she's headed," I said.

"I told her in the letter that I couldn't live like this any longer and that the kids could stay with us until she straightened her life out."

"We'll have to see what happens. If I hear from her, I'll call you," I answered, hoping that Debbie's decision to put Lori out of her house would work out as we hoped.

Debbie called a few hours later and said Lori had called her when she found her things on the porch. She was stunned that her sister had kicked her out of the house. Even though there was a valid reason for her action, Debbie felt awful. I sat home praying Debbie had done the right thing and for God to protect Lori no matter where she was or what she was doing.

Bringing Lori Home

For four months, Lori bounced from staying at the Motel 6 in Somerset, to a residence in Rhode Island with a male friend she had met while he had been a patient at Butler Hospital. I didn't know this man, but she had spoken about him in the past. She informed me that he had been admitted for drugs. How could I not think he was supplying her with them while she was spending time at his place? Maybe she took them while she lived with Jimmy when she was single; I had no way of knowing.

I kept getting the strongest urge to go to this motel and bring her home. Friends were saying that she had to reach "rock bottom." Instead of listening to them, I should have followed my heart and went to see her. Lori probably wanted to call out for help and was too sick. This stays buried deep within me to this day; more guilt to carry.

Lori was in desperate straits, and we gathered that her money would be running out soon. We thought her situation would have had her calling to come home. Our thinking was she'd reach out to her family when she got tired being separated, hopefully, reality would hit her. Maybe our thinking had been just as sick as her actions.

The next thing Al and I heard from Debbie was that Lori missed being in North Dighton and talked her girlfriend, Judy, into letting her rent her second floor apartment. Lori had convinced Judy that she could meet the payments and get a job once she settled into the dwelling. I thought maybe she had money left over from her settlement.

It was November 2005, and the weather was bitterly cold. Lori phoned to let us know where she was staying and that she was all right. It was a relief to hear from her. During the day, she babysat Judy's two daughters while Judy worked, and said that this balanced out the rent payment while she searched for a job.

I was mentally relieved knowing she was back in town. It was easier to keep on top of what she was doing. We were shocked to hear that she had been at Judy's for two months and hadn't visited Joey and Meagan. Judy's was less than ten minutes from Debbie's house.

Al and I were blind to how she had been living, until we got a surprise call one afternoon from Judy. "Mrs. Sequeira, I need to talk to you about Lori."

"Is she okay?"

"She's not giving me anything for rent. We had agreed she could stay as long as she got a job."

Because Lori had told me something different, I just sat and listened.

"I can't keep her here, and I don't want to call the police, but she won't leave."

"We'll come to see her. What's your address?" I grabbed a piece of paper to write the information down. We knew Judy, but we had never been to her house.

"We're going out tonight, but my husband's red, Ford pickup truck is parked out front. You can't miss it."

"Thanks, we'll look for it."

Around five o'clock, Al and I got into the car and traveled forty minutes to Dighton. With the time change, dark had come early. We had to drive slowly because the road had no street lights, and we couldn't see the numbers on the houses.

A red truck caught my eye as we passed a house that was set back from the street behind a few trees.

"Lucky she told me about the red truck, or we never would have found this place," I said to Al.

We parked on the street and noticed that a floodlight lit the backyard. As we walked, we bumped into a toy carriage and other playthings that were scattered all over the front yard. We couldn't see our way around her property; because there were no front lights anywhere. I was surprised that Judy didn't have them on knowing that we were coming.

We walked toward the backyard and spotted Lori's white Pontiac parked behind the house. It was close to six months since I had last seen her and couldn't wait to go inside.

There were narrow steps on the side of the house that went up to the second floor. A dim light above the door on the small back deck gave only a faint glow. The tiny deck could hardly accommodate the two of us as we stood by the door. I had to watch myself so I wouldn't slip backwards off the steps.

I knocked on the door, but there was no answer.

"I don't think she's home," I said. "It's so dark inside."

"She has to be, her car is here. Let me try the door." Al stated.

Al turned the door knob, and it opened.

"Lori?" I waited for a reply and called a little louder. "Lori?"

Still no answer. We entered into a small, empty living room with hardwood floors. I felt the icy cold hit me. Instantly, a chill went through my bones.

"God, it's freezing in here!" I shouted, rubbing my shoulders.

It was a two room apartment with a small stove and refrigerator in the kitchen. Lori's belongings were in a few green trash bags that sat against the living room wall. A bare rocker in the corner was the only furniture. I saw a pillow on the floor with no bedding. Her small 13" television with rabbit-ear antennas sat on the floor. I felt sick. I realized my daughter was sleeping on this hard floor with no blankets to cover her and the heat turned off. How could Judy be so heartless?

I walked back into the kitchen area, and there wasn't one item on the counters. I opened the refrigerator only to discover bare shelves. Not one piece of meat or a can of juice was in there—nothing!

I'd been home, warm, in a comfortable bed with a stocked refrigerator, and she was alone with nothing to eat or drink. *What was she living on? What happened to all her money?* All I thought about was her going to bed hungry and waking up starving. *Why didn't she feel close enough to call us for help?* She never once told me that she had nothing. During one conversation, she had mentioned that Judy had given her an air mattress to sleep on.

Al opened a closed door off the living room. It went directly into a bedroom with twin beds. Dolls were laid out on both beds. I gathered the room must have been her two daughters' sleeping quarters. Once we entered the room, the heat hit me.

"I hear a radio or a television," Al remarked as we walked through the bedroom to investigate the sound.

I followed him to a stairway leading downstairs. We descended into Judy's living room and found Lori lying on a couch watching television. She had a glass in her hand the content of which I assumed was liquor.

"Mom...Al, hi, what are you doing here?" she asked with a big smile, surprised seeing us standing in Judy's living room.

"Judy called me today." I replied.

"She did? Why?"

"She told us that she has been asking you to leave, and you wouldn't."

We could tell by her slow actions, that she'd been drinking. Her eyes were glassy. It had been so long since we last saw Lori that I was happy to see her even in this condition.

"Really! I've been good enough to help her with her kids to save her babysitting money, and now she doesn't want me?"

I studied Lori as she spoke and couldn't fathom how my precious daughter could allow herself to get into this situation because of her drinking. She had lost all her roots and had been stubbornly going from one place to another, when all she had to do was make a call to us.

Why did I go along with the belief that an alcoholic had to reach rock bottom? How much deeper did she have to go to reach it? Why didn't I look for her sooner and take her home?

Al sat on the couch next to her and put his arm around her. "Lori, you don't want to live like this. Let's get your things and get out of here. We want you to come home with us."

I can't describe the emotions that went through me when Al showed so much love toward her.

"I'm so glad you two came for me," she said as she got off the couch trying to keep her balance.

How many months had she been hoping for someone to come for her?

The three of us went up the stairs. When we reached her living room, I asked her, "Lori, what have you been sleeping on?"

"Judy took the air mattress from me."

What did she expect you to sleep on?"

"I don't think she cared."

"Why is it so cold in here?" I asked.

"She turned the heat off. I guess she figured it would get me to leave."

"That's against the law," Al said angrily. "She didn't even give you blankets for God's sake! What's wrong with that girl?"

How did my precious daughter come to live like this? I couldn't believe Judy would treat Lori like this. They had been friends, or so I thought.

Lori grabbed the few trash bags in the corner.

"Are those all your things?"

"This is all I have, Mom. Just these and my television set."

What absolute heartbreak. All my daughter's belongings were in a few trash bags. Her furniture was still in storage. I read and heard about alcoholics living this way, but it wasn't supposed to happen to my child.

We packed her car, and she hugged Al. "Thanks again for coming for me."

"Al, why don't you drive her car home? I'll follow in ours," I said

"Okay." He opened the passenger door for Lori.

"I can drive my car," she said.

"I don't think so. You just sit back and relax while I drive," he said with an arm around her.

When we arrived at our home, we took Lori's bags and placed them in the sunroom. I immediately went upstairs to the spare bedroom and turned on the electric blanket for her. Before we left to pick her up, I had placed a picture of Joey and Meagan on the nightstand by her bed. I wondered how many places this poor girl had landed since she left Debbie's.

I went into the living room, and sat on the couch. It was close to 9:30 pm and Lori came in and laid down with her back against me with her head touching my chest. I wrapped my arms around her and pulled my thirty-eight-year-old daughter close to me; just as I had done when she was a child.

"I'm so glad you came for me, Mom."

She was inebriated, but I didn't care. I held her tighter.

"If you only knew how good it feels with you holding me."

To this day, those words and that moment are embedded in my mind, wondering how many times she had needed my arms and love wrapped around her while drifting from one location to another; not having any family members near her. Lori was very much a family person and loved being in everyone's company. We had left her trying to find her own way far too long.

"It feels good to me too, Lori." I ran my fingers through her tangled hair. It looked like it needed combing. I wondered what terrible and lonely things had happened since she strayed away from all of us.

I prayed the rosary daily for her, and no one could have prayed deeper from the heart. I couldn't understand her suffering or comprehend my daughter having nothing in her life but the bottle.

She asked me, "Why can Debbie drink, and I can't?"

"...because she didn't inherit this terrible disease," I answered.

This cruel demon possessed my loving daughter and turned her into a lost soul. There was a time when she was so happy with life and her family. She loved Joey and Meagan beyond anything and had been so proud of them. Now she was with me with no place to call her own anymore. This illness had even separated her from the close friends she had been with since grammar school. Most of all, her addiction had separated her from her children.

I knew that she felt worthless and guilty for constantly disappointing us. This confusion in her life had her blind to the disease that was killing her. She still didn't identify herself as being an alcoholic. It was the disease that was turning her life inside out. The demon had put a tight grip on her and wouldn't let go. She had no peace and felt no love from any of us. We let her struggle to find her own way instead of pulling her back into our lives. The sad part was that everyone she needed was right in front of her, but she didn't see it. She didn't want to face the reality of what alcohol was doing to her. At this stage, alcoholics need assistance instead of being left to fend for themselves.

We stayed locked in an embrace for an hour. Finally I told her to get comfortable upstairs. I followed her into the bedroom where I had laid out a pair of warm, winter pajamas on top of her heated blanket. She headed toward the bathroom.

"Take a nice, warm bath, honey, and get into bed." I remembered back to the visit to my parents' home in Hull after my divorce. My father had filled the tub with hot, scented water for me to soak my tired body in. After I had felt so lost and alone, his thoughtfulness left me with memories of love for a lifetime.

I went downstairs where Al wanted to talk to me while we were alone.

"I had a good talk with Lori on the way home."

"…What about?" I asked.

"When Lori got into the car, she said, 'I don't know how to thank you for coming for me."

I told her, "You don't have to thank us. All we want is for you to get well, and that would be the best thanks you could give us. You just relax and get some rest for a few days, get your strength back, and then we'll talk about what we'll do. We love you, and so do Brian and Debbie. You've got two beautiful kids who love and need you with them. Just concern yourself with getting better and taking care of you, and don't worry about anything else. You don't want to be like this, nervous and shaky, not being able to function properly and having to depend on strangers. Your family will always be there for you, no matter what the circumstances. Your mother will be stress free having you living with us. I'm sure Debbie, Brian, and the kids will feel better knowing your safe. We know this struggle hasn't been easy for you, not having money coming in, and your mother has been worried sick about how you were getting by. We didn't know the conditions you were living in, we thought you were doing fine."

Al continued, "Lori told me that she didn't know Judy wanted her out. She explained how she had babysat her kids when they went out and stayed in her room most of the time."

"What did you say to her about that remark?" I asked him.

"Well, I told her you never know people until you live with them," and she said, 'Isn't that the truth!"

"So, she seemed content coming here?"

"I think she's happy being rescued."

After a half hour, I went up to see how Lori was doing, and she was getting under the covers.

"Boy is this warm! It's so nice," she said with a huge smile, pulling the covers up to her neck.

I wondered how long it had been since she had a bed to sleep in. I couldn't fathom my daughter going through this turmoil. This wasn't the life she or Debbie had growing up while they lived with me. As much as I had struggled as a single mother, I had food on the table, heat in the house, clothed them both, and had given them support and love.

I smiled back. It was like putting my small child to bed again.

She spotted Joey and Meagan's picture. "You put the kid's picture in here!"

"I want you to look at them every day, Lori. Those are the two best reasons for you to get well. They miss you."

"Thanks, Mom."

I kissed her. "Go to sleep and worry only about getting better. We'll help you through this."

I closed her door; having her with us I felt peace for the first time in years.

Battling the Demons

While Lori was staying with us, Al and I were surprised that she had no withdrawal symptoms after stopping her drinking routine cold turkey. She became energized and started to read the New Bedford Standard Times, the local newspaper, searching for jobs in the area and sending her resume out again.

Al and I took her to the unemployment office in the south end of New Bedford after a few days of letting her relax with us. We explained to her that she needed the assistance to meet her necessities. Lori sat quietly in the large waiting room that contained about thirty people and watched everyone as they were called one by one to sign up for benefits. She felt defeated and degraded, believing the people around her were of a different social class. Her pride kept her from taking any low paying position to get started; she had held a high paying management position and wanted nothing less.

Lori was excited when a nursing home called after receiving her resume and wanted to interview her for an accounting position. It was in New Bedford, and Al offered to take her to the interview because the one-way streets in town were confusing.

New Bedford, Massachusetts, is the world's most famous whaling- era seaport and the number one fishing port in America. It has many fishing fleets and hundreds of fishing boats, many individually owned. This city is filled with unique architecture in its beautiful colonial buildings. The attractions include the Zeiterion Theatre, the Whaling Museum, and many fine restaurants offering the freshest seafood from various fish processing plants located by the water, along with the enjoyment of strolling down the cobblestone streets that bring you back in history. Summertime offers outside entertainment with singers and plays, and many open air festivals. There are also numerous local wineries in the surrounding communities.

When Lori went in for her interview, Al and I sat in the car talking. I felt so strong that she'd get the position with the accounting department in this facility because she had all the qualifications they said were needed to fill this position. She had always wanted to be in the medical field and this position might give her security.

She came out looking confident. "It was right up my alley. I've worked on the whole computer system they have, and I knew their language terms. The woman actually seemed impressed with me."

I felt hope build up inside me. She needed something of her own to fight for again.

Once we pulled into our yard, Lori thanked Al. "I don't think I would have ever found that location if you didn't take me."

It was wonderful hearing her appreciation of our help. I was finally getting the opportunity to be in her life again.

When she wanted to attend the first AA meeting at the First Congregational Church in Marion, our hearts leaped with joy. It was only fifteen minutes down the street from us. She was happy showing me her AA pamphlet that listed where the meetings were in our area.

That night, the sky had opened up with a steady, heavy downpour of rain that flooded the streets. Because it was nighttime and she wasn't familiar with the area, the torrential rain would have been nerve-racking for her trying to find the location. It was hard to see two feet in front of you. Al offered to drive her and pick her up around 9:00 pm when the meeting ended. He was back home by 7 pm.

Having some time to myself, I decided to wash all her clothes that were pushed tightly into the two garbage bags in the sunroom, where they had been since we brought her home. As I started to divide the whites and colors, I came across an empty, 1.75 liter vodka bottle. Digging down deeper, there were a couple more, all were empty.

"Al, look at all the liquor bottles. She hides them in-between the clothes!"

Al came over and looked into the bag. He put his hand in and came out with more. "Here are a few fifths," he said.

By the time we had emptied the clothes basket, it added up to over four gallons of empty Vodka bottles. Al and I decided to check her car out. He found more under the driver's seat and on the back floor in the car. I was shocked. Her car looked like her father's when the vehicle had been left in our yard after his death.

I was shaken to see that she hid liquor in her car and between clothes. The reality of her being addicted this badly to liquor was mind-boggling. Hearing that she had been drinking too much had been one thing, but actually seeing that she was at the point of hiding liquor to sneak drinks was another.

My God, when did she get this out-of-control with her drinking?

Lori was never drunk at family functions. Like her father, she must have done her drinking when she was alone.

Al took the bottles and put them into the recycle bin in the garage, and we didn't say a word to Lori about finding the bottles. This was the same action I had done in my marriage with her father; not talking about the incidents as they had occurred.

I washed, dried, and ironed some of her clothes and put them in the closet in her bedroom. I thought she'd feel better about herself if she could see them on hangers, instead of having to pull winkled clothes out of trash bags.

After a few weeks, Lori seemed happy going to the AA meetings. She talked about the men and women in the group and how much she enjoyed them. A week before Christmas, the group was having a holiday party. Lori went to a bakery and bought a large assortment of pastries. It was the first time she seemed excited going to meet friends.

I pulled out a large, black, heavy plastic party platter that I had put away for an occasion of this sort and this event seemed like the perfect time to use it. Slowly, I started to place the cookies, muffins, and small individual cuts of different flavored cake pieces on it. I wrapped a green, see-through cling wrap around the platter of desserts and twisted the top tying it with a red and white striped, decorative tie. She was thrilled carrying the package out to her car.

Al and I were so hopeful and happy to see that she was excited joining an AA group in our area.

Around ten o'clock, she arrived back, raving about how the members enjoyed the pastry and commented on how professionally wrapped the package had looked. I could see how special she felt. This small gesture seemed to connect her to the new group.

Lori waited weeks to hear back from five companies she had interviewed with. No one called her from other locations where she had filled out job applications. She was especially disheartened that the nursing facility hadn't called. I felt each disappointment for her. She was certainly qualified, having twelve years of experience managing a huge payroll department. I couldn't understand what was missing. Instead of valuing her position and responsibilities, they seemed to be penalizing her for being over qualified.

I started to let my guard down and didn't worry about her drinking while she was staying with us. After all, she was on the road to recovery, or so we thought. One evening, Al and I were talking at the kitchen table waiting for her to come back from an AA meeting. I thought my eye caught her stumble coming through the kitchen door. My heart sank.

"Where have you been, Lori?" I asked.

"I went to a meeting."

"No you didn't. Look at you!"

"Why, what's wrong?"

"What's wrong? You're drunk!" Al said in a disappointing, but quiet tone.

"No, I'm not."

"How can you say that? You can't even stand up!" He remarked, surprised by her denial.

"I'm standing."

"You're swaying."

We were startled that she stood there, obviously inebriated, and *insisted* that she was sober. I felt defeated. She was killing herself. It was the first time Al and I had ever seen her drunk and openly lying about it. She was in denial about her dependence on drinking. I couldn't believe that she had been living this way for years. Since we lived so far away, she could hide the drinking from us. If Debbie hadn't kept us updated, we never would have known the little that we did about her life, including her being an alcoholic.

Seeing her drunk made us feel as if she had taken a big fall backward. I never thought she would drink in front of us, her parents. We knew that discussing the situation with her in her drunken state was useless, so we let her go to bed to sleep it off. I was glad to see that she made it home safely.

The next morning, she came into the kitchen. I'm sure that if she could have sneaked out of the house through some side door without confronting us, she would have done so. I knew she dreaded facing us.

"Lori, you're not trying to stop drinking at all," I said to her as she poured a cup of coffee.

"I slipped one night, Mom."

"You need to get a sponsor; someone who understands this disease."

"I haven't found anyone who I feel comfortable with at meetings."

"Are you asking anyone to sponsor you?"

"People aren't as outgoing as you think when you walk into a meeting."

"You've been telling us how you liked everyone in this group. You're very friendly, Lori, so it's hard to believe that no one will approach you."

"I'll try at my next meeting."

Two days later, she informed us that she was going to Debbie's for a visit. "I have to take Meagan to her annual doctor's appointment today."

"You're coming home after that, I hope," Al questioned.

"I'll call you; I may stay over if Debbie lets me."

"She works, and the kids have school, so why would you stay over?" I asked.

"Please, don't tell me that I can't go to my sister's house and be with my kids. I'm not a child!"

I hated to give her the third degree, but I didn't trust her. She planned things that we knew weren't good. Al and I were trying everything we knew to control her and the drinking. She had her own mind. I was becoming mentally exhausted watching her every step and waiting to see what she was going to do.

I didn't realize how I was back to my old routine of years ago, looking at the clock and wondering if she were coming home and in what state. The only thing I didn't see was any desire or fight to give up the drinking. Not once did she open up about wanting to get out of this dark hole that was swallowing her. This kind of life seemed normal to her.

"I'll be with the kids and Debbie. I'll call you," she said smiling while giving us a kiss and hug before heading toward the back door.

"We're going to plan on you for supper," Al said, hoping to lock her into returning.

"I'll be home by then," she said with a grin. It was hard getting upset with her. She was never rude or disrespectful; if anything, she showed love toward us all the time.

Suppertime came and went. A little after six o'clock the phone rang.

"Hi, Mom."

"Where are you?"

"At Debbie's, but I'm going over to see Paula before I leave."

Two alcoholics getting together—late at night! I knew that Al and I confronting Lori a few days ago about her drinking was enough to send her running to distance herself from us. Whenever Paula and Lori got together, it seemed to lead to a drinking spree, but neither of them believed they were alcoholics.

"I don't think that's a good idea, honey," I said, very upset.

"Why? What do you expect us to do?"

"You're leaving yourself wide open to drink."

"I'm sorry you're upset, but I haven't seen Paula in weeks. I'll let you know, if I go," she said politely.

She hung up, and I knew she wouldn't be home.

"What did she say?" Al asked.

"She's going to Paula's."

"Oh, boy, we won't be seeing her tonight."

"I have bad vibes about this," I said walking out of the kitchen.

Lori called a few hours later. "I'm at Paula's."

"You've been drinking," I could tell by her voice. I hated reprimanding her like a child, but having my suspicions confirmed infuriated me.

"No, I haven't."

"Are you coming home tonight?" She didn't answer. "Is this a guessing game?" Even as I asked the question, I knew I didn't want her driving after she'd been drinking.

"I don't like confrontations, Mom."

"I don't either. The longer you stay away, the worse the situation gets. We can discuss this if you come home."

I heard Paula in the background advising Lori in what to say. I became angry.

"I don't need Paula throwing answers at you. This is between us!" I snapped.

Besides the argument we had had on her wedding night, this was the second time the two of us had openly been upset with each other.

Paula got on the phone and at the top of her lungs yelled, "So, we fucked-up, big deal!"

She went on and on, the foul language increasing as she ranted. Shocked at her behavior, I hung up.

I could feel my insides shaking. I was determined not to call them back. *Let them drink themselves to death.* I was sick of trying to control and watch Lori's every move.

In seconds the phone rang, and I was tempted not to answer it, hoping they'd have some guilt about their behavior. Knowing her father's past behavior, I knew questioning Lori about her actions would have been another excuse to stay out. I controlled my rage, and picked up the receiver without saying anything. I was frustrated and furious.

"Tante?" it was Paula. She always called me aunt in French. "I shouldn't have sworn at you. I'm sorry."

"You're right, you shouldn't have. I accept your apology." I tried to sound calm while my insides were racing. I was frantic, having no control over their drinking and not being able to wake them up to the road they were on; they were heading to disaster.

"Lori's staying over, and we don't want you to be upset. I know we've been drinking, but we'll be okay. Please, don't worry about us. We'll spend the night talking. She'll call you in the morning."

I hung up with tears of aggravation running down my face. I knew Lori had to be in bad shape if she was avoiding the chance to talk to me. I was tired of trying to discipline my child who was now an adult. I was irritated knowing she couldn't see any harm in staying at Paula's, but I knew it was an excuse to drink. Lori was walking head on into a runaway freight train, and was doing nothing to avoid it; so was Paula. I was frantic thinking that we were going to lose both of them.

Lori was constantly making bad decisions and now she was playing with her life. How much abuse could her liver take? She looked at her family as smothering, controlling, and not letting her live the way she wanted. It was rare that Lori ever made the effort to visit Joey and Meagan. I was shocked that her love for them wasn't strong enough to keep them in her life. I believe the neglect of her kids was the most devastating. They were suffering because of her absence.

The next morning, our fears were confirmed. It was ten o'clock and no Lori. I could feel the nightmare starting. I didn't know what else to do to help her. Disappearing and staying out all night had to be the same agony Brian and Debbie were going through day after day, waiting for her to come home.

I called Debbie at work. "Have you heard from your sister?" I asked.

"I spoke to Aunt Anita this morning, and she said they left for her cabin in New Hampshire."

"Oh, no, that means only one thing!"

"We'll have to wait it out," Debbie said.

The family surmised that once Paula and Lori were in New Hampshire at the Lopes cabin, there would be days of non-stop drinking. We heard Paula had broken up with her boyfriend and knew that she had to be feeling depressed. All an alcoholic needs is an excuse. Lori felt she had parents that were trying to control her every move. She had no money, but Paula's parents, Anita and Sonny, owned the cabin, so they were comfortable to stay as long as they wanted.

A few days went by, and my nerves were getting the better of me.

I called Anita. "Did Paula call you?"

"Yes, she hurt her back, and said she can't drive home right now."

"She didn't hurt her back, Anita. They're up there drinking. Why can't Lori drive home?"

"You're probably right. I didn't think of that."

"Well, I guess our hands are tied. I'm not driving three hours to talk to them while they're high." I was mad and had no way of venting my feelings of hopelessness.

Ten days went by before Lori called. "I'm back at Paula's, and I'll be home in a few days."

"Why do you have to wait a few days?"

"I know you're upset, and I don't want to fight."

"Who says we'll fight?"

Paula picked up. "I told her that she has to go home."

I couldn't help but wonder if Paula's boyfriend had come back. Lori had told me that, during their relationship, it had been a normal routine for them to break up and then get back together. That might have been the reason why she now wanted Lori to go home.

Paula continued, "We talked a lot over the week, mostly about how close my mother and I are. You know, all week Lori kept saying, 'I wish that I had a mother that I was....' *Click!*

The phone went dead. I knew Lori had hung it up on Paula. She must have panicked thinking Paula was going to finish by saying, "...that I was close to." Stunned, I sat in the kitchen chair. I felt so much pain, thinking she felt no closeness to me. I couldn't even tell Al what she had said. The remark was so cutting it broke my heart.

Did she actually hate me? I was always there if she needed me!

I never stopped worrying about what she was doing to herself? This time I didn't blame the liquor for her remark.

The next day, Lori pulled into the driveway.

"Lori, you look awful." Al stated when she walked into the kitchen.

"Thanks, Al," she answered sarcastically.

"It's true." Al stated. "You don't look good at all, Lori. You've been drinking for nearly two weeks straight, and it's obvious that you can't control it. You're going to have to go to a detox center again. You need professional help because we aren't reaching you."

"Lori, you have to get back to a rehab so they can help you," I said.

"I know, but I want to go to Gosnold. I won't return to Butler Hospital." She never fought being admitted to a rehabilitation center. I could see the physical damage nearly two weeks of drinking had done to her. She was pale and extremely thin, and her eyes seemed sunken in with large brown circles under them. There was no denying her organs were being damaged. She needed help, and fast.

"That's fine, Lori, we'll call," I said.

Al and I never raised our voice to her as she had feared. That afternoon we called Gosnold Rehabilitation, and the girl in the admission office said we could get her into their facility in three days.

Fortunately, she was still insured as part of her divorce settlement. She spent the whole day on the couch watching television. I'm sure that she wanted to detach from us. I wouldn't be surprised if she hated herself for falling again and disappointing us.

Thinking back, it was another moment in my life that I wished I could have lived over. I should have sat with an arm around her telling her how much I loved her to give her assurance. I should have asked what she feared, what she felt, or what she needed and wanted from me.

We needed to communicate. Instead, we sat on opposite chairs in the living room, in silence, watching television for hours. A day ago, I had heard that she didn't feel close to me, and there I was sitting, making no effort to reach out to her and show her the complete love that I had for her. As unbelievable as it may sound, I was waiting for her to have the desire to reach out to me. I didn't want to push her, but I should have.

Oh, the mistakes we make in life in loving relation-ships. Everyone waits for the other to make a move. We let precious moments pass that would be better used showing the person how much love we really have for them. We are human beings who need to love and be loved to survive. A person living without these needs fulfilled can drown in depression and hopelessness.

I should have been showing Lori that I was there for her emotionally. I let too many moments go by when she felt emptiness and needed me to listen to her. I didn't fill that need that day or on so many others. Maybe she didn't talk because she was scared or because she had no desire to share her feelings. Her fears were held deep down inside.

Lori and I slowly followed the same unresponsive path that her father and I had taken by not talking. She never argued, fought, yelled, or swore at me or any other family member. She had the greatest personality. After an incident, she'd admit that she was wrong. We couldn't get mad at her. That's what broke our hearts. She was such a sweet girl. It was the disease that controlled all of us. We knew that she couldn't get well until she wanted to fight and ask for help.

I was blind in not seeing that Lori had reached the point of not only just wanting a drink, but also of being alcohol dependent. By now the alcohol held power over her. She was probably increasing the amount of drinks because it took more alcohol to relieve or avoid withdrawal symptoms. Drinking would stop the shakes or quell a hangover.

I was denying Lori emotional support without realizing it. I was the one who should have talked to her. She needed all the love I could have given her instead of my asking her *why* she kept drinking or *why* she wasn't going for help. The demon had wrapped itself around her and had drained her of the strength to fight back. It owned her.

She had lost her father, her first real love, Jimmy, and two husbands. All the men she had loved were gone. Her family seemed distanced from her. She had separated from her children, lost her home, job, and close friends. Everyone who meant the most to her seemed out of her reach. How alone that poor girl had to feel. She used to be the life of the party. That world we call *normal* had disappeared from her life. She had been such a happy girl who had lit up a room when she entered.

It's not easy for me to admit my faults, realizing too late, that the doors were open for me to do more to help Lori get better. There might have been more of a chance for her to have the desire for recovery seeing and feeling her family supporting her. We should never give up on our children when they need us, especially with a disease they can't control. Parents need to show the love. Don't hide it. Show your fear of losing them. Do everything humanly possible to get them help.

Paula and Scott

Paula

The Emerson House

I accompanied Al as he drove Lori to the Gosnold-Thorne Clinic in Falmouth, Massachusetts. We walked her inside the building, but when the aids came for her, we weren't allowed to go any further. We kissed her and watched her through the glass on the swinging doors as she walked down the long corridor. She was again alone to fight her demons.

My heart was breaking. She was so sick. Her everyday normal routine was gone. Attending and enjoying family events and social functions like any normal woman had disappeared. Now, her days were spent behind closed doors at a hospital all alone without anyone by her side. I can't imagine the feelings she must have had at night, lying in the dark, locked up, wondering what had happened to her. The last three years of her life had been a nightmare.

This was her second stay at Gosnold and her third time at a rehabilitation hospital. I wanted so badly to get into counseling with her. I planned to ask this time.

I feared the doctor's prediction of her dying from liver failure. It had been two years since the doctor had told her how serious her illness was. I knew that the two weeks in New Hampshire affected her health negatively, and she was now in an extremely dangerous situation. How was a week's stay going to cure her? There had to be more deeply rooted problems that she felt she couldn't share with me. I felt strongly that there were emotional issues eating at her, but something was keeping her from talking about them.

Officials kept her for a week in the detox center and wanted to send her to the Emerson House, a rehabilitation facility on the same grounds for women.

When Al and I tried to schedule a family meeting with her, Barbara, one of the counselors, called us and said, "I'm sorry; she doesn't want a meeting."

"Why? How can we help her if she pushes us away?"

"I can't force her into allowing you to attend her counseling."

"She never opens up with me, I can't understand why." I said.

"Lori has told me that she has been scared since she was little and has no idea why."

The news felt like someone was tearing my heart out with a knife. My daughter had been suffering silently, being frightened since she was a child, and I never knew it. Lori always acted upbeat and in high spirits. Her friends filled our house daily when she was growing up. She never moped around the house or stayed home. I couldn't fathom her being sick back then. How was I to know? She never talked to me about her fears, about drinking too often, or being scared.

Barbara continued, "The Emerson House is where the women go for heavy counseling. You're daughter is really sick and has deep emotional problems. Her insurance is willing to pay for it. We're trying to convince her that she needs to stay more than a week. The longer we keep her, the better chance she has of fighting this disease."

How can I explain the deep terror when Barbara said those things, and my daughter didn't want to share them with me?

"I'm worried about her drinking. She's been in rehab three times, and I'm afraid that she'll die from this," I said breaking down into loud sobs.

"I spoke to Lori today. I truly believe that she belongs in long term care. It's a three month program. I sent her to the administration office to fill out the papers. I feel that she is illegible to have the insurance pay for it."

"We'd love her to be in a program that long, Barbara, the longer the better."

"I find that Lori is very fragile and has a lot of issues to deal with. She needs to stay here. We can't force her. She's fighting to do it on her own."

"I'm the one with the answers that she's probably looking for; I lived that life. I'm afraid that she'll refuse the help."

"She may not agree to this. If she doesn't, there's only one other solution. If you consider her to be harmful to herself by not being able to give up drinking, we can go to court for a Section 35."

"What's Section 35?"

"We would show the court that her liver is in danger of not functioning and that the three rehabilitations did nothing to help her. That would be reason enough. We could fight for a longer stay than the 30 days."

"That wouldn't be hard to prove."

"It wouldn't be easy going forward with court action. I want you to be aware of what it entails." She took a deep breath and continued, "She'd be picked-up by the police and handcuffed. They'd send her to a facility, and she'd be with some tough women."

My heart sank. "Do you think we have to take this drastic step?"

She'd hate us forever. What if someone hurt her in there? My head was spinning.

"Let's wait and see if she signs the papers because we're shooting for three months, and we'll go from there.

Being able to wait to make such a serious decision took some pressure off me. The action might have to be taken to save her life if she refused the stay.

Barbara added, "If you fear her dying from this disease, this next action is for the best. Lori may not think so at the time. Talk to your husband about this, and I'll see if Lori will have a meeting with you two on Wednesday. I'll call you tomorrow."

"Why is she too scared to talk to me?"

"I can't tell you about the conversations I have with Lori, they're private."

"You can tell me that she's scared, frightened, and fragile, but I can't have any part in helping her recover."

"I'm sorry, Mrs. Sequeira."

"You're sorry? I never knew Lori had been this sick emotionally all her life. You'll never know what this is doing to me, not being allowed in any of her counseling sessions. I feel this is the only way she'll get better."

"I'll let you know what Lori decides in the morning."

The next day, Barbara called. "Lori doesn't want a meeting with you."

"Why is she so petrified to meet with me? I don't understand it! I can't help her with these issues if she rejects me."

"There's some good news. Lori has agreed to go into a long term session, if it's approved."

Within a few days, Debbie called from Lopes Construction saying their company insurance was going to pick up Lori's stay. All of us were thrilled; they had approved three full months. I was hoping during that time, she'd agree to go to a meeting with just me and the counselor.

Debbie took Kerri, Michael, Joey, and Meagan to see Lori after she had moved to the Emerson House. Al and I alternated the times of our visits with Debbie, so that Lori would have more visits with family members. Lori made sure we weren't alone to have private conversations or to allow me the opportunity to cover subjects she didn't want to talk about. Because she had prevented herself to open up to me, our talks were light and didn't give us a chance to talk about her pain and fears.

Once we entered the Emerson House, I could understand why Lori wanted to come back there. Butler Hospital in Providence, Rhode Island had a state hospital atmosphere while Emerson felt more like a home. All the girls' bedrooms, which we weren't allowed to see, were on the top floor to give them privacy. They had a large kitchen with tables and multiple chairs, and there was a very relaxed atmosphere in the large living room. There was another small room near the entrance which was used as an office for the girls to report to before being admitted, or for needing requests filled.

Many black, trash bags and small suitcases containing the girls' belongings were on the floor near the office. I had let Lori use luggage to pack her clothes. The front porch was large, and the girls often took their breaks out there. They also had the privilege to walk on the grounds near the house. The location was on a main road in Falmouth, but the house could easily be mistaken for a private home.

The girls living there were very friendly. Lori seemed to be happy being with everyone. She was still acting like a leader instead of a follower. You would never know, from her actions, that Lori had any problems in her life.

She passed out copies of a prayer that I had given her. She had hand written it for the girls. The prayer is called *Come Holy Spirit;* I had given her the prayer card a few years back hoping to give her comfort. She loved it and so did the other women. On my next visit, I donated 500 of the prayer cards to the home. The girls were lined up to take them before I could get them out of the box. Lori helped me pass them out.

The prayer card reads:

"Come, Holy Spirit"
my Light, my Life, my Love, my Strength,
be with me now, and always:
in all my doubts, anxieties and trials,
Come, Holy Spirit;
in the hours of loneliness, weariness and grief,
Come, Holy Spirit;
in failure, in loss and in disappointment,
Come, Holy Spirit;
when others fail me, when I fail myself,

Come, Holy Spirit;
when I am ill, unable to work, depressed,
Come, Holy Spirit;
now and forever in all things.

When we left, I felt that Lori would be getting the proper help at last. Debbie called around 6:00 pm to tell me that Lori had phoned Brian and spoke to him for a long time. Debbie told me of the conversation.

Lori told Brian, "I was in my group meeting today, and I was scared to talk."

"Why?"

"Brian, I'm afraid of breaking down and crying."

"You've got to open up and get rid of your hang-ups," Brian said.

"The girls in the group asked me why I didn't want to stay at the Emerson House. I couldn't find an excuse so I said that I needed to get my mail."

"What did the girls say?"

"They laughed their heads off. They said it wasn't a reason, it was an excuse to get out, and that they knew my reasoning."

"Take things slowly, Lori. Open up a little. Talking will get easier the longer you stay."

"I'll try. Tonight a group of us are going to an AA meeting somewhere in Falmouth. A bus is taking us."

"You take care of yourself and listen to what they say."

"I will. Talk soon."

Lori loved Brian. He was so easy for her to talk to on any subject.

One afternoon, Debbie went to see Lori with Joe and Meagan. They stayed forty-five minutes.

"Lori had a different attitude today, Mom. She finally talked to the kids about drinking and drugs, which was a big step for her. It was the first time that she talked to her kids about her illness."

Lori told Debbie, "I learned a lot about what happens to certain cells in the brain from drinking. I made a huge mistake going to New Hampshire to the cabin with Paula."

"At least you know it now," Debbie said.

"I told the group that I felt smothered by Al and Mom."

"What did they say?"

"Someone told me that it's normal for parents to worry."

"They're scared that you won't get better, Lori."

"The counselors told me to write two pages on what dramatic things happened in my life and another essay from my birth to the present," Lori said.

"That's good. Don't be afraid to open up," Debbie told her, trying to get her to find the strength to talk about her past.

Debbie told me that it had been the first hopeful sign she had ever seen of Lori talking openly about the disease and seeing things differently. Lori wanted to learn to stand up for herself and not be afraid to say what she thinks about something.

I was heartbroken that she didn't want to open up with me. I couldn't understand why she was afraid of me. I had so many answers about her past that might have helped her. I couldn't imagine what I could have done to her in the past that she would put up a shield between us. I realized then that I never should have let years go by without talking to her about the past when we did have moments alone.

The following day, Debbie took only Kerri and Meagan to visit Lori. The counselors allowed Lori to go with them to downtown Falmouth. Lori had four hours allotted to her, so they spent the day having their nails done, shopping at a jewelry store and eating at a restaurant. It was a girls' day out. Debbie said everyone had fun. I actually felt jealous that Lori shared her inner thoughts and pain with Debbie and locked me out.

A week later, Lori asked me to bring my cream colored blouse for her to wear to a party they were having for the women in a few days. We dropped it off, and Al and I thought it was a private affair and left after spending some time with her.

Two days passed before she called me. "We had our event this morning. I wish you had come, Mom."

"You didn't say anything about us being allowed to come. We thought it was a private party at the home."

"For the first time I got up and talked about my life."

"Oh, Lori, why didn't you invite us? I would have been thrilled to hear you talk."

My daughter had opened up about her life, and I had missed it. Nothing could have saddened me more.

"A girl came up to me and asked me questions about my life with drinking. It felt so good that someone would turn to me for help." Lori was so excited.

"Why not, Lori? You have a lot of compassion in you."

"It made me feel so good, Mom."

"It should. We're proud of you."

"Well, I've got to run. We'll talk later." She sounded so emotionally stable.

I hung up the phone feeling depressed. I had missed hearing my daughter talk about her fears. I might have gotten some insight about some of the things she kept hidden. She might have felt more comfortable to go into counseling with me. Maybe we could have moved on together in this battle. I told Al about her call and her talking in front of the girls.

"If you were there, she may not have felt free or comfortable to talk about those issues. Maybe it was for the best that we weren't there. She opened up. That's a healthy sign."

I thought that he might be right. Lori never opened up to me in private, so why would I think that she would in a room full of strangers with me present?

Halfway House

Three weeks passed, and my hopes went sky high that Lori would face the reality that she was an alcoholic and would work seriously with her counselors. She finally agreed to have one family meeting with Al and me. I was surprised she wanted Al in the meeting, but I think she feared being alone with me.

I wanted only to concentrate on the fact that she was welcoming me and was ready to share her past. She had another two months of counseling, and her recovery looked promising. She had come a long way in less than a month.

When we arrived and entered the counselor's room, I could see that Lori was uncomfortable being with us, or maybe just with me. She sat in the far corner completely separated from us and the counselor; her hands were shaking on her lap. I think back to that day and wonder how I could have again let an opportunity pass to question Lori about why she had the need to be so far from us. I had never been abusive to her, but it was obvious that she was scared. Why would she fear someone who has always loved her?

The counselor spoke first. "Lori has come a long way but still needs counseling. She has at least two weeks left before being evaluated. The director will be able to see if Lori wants to stay longer."

"What do you mean—if she *wants* to stay longer?" I could feel a panic alarm starting to go off inside of me.

"We're going to give Lori the option of going to a halfway house."

"I'm not comfortable with this," I replied.

"Why?" the counselor asked.

Lori sat without adding any comments. She depended on her counselor to do the talking to us.

I said firmly to the counselor, "We understood that this was going to be a long term stay, involving a full three months program. If she leaves, she's open to drinking again. This short stay isn't going to help her. Once she leaves here, she'll be right back to drinking."

We're giving her the choice to go to the halfway house."

"She has a home once she comes out," I remarked.

"I need to do this on my own," Lori stated, looking petrified at defending her decision.

"I'm not happy with this decision," I answered putting my head down in despair.

"Why, Mom? I'll be learning to stand on my own two feet again," Lori said.

"I think that the homes are good for people who have nowhere to go. You have a family."

"I have to do this alone."

"I don't believe that you can do any of this on your own. That's why you're back in rehab a third time. This disease is stronger than you realize." I didn't raise my voice or show anger. I kept myself calm. I didn't want her to be afraid to open up with me.

I continued, "Lori, if you were in this program three full months and then decided to go to a halfway home that would be different. Three weeks is not enough time, honey."

"I'm going to look for a job."

"You can do that living with us."

"I want to do it on my own."

"That's her choice," the counselor replied cutting in.

"Is it free to stay at the halfway house?" Al asked.

"It's $110 a week."

"And how does she get the money?" I asked the counselor, knowing Lori had nothing.

"She can get a job while she's living there."

"And what if she can't find one?"

"There's always someplace looking for help, whether its being a waitress or working at McDonalds. It's not about getting a high paying job. They have to start getting out in the working world again."

"If finding a job had been that easy, Lori would have had one already. She had a good paying job at Lopes Construction but doesn't want to settle for anything less."

I didn't want to knock Lori, but I knew the game she was playing. It happened too often. She wanted out so her counselor would stop digging into her past. She didn't *want* to talk about those events nor did she *want* to give up drinking. She had told Debbie that she was a social person and couldn't picture her life without a drink.

"There are rules that they have to follow, or they're kicked out," the counselor said. "If they can't meet the monthly payment, if they drink, or if they come in after curfew, they'll be asked to leave."

"And we start all over again," I stated, feeling strongly that was exactly what would happen.

"Where do you expect to get the money for the monthly payment, Lori?" Al asked, looking in her direction.

It was uncomfortable and odd to be talking to our daughter cuddled in a corner off in the distance of the room. Why wouldn't the counselor want to discuss this fear Lori held inside her? Wouldn't that have been a start to recovery? This meeting was an opportunity to open up as a family and reach my daughter.

"Well, I was hoping you'd pay the first week, and I'd pay you back when I get a job."

Lori was waiting for an answer. We both wanted to say no because the vibes were so strong that she wasn't going to stick to the rules or stay there. She wanted to go anywhere to get out of counseling, and the halfway house was the perfect opening. Lori may not have talked much to us, but Al and I knew her thoughts, yet we wanted to be supportive. We knew Lori loved us, but we also knew she was using us. An alcoholic will do anything to anyone to get the freedom to drink.

"We'll expect you to keep that promise," Al said.

"I have to go look at two locations," Lori said. "One is in Fall River, and the other is in Buzzards Bay."

"I'll take you when I pick you up," I stated.

I wasn't happy at all with her plans. I was angry that the facility was letting her out before the three months of rehabilitation were completed. If the counselors didn't offer Lori a choice, she would have accepted her long term stay. We knew that much about her. The treatment program didn't even begin to reach Lori about why she kept drinking or how serious her condition had become. I was starting to feel that finding out the reason for her continued drinking was more important than the abuse of alcohol.

Nothing gave me comfort, especially the fact that the home was releasing her to a halfway house. There was no way the liquor was out of her system. I remembered hearing Dr. Phil say on his television show that the effect of alcohol takes a full year to leave the body. Lori wanted out, and going to this halfway house was the perfect answer to leaving the stress of counseling and meetings. They handed her a perfect opportunity to get out of her rehabilitation commitment.

After our talk, or should I say, the *informative meeting* to let us know her plans and get our approval for her first halfway house payment, Lori didn't feel the need for any more meetings with us. She wanted to be sure we would give her the money. I knew Lori had agreed to the get-together because the counselor was backing her decision. She had no intention of having a family meeting. That hour was to inform us that Lori would be leaving the rehabilitation center. Not keeping Lori in the full three months recovery program, made me uncomfortable, fearful, and angry. She needed more time to talk about her past and share her fear of trusting me. The counselor didn't have any plan to bring them up either. Didn't the counselor see that this meeting was the perfect time to talk about these topics? Did she realize that not discussing Lori's fears only helped push her past deeper inside her?

Once Lori knew we'd pay for the halfway home, the counselor continued, "Lori has earned an overnight at home. She didn't want to go this weekend because Lopes Construction is moving to their new location, and Debbie will be busy with the move."

"She's welcome to stay with us."

"If I go to Debbie's, I'll be with the kids."

The counselor tried to show her appreciation of our visit. "It's rare that family members want to be involved with the alcoholic's program. I think it's wonderful that you two wanted to be here."

"We'd do anything to help her," I answered.

I wanted to scream at what was starting to unfold. They were putting her back into the world of drinking without any thought to the consequences of their decision. Rather than *insisting* that she stay the full three months, they made it easy for Lori to return to her old ways.

"We'll discuss the halfway house in a few weeks," the counselor replied, but I knew that we wouldn't be invited to another meeting before Lori left.

I walked out feeling defeated. I was angry with the board of counselors for agreeing to let Lori out after they themselves had told me that she was emotionally sick and that she couldn't give up drinking.

As we were leaving, Lori introduced us to the girls, who were on their way out to the porch for a break. Most of them were digging into their cigarette packs for a smoke. *Something else to kill them*, I thought. By now, I was bitter. I knew deep down that this long term stay was the last hope to save Lori.

A few days later, I received a call from Lori to pick her up. After getting an okay to leave her program, she didn't want to stay and complete her next two weeks for her evaluation. Lori wanted out, and we knew that decision was final. I didn't believe that anyone who drank for over half his or her life could be mentally and physically healthy to get out of a rehab in such a short time. I had no control over her choice to leave the recovery program.

I put off the decision of going to court to have Lori arrested because we were giving her one more chance, just in case we were wrong. Maybe she would do this on her own, and the group of women at the halfway house would support each other.

When Lori was on the phone, she told me about a woman who had demanded to leave the Emerson House the night before.

"It was around 9 pm, and she stood out in the driveway with her bags of clothes with nowhere to go. I felt so bad for her," Lori said.

"Then she should have stayed with the program as long as she could." I was firm with the remark.

"Her family doesn't want her, how sad," Lori said.

"That's why you're lucky, Lori. We all love you. You can come home to any of us anytime."

I was hoping she'd realize how fortunate she was after seeing the other girl as an example of having nowhere to go. Instead, she felt that Al and I were suffocating her.

"I'll be there in the morning to get you," I said feeling every fiber in my body wanting to fight this decision.

"Okay, I'll be packed," she answered, all excited.

At ten o'clock the next morning, I arrived at The Emerson House in Falmouth. Lori had her small, overnight bag repacked. It was May of 2006, and the weather was warm. She was neatly dressed in a pair of black, summer slacks and a white, feminine blouse. Her hair was pinned up; she rarely wore it down. She was running around hugging and saying goodbye to all the girls. I'll never forget that moment, watching her smiling and looking so happy. Lori hid her pain so well, but I knew she was suffering deep inside.

We put everything in the car, and I looked over at her. "Lori, you look beautiful."

"Thanks. You say that because you're my mother."

"No—you're beautiful inside and out. You have never realized that about yourself."

She continued without replying to the compliment. "I've decided what I want to do with my life. I want to be a counselor."

"That's great!"

"I'm serious, Mom. I want to help women who are struggling like me."

"I believe you. The first thing you need to do is help yourself so you can be of assistance to them. Maybe you can talk to one of the counselors when you're stronger. You have so much love and compassion that you'd be good for other women. I'm happy with your decision."

It was the first sign of her having a goal in years. *She found her niche in life*, I thought. Many abusers move into the field of counseling other alcoholics after they've overcome the pain and suffering of their own disease.

My excitement for her changed to despair in seconds. She looked at me, while I was driving and said, "I still don't understand why I can't drink."

My hope for her recovery plummeted. "If you don't understand, after being in a rehab three times and seeing your father die from drinking, you're in big trouble."

I knew at that moment that letting her out of the Emerson House was a huge mistake.

I was shocked at her question. How could she not see that her actions were the same ones that caused her father's death? The girls and I didn't witness Richie's last years of heavy drinking while he lived with Sara. We didn't see all the warning signs of cirrhosis of the liver that had developed in him. Anita was the one who had first noticed his large stomach and yellow skin.

At times, family members and outsiders had noticed that Lori's corneas were yellow, but Lori would look close into a mirror and say, "I don't see any yellow."

Lori informed me that she had gone to Fall River to check the halfway house out with Jeff, another counselor. She stayed at our house, and I made plans to travel with her to Buzzards Bay the next day to look at the other location. It was a thirty minute ride from our house in Rochester.

The halfway home was on a side road off the rotary before the Bourne Bridge leading to Cape Cod. The home looked like any residential two story home. They were lined up close together on the street, and we could see the Cape Cod Canal at the end of the road.

I choked back tears. *Why is she doing this?* I just couldn't understand her decision. *Could I be wrong being against this move?* I feared that someone living there could get drugs or alcohol, and supply Lori with them. I was trying to give her room with her life, but deep down I felt that she was too sick to be on her own.

We pulled up to the address and got out of the car. The entrance was on the side of the house. I didn't like the home, it wasn't well kept. It had cedar shingle siding and many panels were loose or missing, and it was also in dire need of new paint. It wasn't an impressive place at all. The Emerson House was like a mansion compared to this location.

We knocked, and someone yelled, "Come in."

The kitchen was very small and held only an unusual, misplaced, tiny table and two chairs. A miniature refrigerator was against the wall. It was a tight fit to walk through. Two girls sat in the living room on a worn out couch that sagged in the middle.

"Is the director here?" I asked.

"Director?" a girl asked looking surprised.

"Whoever is in charge of running the home?"

"No, she isn't," one girl replied biting into an apple.

"Do you expect her soon?"

"Who knows? She's hardly ever here."

I felt my stomach churn. The girls were free to roam or leave at anytime. Lori wouldn't be supervised. The counselor at the Emerson House had informed me that an authority figure would be staying with the girls. I didn't relish the idea that there wasn't a responsible person in charge.

"I'm supposed to decide if I want to stay here." Lori said to them.

"You're free to look around," one said as she bounced up to turn the volume down on the television. There are only two rooms available. They're right upstairs. Pick any one you want."

We walked up the steep, narrow stairs and looked into the bedrooms. There were four, each containing a single twin bed. The girls' personal belongings consisted of family pictures, colorful flowers placed in vases on their nightstands, and clothes everywhere. It looked much like a college dorm room, with every bed unmade and individual possessions scattered all around the room, lying on chairs or on the floor.

We looked into the two empty rooms. "There's not much privacy here," I said to Lori before we went back down the stairs.

How could Lori want to live here after being at the Emerson House? I wondered. It had a healthy atmosphere with daily management compared to this location.

"Thanks," Lori said to the girls as we headed out the door. No one replied. They showed no interest in a newcomer.

We got to the car, and I couldn't hold my emotions any longer. Tears rolled down my checks. "I don't like this, Lori. *Please*—I'm *begging* you to come home. These places are for women who have nowhere to go. There is no control here, and honestly, the place looks like a dump. I love you and can't see you living like this."

My heartbreak didn't seem to bother her.

"I liked the halfway house in Fall River better. I'd be closer to Debbie, and the short ride would make it easier to see the kids."

She used the kids as an excuse every time she wanted to do something against anyone's judgment. Yet, she didn't visit them often.

"I'd like to go with you and see the place, I said."

"You don't have to, Mom. It's nicer than this location."

"You're not going to change your mind about this?"

"I'll be fine. Jeff is the counselor who runs the halfway house, and he goes there everyday. They'll probably take me within a few days."

I drove home wanting to drag her into the house, lock the door, and hide the key.

I went out the next day and spent over a hundred dollars buying groceries that I thought she would need. I purchased everything from bread, milk, cereal, microwavable meals, snacks, cold drinks, and even condiments. I bought the largest boxes so the food would last for a long time. I didn't know how any of the girls could separate their own food items from the others staying there. Lori told me there was one refrigerator they had to share.

After purchasing the food, I went through my closets and dug out a comforter, twin sheets, and a new pillow, still in its wrapping. My next trip was to the bathroom to collect the extra toothpaste, a toothbrush; personal hygiene items, and toilet paper. I put the items inside large, oversized trash bags.

A room became available the next day, and Al and I helped pack Lori's car with all the clothes and food. It was such a tight fit that we had to push the bags in hard with both hands to close the door. We worried about her not being able to see out the back window.

We kissed her, and I didn't want to let her go. It still didn't feel right. Al gave her the first check for $110. She hugged and kissed us with an expression of joy on her face.

"Don't worry about me. This move will get me back on my feet."

I watched her close the driver's door, and she gave us a huge wave as she slowly backed out of our driveway. The highway, Route 105, ran directly in front of our house.

As we stood there waving back, Al said, "I didn't feel good giving her that check. It's like we agreed to this arrangement. I hope we're doing the right thing."

Lori disappeared around the bend.

"We made it too easy for her to leave," Al stated, wanting to stop this decision.

"I can't believe the rehab didn't keep her for the other ten weeks. It could have made a big difference in her recovery. Maybe there would have been a chance for me to join her in a meeting. I hope she gets counseling there. We never asked," I said fighting the ache that was crushing my chest.

A week later, on a Friday, Lori came to the house and gave Al a Father's Day card that contained a written loving note inside. She stayed a while talking about looking for work and how she was doing. The conversation was light, and we didn't press her for information about the halfway house and the girls living there. Al gave her a second check for the following week; we knew it was the main reason she had stopped to visit.

Kicked Out

Tuesday morning arrived, and Lori called. "Hi, I thought I'd tell you that I'm at Aunt Anita's."

The news stunned me, and I couldn't say anything at first. "Are you visiting her?"

"I'm staying here."

"Why?"

"I got kicked out of the halfway house. I was only an hour late for curfew. I couldn't believe that Jeff would do that to me. Can you imagine?"

"Why were you surprised? They had rules, Lori. You were aware of that when you went there. They're not going to treat you any differently than any other girl."

I was so angry at her actions and more upset that Al and I had given in, knowing the decision wasn't healthy for her. It had ended the way we feared. My world crumbled. I shouldn't have been surprised, but I was.

"Why didn't you come here? Why didn't you call us?"

I was fuming with her doing anything in her power to get away from help. By now, I was mad and tired of giving support. She didn't want anyone to question her actions or to be responsible for them.

I could tell by her shaky voice that she had been scared to death to call. She knew we'd not only expect her to come home after being evicted, and that we knew her behavior was wrong.

"Did you take any of the things that I gave you, especially the bedding?" I really didn't care about the food. I looked at it as a donation for the girls that were there. It would take care of them for months.

"No, I'm sorry. I didn't have time to collect them. We can talk later. I wanted you to know where I was."

I hung up with more aggravation. I was livid beyond belief that she lost the good bedding. It sounds selfish of me, but she never concerned herself about items given to her. Al knew by my expression that it wasn't good news. I told him the story.

"You've got to be kidding me!"

He was just as upset. Two hundred and twenty dollars, not including the food and bedding, flew out the window. Our payment for her second week had only covered two days, and being kicked out didn't faze her in the least, neither did our investing the money to help her. It wasn't the expense that bothered us, just the fact that she had walked out without trying to put her life together. We surmised that she had been drinking and missed her curfew. She had no intention of staying there.

Sonny and Anita had serious health problems. They didn't need Lori living there with a drinking problem to add to their situation. Her aunt and uncle had been hospitalized recently with heart procedures, and we were embarrassed that they'd be burdened with problems that should be ours. We had no idea how she had ended up there.

In a few days, we decided to visit Anita. It was something that we had done often so a visit from us wasn't out of the ordinary. When we arrived, Anita told us she had given Lori the freedom of having the whole downstairs of their home. It was one large room with a double bed, a television set, a sink, a kitchen table, a refrigerator, and a private bathroom. What more would she need?

We walked down the stairs to see her. A man was sitting on the couch with her.

Al and I walked over and gave her a kiss.

She introduced us. "This is Tom. We've known each other since I worked at Lopes Construction. He's still working there. Tom, this is my mother and stepfather, Al."

When did this man come into her life? She had just left the halfway home a week and a half ago and no man was in her life that we were aware of. She had never spoken about him. Was she jumping into another relationship too fast?

"Hi, Tom," I said, cautiously.

Tom was about 5 feet, 8 inches tall with a medium build. He had dark brown hair which was cut short, almost in a crew-cut. He seemed to have a serious demeanor, which was only an assumption on my part, since I didn't know him when we shook hands.

Tom looked directly at me and said, "I'm going to take good care of your daughter."

I couldn't believe the remark. I had no idea who he was, and he was already talking about taking care of her. The conversation lasted ten minutes because Lori said they were going out. She seemed uncomfortable being in our company for any length of time. There had been a time when talking and laughing with her had always been easy and fun. When they left, Al and I went back upstairs to talk to Anita.

She started to explain how Lori's arrival at her home came about. "Last Saturday, Paula and I were on our way to my sister Loree's house in Fall River. Paula got a call from Lori on her cell phone; she wanted us to stop by and see her at the halfway house. When we got there, Lori was outside with some other residents. We drove over to her, and she said that she had just been evicted for missing curfew. Paula said to me, 'You have room, Mom, why can't she stay with you?' Paula convinced me that Lori was doing better so I took her in. To be honest, I didn't want Debbie to be burdened with her sister."

"I don't know why she didn't call us," Al said.

We knew that Lori wasn't doing better or was even in control of her drinking. It might have been Paula's way of giving Lori a place to stay. Maybe she knew about Lori's termination before they went to the halfway house. I was embarrassed that Anita and Sonny were going to be facing problems with *our* daughter. Anita lived about seven minutes from Debbie's house. I wondered if Lori would be visiting her kids.

It took less than a month for Anita to start being confused with Lori's actions. "Lori isn't here much. She's downstairs when I get up, but leaves when I go out. She's coming in at all hours of the night or not at all."

What else was new? I was furious! Everyone was trying to help her, and here she was lying to her aunt and not giving her the courtesy of letting her know if she'd even be home at night. Al and I assumed that she had been dating Tom when she was at the halfway house and probably went out with him, thereby missing curfew hour. Lori never explained what really happened. She never did explain her actions.

A week later, Lori left Anita's home without giving any notice or explanation as to why. She found out later that she had moved in with Tom. There wasn't even a goodbye or thank you to Anita or Sonny. All her belongings were left behind. I was so disappointed that Lori had shown no consideration for all the help she had been given. Tom finally came by Anita's and took Lori's things to his place.

It was rare that I heard from Lori. She used Tom's cell phone when he went to work to make her calls. The next time we saw her was two weeks later when we went to a cookout at Debbie and Brian's. The event was just a typical family cookout with cousins, uncles, and aunts attending. Lori came with Tom and seemed like her old self with the family. I could see that Tom really cared for her. He couldn't do enough for her.

Lori had on a red, sleeveless, summer dress. She wore her hair down, which she rarely did. Her curls fell loosely on her shoulders. She looked beautiful and I told her as I hugged her.

Joey and Meagan didn't spend time with Tom. I assumed they were still angry that their mother had walked out on them and was now living with a man they didn't know, spending time with his two teenage daughters and not them. They had been invited to Tom's home in Tiverton on several occasions, but they never went.

A month later, Lori called with news. "Mom, I've got a surprise for you."

"Really?"

"Tom asked me to marry him."

I was silent, the announcement was a shock; to my knowledge they hadn't been dating that long. She was seeking my approval.

"Mom, are you happy?"

"Are you? That's what's important," I asked.

"Of course, but I want you to be."

"Lori, we don't even know Tom. We haven't spent much time with him. Isn't this happening too fast?"

"We're going to get married next year."

"That's a smart move. That will give your kids and family time to know him."

Lori's children needed time to redevelop their relationship with their mother again before she brought someone else into their lives. How could she fall in love with someone who seemed to come from out of nowhere?

After her news, we had a short talk. I wanted to be happy for her, but I really didn't feel that she was over Mark. I didn't think it was a good idea to jump into another marriage before healing from the last one. It had nothing to do with my feelings for Tom, I hadn't been in his company long enough to form an opinion. I believed he wanted to be with her. Lori didn't seem to have any excitement in her voice. I couldn't help but feel she just wanted to have a place to stay and someone to take care of her.

July 29, 2006, Lori's thirty-ninth birthday arrived. It seemed that she had disappeared from the earth. She lived almost an hour away at Tom's home in Tiverton, Rhode Island. I prayed she was happy, although I was still traumatized by her separation from her kids and family.

I called to take her out for her birthday. It was hard to reach her, but finally, a few days after her birthday, I did.

"I'd like to take you out for your birthday."

"I'm busy right now. Where did you want to go?"

"Anywhere you want. I'd like us to go to LaSalette Shrine in Attleboro afterward, so we can walk around. It's so peaceful there."

La Salette Shrine, located in Attleboro, Massachusetts, is run by the missionaries of Our Lady of La Sallette, it's a major seminary. A constant flow of people visit this location, praying daily to Our Lady for healing and hope and to find answers for their struggles in life. Their Christmas display is among the best anywhere. Secretly, I wanted to take Lori to the shrine with the fervent hope that Jesus would get rid of the demons that had a hold on her. I felt it would make up for my not taking her to Medjugorje.

"I've got a lot of things going on, but I'll call you, Mom."

I called Lori numerous times, and she found every excuse why she couldn't go. I just assumed she didn't want to be with me.

Debbie called me. "Lori has been calling me and is nervous wondering why you want to take her to LaSallette."

"Lori's nervous with anything that's religious. If she's that uncomfortable about going, we don't have to go. Why can't she talk to me about it? My God, is she that afraid of me? All she has to do is say she doesn't want to go."

I couldn't believe that she had to call Debbie rather than coming out and asking me. It was no big deal if we didn't go there. I just wanted time with her.

After not receiving a call, I made one more to her.

"Lori, I miss you. Why can't we go out for lunch? This is crazy. Your birthday passed a month and a half ago. Do you want me to take a ride out to see you? We can go somewhere in your area."

"No, I'm not up to it right now."

"I love you, honey. I don't like this much time passing without seeing you."

"I'll call you. I'm fine. Don't worry about me."

"You're always saying that, but I never hear from you."

I could feel the distance. Finally, I gave up calling and waited once again to hear from her. I didn't know what else to do.

Lori Rushed to Charlton Memorial Hospital

On November 11, 2006, a Sunday night, I was getting ready to go to the Zeiterion Theatre in New Bedford with my friend, Rachel Constant. Al was going to watch a Patriot's football game with her husband, Bob. I also had tickets for Al's son, Alan, and his girlfriend, Donna. We planned to meet in the lobby.

As we were about to put on our coats, Debbie called. "Tom just called me and said that he's trying to get Lori to go to the hospital, but she won't go. He has the ambulance there."

"…An ambulance! What's the matter with her?"

"She has been hemorrhaging but says it's from hemorrhoids. He said she looks awful. She's been sick, but refused to go to the doctor."

"I've been calling her for months, Debbie, and she never mentioned that she wasn't feeling good."

"She didn't tell me, either. The police are there, they said the only way they can transport her to the hospital is if a family member makes the decision. Brian and I are on our way. Can you meet us there?"

"I don't believe this," I said as I explained the situation to Debbie.

"Maybe I can give the tickets to Rachel and Bob, and they can find Alan and Donna."

I was going back and forth in my head trying to figure out how to arrange getting the tickets to everyone; they'd all be waiting for *me*.

"Mom, go to the show, and I'll call Al on his cell phone if her condition is serious."

"Okay, I'll have mine on vibrate so it won't ring and disturb anyone during the show."

We arrived at Rachel's house, and I fell apart. "Do you think we can call the prayer line members and put Lori on it?" I asked Rachel.

"Of course, we can," Rachel said as she dialed the number to our group.

"Relax, Alberta. If Debbie's concerned, she'll call me," Al said. "If she does, I'll call you."

"I'll take my car, Alberta," Rachel said. "This way Al can meet you there with your car, and I can go home alone. You'll be about fifteen minutes from the hospital."

We arrived at the theatre, and within twenty minutes, Alan and Donna arrived. I told them about Lori. I couldn't relax. I feared something could happen to her. I had no idea what the outcome would be after she was examined.

Donna leaned over and whispered, "Maybe you should go to the hospital."

"Al's going to call me as soon as he hears from Debbie. If it's serious, he'll pick me up here, and Rachel has her car to get home. Charlton Memorial Hospital isn't far from here."

Before the show started, my cell phone vibrated. The orchestra was warming up.

"They got her in the ambulance but not without a fight. The police had to get a woman police officer to the scene," Al said.

"Al, pick me up."

"Debbie said to stay put, and she'll call once they get her to the hospital and the doctor talks to her."

"Okay, but call me right away." I sat, but my body wanted to get up and run out the door. *What could be so wrong that she had to go by ambulance?*

We sat through the entire show to the end and no call came through. I felt better. I couldn't wait to get to Rachel's and get home. She knew how anxious I was, so we didn't stop anywhere on the way back.

We arrived at Rachel's at 10:30 pm, and Al and I headed straight for our house. We were getting ready for bed when the phone rang at eleven.

Debbie was on the verge of tears, "Mom, the doctor just told us that Lori's kidneys and liver were shutting down."

"Oh, my God, we'll be right there," I screamed.

We got dressed in a hurry and left for the trip to the hospital.

I realized that I should have gone to the hospital in the first place. Al drove on Route 195 as fast as he could without being stopped. I grabbed my rosary beads from the compartment and held them in my hand. I couldn't concentrate enough to say the prayer. The drive was about twenty-five minutes to the hospital from our house, and I was scared something would happen to her before we arrived. I'd never forgive myself for not going as soon as we heard.

I became angry thinking about the last four months that I had been calling her, and she never once said that she was sick. How could I have gone that long without going to see her? No one had seen or heard from her. I thought she was happy with Tom, and that everything was fine. Again, guilt was choking me.

Finally, I opened up to Al in sobs. "I should have called her more, checked on her situation or never left her alone this long. I should have done more for her."

"Alberta, stop putting the guilt on yourself," Al said, upset. "How many times have we tried to get together with her? Either she wasn't going to be home or wouldn't answer her door or the telephone. Everyone offered her a place to stay so she could get her life together. She left everyone of them for the freedom to drink without anyone questioning her. We offered to go to doctor appointments and counseling with her and she refused. It was her decision not to stay with counseling or attend AA meetings. We did everything to help her so stop doing this."

We drove in silence while I was still feeling a mother's responsibility of not helping her child.

It was midnight, and the hospital parking lot was empty. We rushed into the emergency room.

I ran up to the reception window. "Our daughter, Lori Cahill Nadeau, was rushed into the hospital about a half hour ago. Can we see her?"

I wasn't sure what name Lori registered under because she had been talking about changing her married name, Nadeau, back to Cahill for the kid's sake, after divorcing Mark.

"Your other daughter is with her," a nurse said. "Let me get her first."

Debbie came out through the closed doors and sat next to me. "Lori doesn't want you to see her this way, Mom. She has IV's all over her and tubes going into her nose."

"I don't care what she looks like. She is my daughter, and I want to see her."

I couldn't believe it. There was no way that I was going to stand by and allow them to stop me from seeing her as I had been stopped from seeing Richie.

I broke down uncontrollably. My heart was completely broken. I wanted to get the tears out of me before going into Lori's room. I had to be strong for her. Debbie put her arm around me without saying a word.

I couldn't help but feel complete bitterness that Debbie was with her and so was Tom. I was her mother!

What's wrong with Lori? How can she be doing this to me? Please, please, God don't take her.

"Let me go and ask her again," Debbie said as she disappeared behind the same closed doors.

Al sat across from me not saying a word, just staring. Within five minutes, Debbie came out.

"Lori said it's okay but not to stay long."

I wanted to scream at the top of my lungs. It was my turn to feel smothered with people telling me what I could and couldn't do. Everyone had the right to be with her, and

179

again, I *needed* permission. I was so sick of this Patient's Privacy Act.

We walked up to a white curtain. Debbie pulled it open. My world collapsed when I caught sight of Lori. There lay my daughter with four IV's in her arms and tubes going into both nostrils. Medicine was going in one, and the blood from her stomach was coming out the other into a bag behind her bed. Lori tried to act calm and in control in front of me.

Every part of her skin, from her forehead to her feet, was a deep, gold tint. The color was so visible that it frightened me. There was no white left in her eyes. Her once beautiful tan had faded into a sickly golden hue. I gave birth to her with jaundice, and now it was choking her liver.

Oh Lord, just like Richie. He had died the same way. *Don't let this be happening again. Please make this go away!*

There were so many tubes and IV's in her that it was hard to get an open space to lean over and kiss her. I fought my way to the headboard and gently pressed my lips on her forehead. I was fighting to hold back tears.

"Hi, honey. Looks like you're having a rough time here," I said gently rubbing her hair.

I didn't want to blame Tom for her condition; I knew that he was hurting too. I just couldn't understand why he had waited so long to call her family. *God, for months I had been calling to see her.*

The four of us encircled her bed in the emergency room. She had feared dying like her father, and here she lay, in the same condition as he had been in when he left us.

A nurse came into the area. "We'd like to get her ready to go upstairs for a gastrology procedure."

Lori panicked. "What's that?"

The nurse started to disconnect certain tubes. Without looking at Lori, she answered. "It's a procedure where they put a tube down your throat into your stomach."

"Will I be awake for it?"

She gave Lori a warm smile. "You'll be asleep. There's no pain after it."

"Do they have to do it tonight?" Lori asked hoping to avoid the procedure.

"They have to find out where you're bleeding from, Lori," she said.

"You'll be okay." I replied.

I wanted her to think positive about anything she would be going through. How was I going to handle the news from the doctor if this was as serious as it looks? The lump in my throat was sharp. Debbie, Al, and Tom seemed to be in control of their emotions. Maybe they were hiding them, but I felt the same uncontrollable fear that overtook me at Butler Hospital when we had admitted her.

Lori requested to use the bedpan so the four of us left the area.

We paced around each other outside the curtained area. Tom started to tell us about what had happened to Lori.

"She's been in bed sick for over two weeks. I asked her continuously if she had been eating anything, and she said yes. She kept insisting that she felt better."

Debbie said, "The doctor told her that they had to do an endoscopy to stop the bleeding. If they don't find where she's bleeding from, she's going to bleed to death."

I suddenly felt weak and faint.

My thoughts went back to when Richie's veins were all breaking in his stomach before he died. I didn't want to think of her dying, but logic was trying to overrule my unrealistic thinking. She looked awful. I couldn't picture how it was possible for her to rebound from bleeding so badly inside and the skin all over her body being completely gold.

The hospital had named Debbie as the contact person. They didn't want a large number of people calling to get information.

We returned to her bedside in the emergency room and stayed with Lori while they prepared her. Tom was scheduled for day surgery the next morning; it was a minor procedure and was taking place in the same hospital.

"How are you going to get up after being here all night?" I asked. "It's after midnight."

"I'll be okay. My daughter will bring me in for noon-time. We only live fifteen minutes away."

The nurse was ready to take Lori into a surgical area to do the procedure. We all kissed her, trying to avoid the wires that were connected to her.

The nurse turned toward us, "I think it would be wise for you to go home and get some rest. She'll be doing a lot of sleeping when the procedure is done. We'll call Debbie if anything changes."

Once she went on the elevator, we hugged each other and left for the night.

I cried off and on the whole way home. Fear overtook me as I thought that something might happen to her during the night. I didn't want to leave.

I couldn't sleep and tossed and turned all night. I got up and went into our guest bedroom and knelt in front of my Blessed Mother's statue, which was on a small table in the corner of the room. I prayed under the Crucifix of Jesus on the wall above her. Our Lady knew my pain; she too, had watched her Son die a horrible death.

Please, God, don't take her. Let this terrible family disease stop with her.

I swore that if she came out of this that I'd never lose touch with her again. Never would I let this much time go by without checking up on her. I promised to have a better relationship with her. I wouldn't wait for her to open up to me. This time I would lovingly and gently talk about our past as a family so she would only have to listen. Maybe she wouldn't feel so threatened. *Please, God, give me time for all this.*

Our Hopes Build

Monday morning I woke up exhausted; I had slept restlessly at best. I hesitated about going for an hour to Adoration at the St. John Neumann Church in East Freetown. It was something I had done every week for years. After forcing myself out of bed, I attended the 7:30 am Mass before going to Eucharistic Adoration in Mary, Mother of All Nations Chapel to pray. I offered up the Mass and Holy Communion for Lori.

It was God I needed at this difficult time, for He's our Healer. I pushed myself to go to Adoration instead of going home. I sat reading the passage from *Matthew 5:4: Blessed are those who mourn, for they will be comforted.* I needed my faith.

Marlene, a friend from church, came into the chapel to pray and saw me looking unusually sad. I never go without saying hello to anyone, but I couldn't bring myself to talk at this time. If someone should give me a soft touch or express sympathy, I knew I'd fall apart.

Marlene came over to me. "Is everything all right with you?"

That's all I needed. I broke down sobbing and told her about Lori.

She put her arm around me. "When my son had his brain tumor, I would come here and pray. I wanted to be alone so I'm going to give you private time and not stay here this morning."

She left, and I prayed for an hour from the depths of my soul. I tried to put Lori's health in God's hands while still asking Him to let her live.

After the hour, I rushed home for a scheduled interview for my first memoir, *A Healing Heart; A Spiritual Renewal* that had just been published on November 6, 2006. Tony Lewis, an editor of The Standard Times newspaper of New Bedford, came to my home. It was the same day that my book had been released from the publisher.

I debated about canceling the interview, but I knew that Lori would want me to keep the appointment. Tony was wonderful and so down to earth. He made me feel comfortable from the very start. I didn't mention my daughter being in the hospital. I tried to avoid anything that would upset me. The interview went better than I had expected. Tony said it would be in the Sunday newspaper.

After the interview, Al and I went to see Lori in ICU. Debbie and Tom were already there. It was close to 2:00 pm, and Tom had had his surgery.

"I can't believe you're here. Did they cancel your surgery?" I asked.

"No, I was done by 1:00 pm."

"And you're here already? How do you feel?"

"I'm fine. I have a little discomfort, but not much. It's more important for me to be here with Lori."

Lori's eyes were half open as she sat up straight with a pillow behind her back. She was heavily medicated. There was a full lunch tray in front of her. She looked up at me only half aware of anything going on around her.

"I look a lot better today, don't you think, Mom?" She slurred her words and spoke in slow motion.

I mustered all my strength and control not to break down. "Yes, you do," I said giving her a kiss.

She was so drugged that she struggled trying to get soup from a bowl with a spoon. She couldn't focus her eyes. They must have sedated her before we arrived.

"Let me help you, honey." It was as if she was a child again, and I was feeding her. For the first time in years, I felt like she needed me. I was constantly fighting my emotions.

After a few tablespoons of soup, she wanted the Jell-O on her tray. I gave her small mouthfuls.

My insides shook so much that I could feel my nerves jumping in my body. I thought that I was going to have a breakdown.

Tom had two weeks of medical leave before going back to work. He hoped that Lori would only be there a week so he would have a week to take care of her.

"Lori, you do realize that this is your last chance at getting better?" Al asked.

"I'm not going to do any more drinking. This is it," she said.

"You can't pick up one drink, or you'll destroy your liver," I stated.

"Oh, she knows," Tom replied. "We've been talking about her drinking. I want us to see our grandchildren grow up."

Anyone looking at him had to be blind not to see his love for her. I just hadn't had the time to get to know him.

"It's not worth going through this," Lori said, half awake. "If I do well tomorrow, they said that I can go to a private room."

"That's a good sign, Lori," I said hopefully. I looked over to the window and spotted my new memoir *A Healing Heart* on the window sill. "Lori, you have my new book here."

As silly as it may sound, I felt her love, something I hadn't felt during her counseling.

"I'm reading her a few pages at a time," Tom said.

"Thanks, I appreciate that." I was thrilled she would know the story of our family.

We could see her drifting in and out of sleep, so Al, Debbie, and I decided to leave. Tom wanted to sit with her while she slept.

The following day, we headed for the hospital after Al returned from the health club at the Holiday Inn in Taunton. Lori had been moved to a private room and looked happy.

Her energy seemed to be returning. I brought her a soft pillow and body lotion from home. I placed the pillow behind her head; she moaned in comfort.

Something so simple touched my heart, knowing she appreciated the gesture. I was craving for her to be pleased with anything that I did for her. Lori was looking for signs of love from me, and I was looking for the same from her. How sad that we had hidden these emotions from each other since Richie had died, twenty-one years earlier.

"That feels so good, Mom. Hospital pillows are so hard."

"I missed your birthday, Lori, so I brought your gifts."

I took each one out to show her. She lit up seeing a short, sleeveless, white and green striped terrycloth robe. It had Velcro straps in the front.

"When I'm up to my showers, I can wear that. Thanks."

"It only took four months to give them to you."

We laughed at how it was normal in our family to be late getting together for birthdays.

We all had such busy schedules and were constantly running somewhere.

"Mom, rub some lotion on my neck, it's been killing me," Lori asked as she picked her hair up to make it easy for me.

After an hour of everyone talking and laughing, Lori started to doze off, but she fought to keep her eyes open. The nurses were continuously giving her pills. Al and I decided to leave her alone.

"We're going to let you sleep, honey," I said kissing her forehead.

Half asleep, she answered, "Okay. See you two tomorrow."

The next day, Lori informed us that the doctor said she had pancreatic problems, and the difficulty had to get better on its own. I got a fast glimpse of Al's expression after hearing the news. His eyes shot up in the air as though he had heard the worst possible news.

I had read once that severe inflammation of the pan-creas is very common in alcoholics. The pancreas is a double purpose gland that lies behind the stomach. It's about six inches long and nestles into the curve of the duodenum where digestion begins. Entirely different pancreas cells produce clear, watery pancreatic juices that contain enzymes that split fats, proteins, and carbohydrates. In general, chronic problems in the pancreas can become a severe and devastating disease, and the prognosis for the patient is poor from the standpoint of longevity.

As long as I didn't hear cirrhosis of the liver, I thought she'd survive and be able to return home. This added problem showed the seriousness of her condition.

"Mom, did I tell you about the ambulance crew picking me up?" Lori asked.

"No, you didn't."

"I kept arguing with them. They repeatedly asked me where I lived. I *insisted* that it was at 1847 Somerset Avenue in Dighton. At the time, I couldn't understand why they had thought that I lived in Tiverton, Rhode Island."

She thought that it was funny and laughed about it. I didn't, because her liver couldn't have been functioning right if she was confused.

Debbie spoke to Lori's doctor every morning and passed the news to the family. One day he would say she was improving, and then the next day he'd report that her kidneys were not operating fully.

After a few hours, Al and I would leave so she wouldn't be too tired when Debbie and Brian came. Debbie called me every night with the updates. It was a ritual we followed each time anyone took a trip to see Lori.

On the fourth day of Lori's stay, Al and I became terribly sick and stayed home. We were afraid Lori might get our colds and develop pneumonia. I wanted to see her, but I didn't dare go. The stress built up with each day that I couldn't go to the hospital. The cold settled in our chests, and we developed deep coughs. I called to tell Lori we wouldn't be in to see her and why. She understood.

Debbie went that night and called me later. "Lori's developing fluid in her legs and stomach."

"What's the doctor saying?"

"They're going to take X-rays later to see why. Her stomach is starting to hurt so they're going to try to take the fluid out with a long needle. They told her that she wouldn't feel it."

The day came and went without them doing anything. They were afraid the procedure would injure the veins in her stomach. Knowing her condition, I was tormented staying home. I was tempted to go, but I would never forgive myself if she caught my cold and had complications from it.

Friday and Saturday, Al and I were still sick with no signs of getting better. We couldn't shake the congestion in our chests and lost our voices due to laryngitis. We didn't see Lori at all.

I called my doctor's office to get some medicine. The girl in the office promised to call a prescription in for me. To hurry the medicine along, I gave her the name of the pharmacy and their telephone number. For two days in a row, I called the pharmacy to find out if the prescription had been filled. They kept informing me that it wasn't called in.

Debbie called after she had gone to visit Lori at the hospital. "A lot of Lori's friends were in her room today. She was upset with everyone trying to get her up and moving or someone trying to force her to eat. She threatened to have everyone kicked out. Lori got so upset that she kept her back to all of us."

"Debbie, she probably doesn't want anyone to see her stomach. It's so swollen. It has to be embarrassing. After all, she has no strength; she's seriously ill. Why would she want visitors pushing themselves on her when she feels like hell?"

"When we first came to visit her, she talked to us."

"Can you imagine what she's going through? She's in constant pain and has been in bed for almost three weeks with no sign of getting better," I said.

I was about to go out of my mind knowing that we couldn't visit her. We called daily so she would know we were really sick.

"The doctor is going to try to take some fluid out of Lori's stomach tomorrow. She's really uncomfortable," Debbie reported.

At 6:30 am, the following morning, Lori called, and Al answered the phone.

"Hi, Lori."

"What time is it, Al?"

"It's almost seven."

"...In the morning or night?"

"It's morning, honey."

"Can I talk to my mother?"

"...Of course." He gave me the phone.

"Mom, they have my arms tied down in bed. They pumped out my stomach today. My body has bruises all over it, and I look horrible. I want to get out of here. I feel like I'm never going home."

"Lori, you can't until you can function on your own. You've been very sick."

I tried comforting her. If I was present with her at this time, she might have felt calmer. I wasn't able to do a thing for her. After I hung up, I called the nurse's station on Lori's floor and told them about her remark.

"Mrs. Sequeira, they didn't drain her stomach, and she's not restrained. Your daughter is talking this way because her liver and kidneys are not working to full capacity, and she's getting confused," the nurse stated.

My heart broke into pieces knowing what she was going through. Loving my child and not being able to help her made me brokenhearted.

In the afternoon, Debbie called. "They think Lori might have pneumonia. They are going to take the IV's out and put a stationary one above her chest. The doctor told me this morning that they're not going to drain the fluid because they're afraid she may hemorrhage. They are starting her on Vitamin K to thicken the blood and give her more antibiotics. If the blood looks good, they may try draining the fluid."

Paula's Visit

I finally called the doctor for Al. He wasn't getting better, and I was scared that he'd get pneumonia since he had a history of the illness. He had developed the viral infection three times the previous year. We got his medicine at Brooks Pharmacy in the late afternoon. Mine still hadn't been filled after two calls to the drugstore.

"Alberta, I called the prescription in myself," the receptionist said.

"Well, they're saying it's not there!"

"I'll check today for you."

I screamed at her, "I need the medicine so I can go see my daughter in the hospital. She may be dying. Just get me my medicine so I can visit her."

I had called Lori's nurse and informed her about our health situation.

"There are facial masks for visitors in Lori's room. They all have them. Come for a visit and use them."

That's all I had to hear. I didn't even think of a mask. We were going the next day. I couldn't stay away any longer. It had been three days.

Debbie called, "I'm bringing Meagan and Joey to see Lori tonight." Joey had the same fear of hospitals as his mother. "The doctor told me that Lori's liver isn't improving. They're giving her plasma today. Her blood is still too thin to remove the fluid. They also want to do a cat scan to see why her stomach hurts so much. The doctors don't want to miss anything."

After her visit, Debbie reported back to me. "The nurse told me that Lori was alert this morning and that she had walked a few times down the hall with them."

Any new achievement gave us hope.

"The doctor told Lori today that she had to fight and have the desire to get better. He has seen patients with stomachs twice the size of Lori's, and they still pulled through. If her vital signs get better, along with her kidneys, it may pull her out of this. She would have to be off alcohol at least six months, and they'll put her on a liver transplant list. After a year they would do the transplant," Debbie stated.

Lori's liver was in serious condition. The good news was that she had a chance. After all, she wasn't in ICU so her doctors had to have hope for her.

Please God, let this incident scare her enough not to take another drink. Let this be her "rock bottom."

I swore to do everything in my power to get her admitted to an alcoholic rehabilitation center once she was strong. I would no longer accept Lori's not wanting me to help her. Debbie and I would assist Lori into seeing that she needed us in counseling to help in her recovery.

After days of being away, Al and I went to see Lori. We grabbed the masks as soon as we entered her room. She told us that Paula had come to visit and Lori was agitated after she left.

"She comes even after I ask her not too," Lori re-marked. "She's forever telling me what to do. Last night she came with two friends, and she had been drinking. She got right into my bed and squeezed me saying how much she loved me. My IV's were being pulled and she was leaning on my swollen stomach. The girls kept telling her, 'Lets' go Paula so Lori can sleep."

I couldn't believe how many people were scared to tell Paula to leave when she had been drinking. There was no doubt in my mind that Paula loved Lori and was upset that she was in the hospital. They were very close, but Lori was fighting for her life against this demon, and Paula shouldn't be visiting when she was drinking.

She had watched her Uncle Richie die from cirrhosis, and now Lori could be faced with the end. Paula was also on the same path and didn't realize it. Maybe the alcoholic is aware of the overpowering control of the disease and finds it easier just to ride with the drinking rather than to fight the addiction.

While we were there, the phone rang, and Lori answered it. Debbie was on the other end telling her about the conversation with her doctor. I gathered, by Lori's questions that they were talking about her kidneys.

Then she asked Debbie, "I'm not going to die, am I?" Her expression was pure terror.

A panic rose in me. *Please, don't let her know anything if she's failing.* I knew that she wouldn't be able to handle the facts. I couldn't stand by and watch her being terrified about death. I knew that if her body was ready to shut down completely, the doctors would tell her. They had told her father when he had been admitted to the VA Hospital in Providence, Rhode Island.

Debbie called me after she and Brian went to see Lori that night. "The doctor took a small syringe of fluid out of her stomach to test for infection."

"They did it already? Did it hurt her?"

"No, and it was done in her room while she stayed in bed."

"That's a relief, knowing she didn't have to go into a surgical room." I knew how my daughter feared procedures.

The next morning, Debbie called saying Paula was supposed to take Anita to a dentist appointment and had asked her friend, Lucy, to take her instead. Paula told them that Lori had been calling, asking her to visit at the hospital. We knew Lori made no such call.

Lori phoned me shortly after Debbie's call. "Paula asked to visit, and I told her I didn't feel good. She said, 'Too bad, I'm coming anyway."

When Al and I got there, Paula was sitting on a chair close to Lori's bed, rubbing her arm. I could tell Lori was irritated; she was rubbing her eyes with her hands, frustration showing on her face. Lori told Paula that she needed some sleep, but Paula never stopped talking.

"I'll rub your back and get into bed with you," Paula said.

Al remarked, "What for?"

"Oh, I've done that before."

"Why?" Al asked, shocked by her statement.

I jumped in, "There's no need for anyone to get into bed with her."

We could smell alcohol in the room. I knew Paula had been drinking.

"We'd like to talk to you a moment, Paula. Could you come out to the corridor?" Al asked.

She walked out of the room. "I'm going for a cigarette first," she said.

We waited ten minutes. "I don't think she's coming back," Al stated.

We then walked back to Lori's room.

To our surprise, Paula came back into Lori's room, and sat in the chair next to her.

"Paula, I'd like to talk to you. Let's leave Lori alone so she can sleep." I said.

We walked Paula to the elevator section. I calmly stated, "Paula, I don't want you here when you've been drinking."

"I haven't been drinking."

"I can smell liquor on your breath."

"That's from last night," she replied.

Her eyes were bloodshot, and the smell of alcohol was unmistakable.

"I don't care when it was, the room stinks of stale liquor. Lori is fighting for her life because of alcohol abuse, and I'm not keen on her smelling and breathing liquor fumes from you."

She got very defiant and defensive. She walked right passed us and went directly back to sit in Lori's room. I hated being put in the position to ask her to leave, but she obviously had no intention of listening to us.

We followed, and she started to rub Lori's arm again.

"Paula, I'm asking you calmly to leave," I stated, getting upset.

"Oh, so you don't think that I've been here for Lori?"

Lori got upset. "Please, I can't handle this fighting back and forth."

"Paula lets go out of the room to talk. Lori doesn't need this confusion," Al said.

Paula still didn't move. I dreaded taking the next step.

I walked into the corridor and confronted a nurse down the hall. "My niece is here, and she's been drinking. We've asked her to leave, but she refuses."

The nurse jumped right on the situation. "We'll take care of the problem."

I went back in, and Paula was still sitting in the chair.

"Paula, I'm not going to ask again," I said.

She got up angrily and said to Lori, "I'll call you later, okay?"

Lori answered, "Okay."

Paula walked past us saying, "You go your way, and I'll go mine." She was angry.

The nurse came down the hall and asked where Paula was going, I said she was leaving. "We just called security," she said.

"I'm glad we didn't have to have her removed. She's a sweet girl, but we don't need anyone in here that's been drinking," I said.

I watched as Paula rushed down the corridor to the elevators.

Book Signings

Al and I returned to Lori's room when we were sure that Paula left the floor. When we returned, Lori was drowsy from the morphine that was given to her. She seemed to be on heavy medication every day. I hated to leave because we rarely had time alone with her because someone else always showed up. I felt like a visitor instead of her parent. There was no chance of having a conversation with her as she slept.

"We should leave now so you can rest. You look uncomfortable," I said.

"I am, Mom."

"Since we're still sick, we can't kiss you. We don't want you to catch this and have something else to worry about."

As we were leaving the room, she looked up at us and put her hand to her lips to throw us a kiss. "Love you two," she said with a smile.

"We love you too, Lori," Al said smiling back.

I called Tom and Debbie and told them that they had to back us up with Paula. "If she's sober, she's welcome to visit. We don't want her in bed with Lori."

When we got home, I called Anita to inform her of what had happened. She was happy that I called. "I wanted you to hear from us what took place in Lori's room."

"Thanks, I'll be prepared if Paula calls and is upset."

At 8:30 pm, Tom called me. "Lori wants to talk to you."

"Hi, honey. How are you doing?"

"I want you to call Joey and Meagan and tell them that I'm going to be in the hospital a couple of days for observation."

My heart fell. She was confused again. She had no memory that her kids weren't living with her and that they were aware of her condition.

"They already know. Debbie told them yesterday," I said.

"Oh, good, I just didn't want them to worry."

"We'll be there in the morning to see you."

"Okay, see you then."

I hung up and cried, telling Al about her request.

"I don't know anymore if she's confused from the morphine or if her liver is failing. One or the other has to be making her talk and think like this," Al stated.

The next day, a Saturday, I was scheduled to do a book signing at a Christmas Fair at St. Mary's Church in New Bedford. I had booked it months before, and there was always a good turnout. I had paid for the booth in advance, but now that Lori was in the hospital, I was reluctant to go.

Al tried taking some stress off me. "You need some time to yourself. It's good to get your book out there. We're going to visit her tonight."

I went, but I didn't enjoy myself. Lori was on my mind, especially after our last conversation on the phone. I wanted to be with her every minute.

I was still sick as a dog from the cold in my chest; I wasn't getting better. There was still no answer from the doctor's office about my medication or any confirmation that the prescription had ever been called in to the pharmacy. I had been so busy running all over the place that I forgot to check as the days went by.

We left for the hospital at 5:00 pm. Debbie, Brian and our grandson, Michael, were just leaving the hospital when we arrived. We met them at the entrance.

Debbie looked hopeful, "Lori was awake the whole time we were visiting her, and she talked without falling asleep. They just gave her a sedative, so she may be sleeping when you go up."

By the time Al and I got to her room, she was sleeping. I was happy we were alone with her. She smiled slightly and tried to stay awake but couldn't keep her eyes open. After a few minutes, she woke up aggravated with the tubes from the IV's that tangled around her arm. She was getting blood, fluids, and morphine at the same time.

"I can't stand these stupid wires," she said pulling on the wire trying to straighten one out. "I can't move without one causing the machine to constantly beep."

Her patience was gone, and she acted unusually irritated as she tried separating the wires to the machine.

She changed her mood to give us a smile. "They're going to drain more fluid from me tomorrow."

She was constantly in a confused state about her care so we couldn't believe everything she told us. Her buzzer to the machine started going off again.

"I just want the buzzer to stop so I can sleep," she said, looking like she was ready to cry.

I tried loosening the wires caught under her bedding. "This should help, honey."

Please, let her get better soon so she can get out of this hospital. I was sick inside watching her suffer with each visit.

Al sat and watched a Patriot's football game on the television set that had been placed high in the corner of the room on the wall. He shut the set off within ten minutes since Lori seemed so irritated.

Tom walked in, and Lori said that she wanted to stay awake to talk to him.

She was very uncomfortable and complained that her back was killing her. She asked to be pulled up more to the top of the bed. Al and Tom gently lifted her. I don't think she really knew what she wanted. Everything bothered her, and she seemed extremely and abnormally restless.

No matter what position she was in, she became angry. I felt she was bothered by us being present. We thought that if we left her alone with Tom, she would calm down and rest.

I never had long moments with her or anytime with just the two of us. Tom was there every day—all day. I knew he loved her and wanted time with her, but so did I; however, I didn't ask for private times to be allotted to just me. I didn't want to hurt him, and I knew Lori was happy when he showed up for a visit.

I thought that once she was released from the hospital, I'd have plenty of time with her. I wanted to take her home for a few weeks so I could take care of her while Tom worked. I was looking forward to the privacy with her. I was determined that we'd both talk about the things that had been eating away at her since she was a child. Maybe I could tell her about our lives during those horrible years. I wasn't going to let this opportunity pass by without giving Lori the answers she had been looking for. Maybe we'd finally have closure on our horrible past.

"Lori, we're going to leave, so you can get some sleep. Tom will stay with you, and we'll see you tomorrow."

Al kissed her, but I held back because of my cough and congestion. I waved and blew a kiss to her this time. She smiled back. I needed time alone with my daughter so I could hold her and try to soothe her anxiety.

It was only six o'clock, and my girlfriend, Sue Schuster, was having a party for me at her home in honor of my new book. The party was scheduled for 7 pm. She had invited all my friends from my former place of employment, Perkins Paper in Taunton, and I was going to autograph the copies of my book which they had purchased. I didn't want to arrive early, but since Lori couldn't relax, I thought it would be better for her if we left.

Sue was surprised to see us so soon before the scheduled time, but I explained the situation at the hospital with Lori. It was wonderful having the support from my friends. They had all brought my book, *A Healing Heart,* and I autographed each one for them. Food and drinks flowed, along with our constant laughter. I was a lucky woman to have kept the friendships with these wonderful women after I left my job for a position in Rochester. Now I worked only two minutes from home instead of traveling forty-five minutes to work.

There was tightness in my stomach as the time passed. I couldn't explain the uneasiness going through me, and I tried to ignore the feeling. Even though Sue's get-together lasted past visiting hours at the hospital, I had an overwhelming desire to return after we had left the party. I tried to brush the anxiety off and didn't say anything to Al. I thought he'd tell me I was being foolish.

Emergency Call

Sunday morning, I woke up feeling very sick. "Al, I can't go to church with you. My chest is so tight with this dry cough and congestion. It'll be hard sitting there at Mass feeling like this. Besides, I don't think anyone else needs to catch this from me."

"Don't worry," he answered. "Stay home and rest. I'll be home in an hour."

"Look, if you want to go for coffee with Bob and Rachael, go. I'll be fine."

"I'll see how I feel after Mass."

He went to kiss me, and I motioned with my hand for him not to get near me. He said goodbye and headed to the 8 am Mass at St. John Neumann Church in E. Freetown.

Al was gone about an hour and a half when Debbie called me in a frightened state. "Mom, I just got a call from the doctor, and Lori's hemorrhaging. She's being rushed into the ICU."

"Oh, God, we'll be right there." I hung right up without saying another word to her.

My body started to tremble and my hands shook so violently that my fingers kept missing the numbers on the phone to call Al's cell. By then, uncontrollable tears flowed down my cheeks.

"Al, come home right away. Lori's hemorrhaging, and she's being rushed into the ICU unit."

"Oh, no! I'll be right there."

I leaped out of bed, grabbed the nearest sweater, threw it over my head, and jumped into my jeans. I pulled a scapular off the statue of the Blessed Mother and ran down the stairs with my sneakers in my hand.

I sat in the kitchen chair bending down to put my sneakers on when palpitations started banging hard in my chest. I knew it was from fear and running down the stairs too fast. My pacemaker, which had been placed in me three years before, was working double time trying to keep me calm.

I took a tranquilizer from my cabinet to keep myself from losing control from the fibrillation. I drank just enough water to get it down. I hadn't taken one in years.

Why did we leave the hospital early last night? I knew something didn't feel right. That must be why she was so aggravated. Please, let her be okay.

Having a few minutes before Al would arrive home, I went into the bathroom and put on the basic makeup to look presentable. I looked as sick as I felt. When Al walked through the door, I completely broke down. My whole body was shaking.

"This can't be happening. She was out of ICU. I'm scared, Al."

He came over and held me. "Okay, honey, calm down. Get what you need, and we'll leave."

I picked up my pocketbook, and we got into the car. It was November 19, 2006, and cold, but my nerves made it feel even colder. Al had the heat on full blast, and I trembled until the temperature got warmer. Our car had a seat warmer, and the device helped to get the chill out of me. We had little conversation the whole twenty minutes to the hospital. The car couldn't go fast enough for me. I looked out my window, most of the time with tears rolling down my cheeks. In between the silence and my prayers, my uncontrollable cries erupted from my excruciating heartbreak and fright.

We arrived at the hospital to find Debbie, Brian, Kerri, Michael, Joey, and Meagan already in the ICU family waiting room. Debbie had already started to call family members on her cell phone to notify everyone of the seriousness of Lori's condition; her situation was now death threatening.

"They wouldn't let us in her room because the nurse said they were still with her," Debbie said.

We congregated in the small room sitting quietly in shock. A television set that had been placed on the corner wall, close to the ceiling, was on, but no one was watching it. Other families were seated around the room waiting to visit their loved ones.

"I'm going to call Joe and his family," Debbie said as she went out of the room.

I went up to Joey and put my arms around him. "When's the last time you saw your grandparents?"

"We don't go to see them anymore."

"Why? That's a shame, Joey,"

"I don't know."

I didn't want to put more stress on him in light of his mother's condition, so I didn't go any further with the subject. We sat in silence, some of us crying, including the kids.

I read and hear about kids dying every day. This can't be happening to us. Please, dear Lord, send us a miracle.

In a half hour, Joseph and Jackie Cahill, Lori's ex-in-laws, arrived. Joe, Lori's ex-husband and the father of the kids, came in right behind them. His two sisters, Lisa and Julie, rushed in to be with the family. They all adored Lori. Joe went over to Joey and Meagan and held them. Then they all broke down.

I watched in shock as the small room filled with family and friends. I didn't want to face what was actually happening. Sonny, Richie's brother, received Debbie's call and rushed to the hospital. He had been visiting Lori for the past three weeks. My brother, Joe, had driven up from So. Dennis, and my brother, Bill and his wife, Sharon, came from Scituate.

Jackie came up to me in a shocked state. "None of us knew that she had been sick or that she was even in the hospital."

She loved Lori, and it wasn't that long ago that Lori had been worried about Mr. Cahill being hospitalized.

"We didn't realize how serious this was either," I said. "When she went from ICU down to a patient room, we thought that she was going to come through this. I didn't even think to give you a call. I'm sorry, Jackie."

I didn't give them a chance to say goodbye to her. Although, she was so sick, I don't know how Lori could have handled more people visiting her each day.

Julie, Lori's ex-sister-in-law, was waiting for her first grandchild to be born in the same hospital. Her daughter was in the maternity ward in labor. *Is God going to take Lori and replace her with a new life?*

The phone on the wall rang. Debbie answered it.

"They said we can go and see her now. They only want two at a time in her room. Do you and Al want to go first, Mom?"

"That's okay. You and Brian take turns taking the kids." I knew how much they loved and cared for Lori during her hard times.

Debbie started down the hall with Kerri, Brian waited with Michael.

They were gone about ten minutes then came back into the room. All of them were sobbing uncontrollably.

Pushing a large button on the wall, Al and I walked through automatic doors that lead to another set of double doors. We went down a corridor that curved around the nurses' station. We were finally going to get private time to talk to Lori. I didn't want to see her in pain.

A nurse pointed out her room to us. We entered, and my heart quickened. She had been put on life support! I expected to see my daughter awake and being able to talk. *Why didn't someone warn me?*

There was a long tube going down her throat with IV's in her right arm. A catheter had been placed in her, and I could see the urine bag on the side of the bed. She lay so still, in a coma. The room echoed with a swishing sound as the air was pumped into her from the machine. Her chest expanded each time the air was forced into her lungs. The heart monitor had the steady, timely rhythm of her heart rate.

I leaned over the bedside railing, and kissed her on the forehead. I fell apart. *This can't be happening.* I gently rubbed my hand over her left arm, holding her hand and kissing it. There were two chairs facing her. Al and I sat quietly and just stared at her.

I focused on her features. My beautiful daughter was being taken from me. This horrible, cruel, hellish demon wasn't happy with just taking her father. She was only thirty-nine years old. There was too much left for her to do. She was supposed to fight this killer.

We didn't stay long because others were waiting to see her. I walked out of the room feeling like someone had kicked me in the stomach. We watched Joe take Meagan and Joey through the ICU doors; the three of them embraced each other. Joe never remarried after he divorced Lori.

In an hour, Dr. Sousa met with the immediate family members behind closed doors in a room connected to the ICU unit. Joey, Meagan, Brian, Debbie, Michael, Kerri, Al, and I sat tensely, fearing the news.

"We're giving Lori a slim chance of pulling through this. The doctor did another endoscopy this morning and placed more elastic bands on her veins. They're breaking in her esophagus, stomach, and colon. I don't know how many times we can keep repairing them."

The same procedures her father had undergone. Oh, God, I'm living this horrible nightmare again.

"Are you saying there is no hope at all?" Debbie asked.

"There's always hope. The next two days will tell us for sure." After five minutes of trying to comfort us, he added, "Why don't we meet tomorrow morning around ten o'clock, and I'll update you on her condition."

We got up from our seats, trying to keep our hopes alive.

"Can we go back to see her?" I asked.

"Yes, there's no problem with you sitting with her."

I could see a gentle man in this doctor by the way he spoke softly and with deep compassion for each of us. He looked to be in his late thirties. How many times during the day did he have to face brokenhearted families to give them bad news? Did he separate himself from this heavy responsibility at night?

We all took turns staying by Lori's side throughout the whole day. Debbie and I debated about staying overnight with her.

When the nurse heard Debbie and me talking about spending the night, she said, "There's no bed for you to sleep on and not being able to rest could make a long night. If her situation gets worse, we'll call."

Debbie and I left the room with the fear that Lori might not be with us the next day. I couldn't bare the thought of her dying without me by her side.

Debbie called me the next morning. "My friend, Jill, and her husband John, wanted to go to the hospital and pray over Lori. Sometimes they talk in tongues. Would that bother you?"

"No, I have a friend who does that. All prayers help. I'd like to be there when they do."

"Jill came into my office today and asked how Lori was doing. Mom, I broke down. She held my hand and prayed with me on the couch next to my desk. That's when she offered to pray for Lori. At first I was taken back because that meant things were really bad, but I also thought it would mean a lot to you if they came and prayed. Maybe their faith will help Lori's soul enter into heaven."

"It's very special for them to offer their time. When will they come?"

"Tomorrow, if that's all right?"

"Sure, we'll wait for them."

At the hospital the next morning, Jill and John were introduced to me. They were both so gentle in their manner and very soft spoken. Jill had short blonde hair and tiny features, and John had a small build and dark, brown hair and wore dark framed glasses.

Debbie and I joined them in Lori's room. We prayed on our knees on the hard, cold hospital floor by her bedside. I don't remember Jill's words, only my private prayers from my heart for her recovery. They stayed about ten minutes.

"Thank you. I feel more at peace because of your prayers," I said hugging Jill and John.

They kissed Debbie and me and gave us long, warm hugs before leaving.

I couldn't believe how Lori's condition had changed. Her hands, stomach, legs and face were doubled in size. I felt sick inside at seeing her in this state. She was losing her normal features.

She was completely swollen because her kidneys were not working and the fluid had nowhere to go. I kept watching the urine bag praying to see it fill, but it stayed dry. Her process of urinating had stopped. Her face was swollen like a balloon. I lifted the sheet and saw that her knees were not even defined, being twice the normal size.

God, take this from her. Give her the strength to fight and come back. My mind didn't want to face what was actually happening. *We need a miracle, God.*

I sat in the chair beside her bed. Yesterday, she had thrown me a kiss and given me a big smile, and now she was in a coma. I didn't kiss her goodbye last night because of my chest cold. How I have regretted that choice.

Her room filled constantly with friends and family. Tom was trying to hold himself together. I could imagine the emptiness he must have been feeling not being able to be completely alone with her at this time; I felt the same.

I rested there thinking about her being all alone this morning in a confused state and hemorrhaging. Then my mind raced wildly, wondering if she had been looking for one of us. *Was she scared? Did she know what was happening? Oh God, I won't ever know.*

She was getting an intravenous morphine drip. I prayed that she had no knowledge of what was happening to her. I couldn't handle knowing that she was frightened. I would have been a mad woman if I saw her in pain or if she had been aware that she was dying. It would have horrified both of us.

I leaned over and whispered in her ear, "I love you, Lori. Please, get well. Fight this and come back to us." I kissed her forehead and ran my hand through her tight curls...curls that I had always loved. The tears poured out of me. I put my cheek against hers. I wanted to hold her whole body in my arms.

Am I ever going to be able to talk to her again? My body felt like it was breaking down from the stress. *Please, God, not two. This is too painful. I'm not that strong. You're asking too much of me. I'm so helpless; I can't do anything for her.*

Dr. Sousa met with the family again that morning. He said their hope for Lori was fading.

"Has anyone been assigned as her health proxy?"

Lori had requested Debbie, but she hadn't signed the paper to make it legal. However; since her whole immediate family was present, he went by our decision.

"Do you want us to resuscitate her if her heart stops? If we do, it could break her ribs."

The same question the doctor from the VA Hospital had asked Debbie and Lori about their father. Now we face this verdict with Lori. I can't handle what I'm hearing. I'm going to come apart. Please, don't let her be in pain. Don't injure her body.

We all agreed to let her go peacefully.

Letting Go

The day was filled with hope as her blood pressure looked good but then it dropped. There was still no urine dripping into the bag. We were on a rollercoaster of emotions, trying to face the fact she was dying and hanging onto hope that she wouldn't.

Lori's ex-husband, Mark, arrived with his son, Terry. He came over and hugged me. Within a half hour, two other men that had been in Lori's life came into the waiting room. Some of them had their children who had grown up to be teenagers since the last time I had seen them.

Don't let me be bitter. Let me show compassion for the ones who walked out of her life. Why couldn't they have loved her and made her happy?

I didn't want to refuse anyone from saying goodbye to her. It was too late for them to say anything to her. They had to deal with their own private regrets and personal pain in losing her. I had known that abandoned feeling from having been denied closure with Richie. The powerlessness was overwhelming back then.

Sitting here in the same circumstances, seeing Lori hooked up to the same tubes, machines, and IV's, and being in a coma, made the day Richie died twenty-one years ago seem like yesterday. I remembered being at the VA Hospital in Providence, Rhode Island, and looking through those drapes of Richie's window that had parted enough for me to witness Debbie and Lori with their father. I thought my agonizing suffering and unforgettable ache had healed through the years. Now, the wounds were resurfacing and being slowly cut open, layer by layer, for me to bleed with the deep, raw, indescribable grief again.

Meagan's girlfriends came to comfort her. All of them had loved Lori and spent so much time with her. How could they not? She loved each one and had welcomed them into her home.

I walked with Meagan to Lori's room. I watched as she sat staring at her mother with a sadness that mortals can't express. My heart ached for her. I couldn't do anything about the loss that was waiting to engulf her.

I put my hand gently on Meagan's shoulder. "When your grandfather died, your mother told me that she wished that she had stayed alone with him. You're seventeen years old; the same age that she was then. So, I'm going to give you some private time with her, I think you need to be alone with your mother."

I kissed her, stood outside the room, and leaned against the nurse's station that faced Lori's room, I watched as Meagan seemed to have no energy to move her body. She sat frozen in the chair, studying her mother's face; trying to absorb every feature. Her eyes didn't seem to blink.

She must have ached to talk to her mother one more time. I, and maybe others, had waited too long to say the things to Lori that should have been said when she was with us. It was too late to ask for forgiveness. No wonder Jesus tells us to love one another. We're never prepared or warned when He calls any of us home. *"No one knows about that day or hour, not even the angels in heaven, nor the Son, but only the Father:" Matthew 24:36.* It's when our loved ones are with us that we're supposed to tell them how much we love them.

We talked with Dr. Sousa a third time. "We're not seeing any improvement with Lori. I think you should all be prepared. You may have to make a decision on whether to take the ventilator off her."

Don't tell me there's no hope, my body screamed, silently. *I'm going to be sick.* I wanted to block my ears.

"What will happen to her if we don't?" I asked.

"She'll probably die of a heart attack."

I felt my stomach in my throat. "I can't do that to her."

He got up from his desk and gave me a soft touch on the shoulder. We all walked out in shock, drained from holding out for a miracle. None of us could make that final decision at that moment. We still hung on to hope.

Al and I met another doctor who had also been taking care of Lori in the hallway.

"Doctor, in your medical opinion, is there any hope, in any way, for Lori?" I asked, almost begging to hear that he thought there was. I wanted a second opinion.

I had hoped that maybe another doctor felt differently. I didn't want to take the machine off her if there was any chance of survival.

"In our medical opinion—no, there isn't."

He took his clipboard and, without another word, walked away. My world crumbled. My mind couldn't accept the fact Lori wasn't going to be in my life, that she was being taken from me.

Debbie and I went into Lori's room. Cheryl, her nurse on duty, asked, "Would you like a piece of her hair to keep.

Debbie replied, "Yes."

The gesture was so final that I couldn't answer. I was in disbelief that Lori was dying. I wanted to stop this nightmare and didn't know how. I wanted to see Lori sit up and hear her beautiful, loud, hearty laugh that everyone loved.

"Could you give us six cuts?" Debbie requested.

I watched as Cheryl tried to put the comb gently through the tight snarls from the back of Lori's head under the hairline. She did it so tenderly. Each one she cut had been placed in a plain, white card so that we could give it to someone of our choice. I couldn't believe we were doing this as Lori lay in a coma.

Stop this. She's not dead. Don't make it final. Oh, that beautiful hair. I wanted to fall on the floor and break down, letting all the pent up emotion come flooding out.

The nurse handed me Lori's cuttings in an envelope. I looked at the locks of curls knowing this was all that I had left of my precious daughter. I felt the panic in my body. I was sitting quietly, but my body was racing in every direction.

The nurse looked at the tube coming from Lori's bladder. "There hasn't been any urine in three days. Her kidneys have shut down," she said, almost apologizing.

By now, Lori didn't look at all like herself; she was bloated. Her knees had swelled and blended into her lower legs. I held her hand while I talked to her.

It was about 8:00 pm, and Deb and I were afraid to go home in case she passed away; we didn't want her to be alone.

Al compassionately stated, "You two would be better off getting two hours sleep at home than none here. There's nowhere to sleep."

We knew that he was right, but our hearts told us something different.

Sonny and Al went in to visit Lori one more time before leaving for the night.

"What a shame," Sonny said shaking his head as he stared at Lori. He had been with his brother, Richie, when he had died, and now his niece was lying before him in the same condition with cirrhosis of the liver from alcohol abuse.

"It really is. It's such a useless death," Al replied. "She was such a beautiful girl. It's really heartbreaking to see her like this."

We decided to go home and come back in the morning. The nurse assured us again that they would call if anything changed.

At 8:00, Tuesday morning, Debbie called. "Did I wake you, Mom?"

"I've been up since six o'clock. I couldn't sleep."

"The nurse on duty called me. Lori is holding on, but her blood pressure is dropping. She advised us to come in as soon as we could."

Al and I got dressed immediately and were at the hospital by 9:30 am. Debbie, Brian, and their two children were waiting. Debbie got on her cell phone and notified Joe Cahill and all of Lori's close friends. Joseph and Jackie Cahill and their girls walked in a half hour later. Joe Cahill was there ten minutes later. We all filled the waiting room.

For the last time, Dr. Sousa met with the immediate family in the doctors' conference room. "Lori's organs have all shut down. It's only the life support keeping her going. The next stage is her possibly having a heart attack, as we talked about. The stress of no organs working is going to cause something dramatic to happen to her physically. In two days, Thanksgiving will be here, and it would be sad to have her die on that day. Any day is bad, but the holiday won't have good memories for you."

How could any of them after this, I thought.

We all knew what he was saying. I believed that she died on Sunday, when she had been rushed to ICU hemorrhaging throughout her body. Here it was Tuesday, and we were selfishly keeping her alive by a machine, only for us. She no longer looked like Lori because of the horrible battle her body had gone through trying to hold onto life.

After an hour, the family decided to take her off life support. We were now hoping God would take her swiftly without any more suffering.

Oh God, how do we do this? Once life support is taken off her, she's gone, never for me to enjoy again. Why didn't you take her Sunday so we wouldn't have to make this decision? I felt like we were about to take her life instead of God doing it.

"Are you waiting for the rest of the family to come? Are both of her children here?" the nurse questioned.

"Joe and Meagan are due any moment," Debbie answered.

"You can have everyone in the waiting room come in and say goodbye to her," she stated. "If you want, I can call a nun to come up to the room, and we can all pray over Lori first."

"We'd like that," I answered.

I held on to the bible's writing: *"Where two or more are gathered in my name, there will I be also; Matthew 18:20." I need your strength, God. Help me let go.*

"I'll call her now, because she had somewhere to go at one o'clock."

Within fifteen minutes, the nun arrived. I was upset that someone had taken the Brown Scapular off Lori's bed post. (The Catholic Scapular is a sign of salvation, a protection in danger and a pledge of peace. Our Lady promises, "Whosoever dies wearing this Scapular shall not suffer eternal fire"). The nun told me she didn't have any with her at the time. I was in a panic since Lori had doubts with her faith. We all prayed for a few minutes, then the nun left the room.

The Cahills were all in the room; shoulder to shoulder, along with us, fourteen of us squeezed together holding each others hands.

I kissed my daughter all over her face and ran my hand through her hair. My heart broke knowing what was coming. I talked to her hoping she could hear me.

"Lori, go toward the light. Go to your baby. Dad's waiting for you."

Debbie leaned over her. "I love you, Lori. It's okay to leave us. Go hold your baby. I promise you that Brian and I will take care of Joey and Meagan and love them like our own. Don't worry about them."

I stood next to Lori's side and put her hand to my lips. Al stood behind me, and Joe Cahill sat in the chair opposite us.

Jackie Cahill came over to me and put a hand on my shoulder, trying to comfort me. I grabbed her hand without looking at her. I knew she felt the deep pain as well. I looked across at Joe, and he was just staring at Lori. She was the mother of his two kids. What a gift she had left him.

Family members took their time to be with her for the last time. Everyone carried pain on their faces along with the continuous flow of tears.

Joey and Meagan arrived and entered the room. We weren't sure if they should be in the room while they took the machine off their mother. They needed good memories with her.

"Are you kids up to this?" I asked.

"We want to be here, Grammy," Joey said.

What torment for them to go through at seventeen and eighteen.

"Are you sure Lori won't know what's happening to her?" Debbie asked the nurse through her tears.

"If you're worried, I can give her more morphine." she said.

She went to get a needle and injected it into Lori's IV. I was hyperventilating knowing that we were going to *pull the plug* on her. I felt that I was killing my baby.

The nurse spoke softly to our family, "There'll be no sudden movements from her, and she'll go peacefully. We can take the ventilator off her, but I'll keep the tube in her throat so you won't hear gurgling sounds. They can upset a family."

I suddenly felt sick and dizzy. Nausea overtook me. Why did she say that to us? My legs were ready to give out. When Al saw my emotional and physical distress, he got me a chair.

"Sit down, honey."

I sat in silence. Brian placed a chair for Debbie to sit next to me. I asked Joe Cahill to hold Lori's other hand. I wanted her to go with the feel of human hands on hers.

The nurse walked over to disconnect the ventilator.

No, don't touch her! Please, God, not her too. You took Richie. I'm not going to live through this.

I was trying not to become hysterical, fighting the desire to scream at the top of my lungs. I fought to control the urge to go over and reconnect the ventilator.

She can't breathe. Put it back on! I was in a state of horror, although, my body was absolutely still, just staring at my daughter.

"It won't take long," the nurse said quietly.

Lori was in the slow process of dying, and the nurse walked around quietly collecting things to be thrown away after shutting everything down. She had no emotional ties.

I watched the monitor as Lori's vital signs started to fall. Her normal heart rate was erratic with short to long wave lengths.

Stop this. Oh, God, her heart is stopping. We're killing her!

I stood up and kissed her, while the tears blinded me. I whispered, "Go to the light, Lori. Jesus is waiting for you. Take everyone's love with you."

She took two deep breaths. Her eyes suddenly opened and rolled back. The nurse came over and closed her eyes so they wouldn't frighten anyone, but she was too late to hide the scene.

I held her hand tight as one final breath was taken. "It's okay, honey, I love you."

"Oh, God, No, No, No!" I screamed. My daughter was gone. I cried uncontrollably as Al held me. The other family members left the room in tears. Debbie, Al, and I stayed.

I sat looking at my daughter, lying so still; no chest movement or sound of her breathing were seen or heard. My child whom I had carried for nine months, the one who moved inside me, the child to whom I had given birth and watched her lungs fill with air to give her first cry. All the memories of love, her laughter that echoed in rooms, were gone. I had watched her take her first steps; watched her go from a child to a teen, to a young woman, to a mother. Even the bad times were good, because she had been with me.

Now, I was there to see her take her last breath. I watched her come into this world, and now watched her leave it. God gives and He takes away, because we belong to

Him. Our children are a gift from Our Heavenly Father. In the end, we all return to our Maker.

I studied her face and was saddened that it didn't look like her. I wanted her beautiful, familiar face embedded into my mind forever.

How am I going to live knowing that I'll never see or hold her again in my lifetime?

Debbie started to leave the room, and Al came over to me. I tried to stand up but my legs became weak. They felt like jelly and gave out on me. I was crying so hard that I couldn't walk.

The nurse came up to me. She helped lead me out of the room.

"Do you need a wheelchair?" she asked.

"No," I answered, but I did. I was ready to collapse.

The nurse helped Al support me as we headed down the long corridor to the family room. Just before the door, I saw Joey sitting on the floor against the wall outside the waiting room with his knees bent up to his chest. He dropped his head into his hands sobbing his heart out. Dr. Sousa was bent down trying to console him.

This can't be happening. She was supposed to fight this damn battle. It was like watching a movie that was happening to someone else.

The waiting room was full of family members, all of whom were crushed by having witnessed Lori's death.

After twenty minutes, I found out that the nurse had asked Debbie if anyone wanted to see her one more time. Debbie had told her no.

"Debbie, do you want to go with me?" I asked.

She shook her head and answered, "No." Debbie was in no condition to handle another visit.

I couldn't leave without seeing her one more time. No one wanted to go with me. As I walked down the corridor, I questioned if I should be doing this.

I came up to her room expecting to see her still on her pillow and covered with a sheet. Instead, she was uncovered and laying flat without anything under her head. I froze in the doorway. She looked like someone who was laid out in a morgue. I couldn't enter the room.

The sound of the ventilator was gone. There was only silence. I wanted so badly to go in and hold her in my arms. There were no features of my daughter at all; I was looking at a stranger. I wanted to cover her up with a blanket to keep her warm.

My stomach felt like it was in my throat. Nausea hit me again, and I had to hold it back. I became dizzy and wondered how I was going to get back to the waiting room. I tried to see if a nurse was in the area so she would take me, but not one was to be seen. I had been so foolish trying to do something so emotionally overwhelming by myself. I needed someone to help me back to the family room.

I was ashamed of myself for not being able to go over to my own daughter. A friend or family member by my side would have given me strength. Why didn't I stay with her after she had passed?

I stayed at the doorway knowing that I wasn't going to be able to handle being there much longer. I wanted to lay my eyes upon the familiar face of Lori; the one that we had all known. If she had retained her features, it would have felt real. Instead, it felt like a bad dream.

I turned to walk away and started to shake all over. For those few moments, my mind was in a whirlwind; nothing seemed authentic. I felt like I had deserted Lori by leaving the doorway and not being able to hold her. I had heard that the dead can hear for a half hour after passing. She needed to hear my voice, but I couldn't go over and embrace my child. I felt the lightheadedness that comes before passing out.

I used every ounce of strength in me to walk back to the waiting room. I felt my stomach turn for leaving Lori on the empty bed, a scene I should not have allowed myself to witness.

Funeral Arrangements

When I returned to the waiting room, everyone was ready to leave. No one commented about me having left the room. I went unnoticed because each person was trying to deal with the loss of Lori. Our grandkids had already left. We agreed to meet at Debbie and Brian's home in Berkley to make the funeral arrangements.

Al and I had parked our car in the back parking lot behind the hospital. I could hardly feel my legs as we walked slowly past the ICU doors to the elevators. My daughter had been breathing moments ago in that unit. My whole emotional system shut down. I was in a fog, just going through the motions to get to our vehicle. Al and I barely spoke as we drove to Debbie's house.

Debbie's home started to fill with friends and family; but this time, it wasn't for a happy event. We went about in shock, greeting people as they offered condolences.

I watched as everyone conversed normally, as though nothing out of the ordinary had happened. An unexplainable panic hit me each moment the reality of Lori being gone swept over me. I acted normal in front of family, but my heart was completely broken. My mind was fighting an unfamiliar degree of emotional pain, as I battled to keep my sanity.

Jackie Cahill had retired from Shaws Supermarket in Taunton. She phoned former co-workers to prepare a few sandwich and meat platters. She was such a thoughtful, compassionate person who had loved Lori dearly.

I sat immobilized on the couch. The reality of Lori being dead completely drained me.

My chest was tight with the congestion that was still with me from the cold. Being so sick and having laryngitis didn't help my emotional state. I got up to call Brooks Pharmacy to see if my prescription had been called in after four days. The girl checked the files and came back to the phone to tell me it still wasn't in. Furious and outraged, I called my doctor's office.

The receptionist answered. "Dr. Blake's office, may I help you?"

"I would like to speak directly to the doctor." My anger had to vibrate through the phone.

"She's with a patient right now," she replied.

"I'll wait."

She put me on hold and after a few minutes came back on. "She's going to be tied up awhile. Can you tell me what it's about?"

"It's about my prescription, which I asked for four days ago!" I screamed at the top of my lungs.

"Didn't you get it? It was called in."

"I have been calling Brooks Pharmacy, and they haven't had a call from your office."

"Let me check."

She got back in a moment and said, "The doctor called it in to CVS Pharmacy."

"Why? I have never had a prescription filled at that location," I hollered.

"The doctor must have made a mistake."

By now, I was livid to the point of no control. All my anger and hurt from losing Lori had built up on top of my frustration with their stupidity in the doctor's office.

"No, Judy, *you* made the mistake. When I asked for a prescription, I told you what pharmacy and even took the time to give you their phone number."

"Well, can you give it to me again?" she asked in a quiet tone, sounding like she was patronizing me.

"Isn't their telephone number on record? Are you that disorganized?"

I tipped my pocketbook upside down, throwing the contents of my pocketbook all over Debbie's dining room table. Some of the items landed on the floor.

Al came up to me. "What's wrong?"

"This stupid girl gave the doctor the wrong pharmacy after I not only gave her the address but also their telephone number. She is constantly doing this." I felt the tears building up again.

Everyone noticed me unraveling. No one ever knew me to lose control. I knew Judy could hear me on the other end, but I didn't care. I wanted her to feel awful about what she had put me through. I wanted her to suffer for this tragedy that had happened to me. Every day that went by without her calling in the prescription was one more day that I wasn't able to go see Lori. I was now blaming her for taking those days from me.

"I can't find it right now," I yelled. "It must be in my other bag at home."

"I have to have the telephone number to call the prescription in again," she said sounding calm, as if the whole ordeal was nothing. She ignored my rage.

I think if she had been near me, I would have been fighting the desire to strangle her. She showed no compassion, and it angered me more. I needed someone to take my pain out on, and she was the one who deserved to feel my hurt.

"You work in the doctor's office, and you don't have Brooks Pharmacy's telephone number on record?" It infuriated me more. "Don't bother," I said slamming the receiver down. I had never misused anything someone else owned.

Jackie came over and tried to settle me down.

By now, I was sobbing uncontrollably. I raved on and on. "I just lost my daughter—I've been so sick for two weeks and this *idiot* can't get things straight; another day without medicine!"

If it wasn't for such a heartrending occurrence, the sound of my voice going from loud to soft, and words breaking up because of the lingering laryngitis, might have made everyone laugh.

Jackie Cahill left to get the food platters, and it wasn't long before Sonny arrived at the house.

"I went to the hospital to see Lori, and I saw no one in the waiting room. I was in complete shock when they told me she had passed away." You could see the emotion in him as he shook his head.

"I'm sorry we didn't call you. I wasn't thinking," Debbie said."

He hugged her, and she fell into his arms.

I looked at her and my heart broke. Lori was her only sibling, and now she would be without her the rest of her life. They had been so close before Lori got so sick. There were times that Debbie went to her for advice, especially when the kids were very young. It was such a terrible loss.

Debbie called Crapo-Hathaway Funeral Home in Taunton to make the funeral arrangements. The director, Jay Moran, asked us to meet with him in a few hours and to bring a picture of Lori for the newspapers. Our family albums were scattered all over the living room rug, as we looked through the pictures. I asked for Lori's high school graduation picture because she hadn't changed that much. The tears flowed as I rummaged through each picture seeing my daughter's life pass before me. The memories tore at my heart. The loss was so raw. After an hour, Debbie found the special picture for the newspaper.

We left people at the house while Brian, Debbie, Al, and I went to the funeral home. None of us thought it would be good to take Meagan and Joey with us. The funeral home might have added more stress for them.

Jay was wonderful and made all of us feel relaxed when we went into his office. It was my first time making plans for a family member's funeral. Being my daughter, the planning was agonizing. My three brothers had handled my father's arrangements.

We gave all the information that was needed for the obituary in the newspapers. A birth certificate and official papers were given for the death certificate. I wanted the announcement to read that her death was from alcoholism, but the family didn't want to advertise her sickness. I wanted the world to know about this disease. People needed to see a death in the newspaper from that particular demon and know that death was a reality of this killer.

Once the paperwork had been completed, Jay stated, "We need to pick out the casket. First of all, make a decision with your mind and not your heart, since she doesn't have any insurance. Don't get yourself in debt."

We went down the curved stairway, and my heart dropped when I saw nothing but caskets facing me. My knees became weak as I thought of putting my daughter into one of them.

My coloring must have scared Debbie when she looked at me, for she asked, "Are you all right doing this, Mom?"

"I'm okay," I lied, hoping to keep myself together.

We were torn between two caskets, a pink one and a powder blue.

Jay made our decision when he commented, "I have a woman who comes here and keeps asking to save this blue one for her. She calls it the *Blessed Mother Casket* because of the color."

He was right. The same beautiful blue that I had seen Our Lady wearing in pictures at Medjugorje. There was no doubt; this was the one. After finalizing our decision, we went back upstairs to his office. He talked to us for over a half hour learning all he could about each one of us.

We went back to Debbie's to eat, and to thank the family and friends who came to support us. Jackie came up to me with my medicine. She and her daughter, Lisa, went to CVS pharmacy to pick the prescription up for me. Their thoughtfulness touched my heart, and I cried harder.

An hour later, Al and I left to go home. I felt so many emotions flowing through me as he drove. My daughter was gone; she was no longer breathing. It didn't seem possible. The tears rolled down my cheeks as I stared out the window, thinking how senseless her death had been.

Thanksgiving – Black Friday Shopping

Two days later, Thanksgiving arrived. Al and I had planned to go to his daughter Lynne's home. Our son-in-law, Ron, was the chef in his family and was preparing the meal. I had no feeling of celebration in my heart and wasn't looking forward to breaking down with each warm hand that might be laid on my shoulder.

I wanted to send Al alone so that I could be by myself. I desperately wanted to disappear into the living room with a pillow and blanket and not move all day. I knew that it wasn't fair to Al because he felt the loss too. We didn't speak a word about our emotions or Lori's death. We tried to embrace Thanksgiving like we were okay with this tragedy.

I forced myself to get dressed for the occasion. My mind raced with thoughts of Lori never being with us for any holidays again. It was so painful. When Al got dressed and went downstairs, I stayed in my bedroom and cried in private. The flood of tears relieved some of the pressure.

We arrived at Lynne's close to 1:00 pm and Al's other daughter, Carol, greeted us when she opened her sister's front door, she lived in Maine and had driven down to be with us for the holiday. She came and gave me a long hug without talking. It choked me up, and I couldn't say a word to her. I smiled through tears. I braced myself as Lynne, Ron, and the grandkids gave me a kiss. All of them loved Lori and had spent time with her through the years. Al and I never thought of the girls as stepsisters. They were all our daughters. I smiled and didn't add much to the conversations going on around me. My mind was a thousand miles away. I didn't want to be there or anywhere else.

Two days after Lori had passed away was too soon to celebrate any holiday, especially a Thanksgiving dinner. She wasn't even buried yet. Life had to go on, but I didn't care about it because mine had stopped. I didn't want to smile, hug anyone, or put a spoonful of food into my mouth. I knew I wouldn't be able to swallow it. Talking took every ounce of strength that was left in my body. If someone asked me a question, I was too emotionally distressed to use my brain to think of a reply. I simply couldn't function.

The table was set festively with gold, red and orange decorations and linens. Lynne always had a wonderful touch with coordinating themes for the holidays. The family sat at the table, and I wondered if someone would say the blessing. I was the one who usually did. My throat felt closed.

Suddenly, as if Al knew, he asked, "Are you up to saying the blessing, honey?" Without looking at anyone, I put my head down. It was a miracle that I didn't go into pieces. The tears flowed without any sound of cries from me. Even praying was too much of an effort. How could I thank God for my blessings at that moment?

Al made the sign of the cross. "God, bless this food that we're about to eat, bless the people who can't be with us today, and most of all, have Lori in your eternal peace, Amen." He said it without falling apart, but I knew that he felt differently inside.

We stayed until 4:00 pm, which felt like forever, and then left to go to Debbie's. If we stayed later, it would have been too much for me to go at all. Al pulled into her driveway, but I wanted to stay in the car. Facing more people was agonizing. This would be another moment of putting on a strong act for someone else.

Lori had been a part of her sister's home. I felt her before I opened the front door. I could picture her inside with her kids. Now they were here alone.

"We're running late, Mom. The turkey won't be ready for another half-hour. We planned on an earlier dinner," Debbie said as she greeted me with a smile and hug.

My God, how does she do it? Her world has come apart, and she's taking care of a house full of people while I'm fighting to keep myself together. I just want to be alone.

"That's fine. Al and I are full after eating Ron's great meal."

We didn't have plans to eat again, but I needed to be with Debbie and the grandkids. I felt close to Lori in their company.

Brian's parents, Larry and Merlyn, were sitting around the kitchen island. They came over and hugged me. Again, I could only smile. I didn't want anyone, especially Joey and Meagan, to see me cry, fearing they would be upset. The pain in my throat was suffocating me. I wanted to put my head down and cry until I went dry. It wasn't long before Brian's sister, Cheryl, her husband, John, and their daughter, Gina, walked into the house.

I started to help Debbie prepare some of the dishes and place them on the dining room table. I had to be doing something in order to avoid conversation. A huge, gorgeous centerpiece with the same holiday orange, gold, and red flowers as Lynne's stood out on the white table cloth, which was colorfully decorated with embroidered green leaves.

Once the family sat down, Al went into the living room to watch the football game. I couldn't just sit, so I strolled back to the kitchen and started washing the pots and pans that had been used for cooking. It felt good being alone.

Debbie called from the dining room, "Leave the dishes alone!"

I ignored her and cleaned the whole area and placed the dishes, used for preparing the meal, in the dishwasher. I couldn't understand how Debbie had the strength to put the dinner on in the first place.

Cheryl had offered to do the dinner, but Debbie insisted she was all right with having the day at her house. The next morning, she admitted that she was mentally exhausted. She took responsibility seriously and fought through her own agony.

We made it through the occasion, and I could sense the depression in all my grandchildren. Everyone was quiet. Joey and Meagan had to be feeling the emptiness. They left to see their father at their grandparents' home. They went together in Joey's car. Al and I left at seven o'clock; it had been a long, stressful day.

The next morning, I met Debbie at her house to go through Lori's clothes. We had to find an outfit for Lori, but nothing looked presentable.

Debbie called Jay at the funeral home to see if Lori's stomach had shrunk. He informed her that we should get big sized clothes as she was still swollen.

"Debbie, let's just go to JC Penny's at the Taunton Galleria Mall and buy her something nice," I said.

We arrived at the shopping mall without realizing that it was the day after Thanksgiving, "Black Friday," the biggest shopping day of the year. The parking lot was jam packed with cars. We grabbed a space that Debbie spotted as someone was leaving. This wasn't a day for politeness about parking, so I rushed over. People were focused on sales and flocked to the entrance.

I didn't want to take my winter jacket off inside the Mall because of my cold. I wore a light-blue, flannel shirt underneath it. Every inch of floor space was taken up with shoppers in every aisle. People were bumping into one another as they sought out the specials in the mall stores.

Slowly, we rummaged through the clothes on the racks. I had a hard time concentrating. I spotted an outfit that had a long, cream colored skirt and a matching short-sleeve top with a silk collar. We both studied the shade and thought it would be a good color against the blue casket interior and Lori's dark, black hair. It wasn't something that Lori would normally wear, but we both liked the set. Lori didn't wear anything this formal, except for special occasions.

We looked at the sizes and Debbie said, "I think we should get a size 14, Mom. She usually wears an 8."

Because of the short sleeves, we decided on a designed, matching, cream sweater to cover-up her bruised arms from the burst veins. We were so glad that we had found the outfit in ten minutes.

"We have to get nylons, too," Debbie remembered.

"Why?"

"Jay said the funeral home requests it. We also have to get shoes."

"Shoes...I think that's crazy, no one will see them," I said, frustrated at not having a choice.

We grabbed a pair of queen size pantyhose. "I don't want a small size that would cut into her enlarged stomach," Debbie stated. Our minds erased the reality that Lori would not feel anything.

We ran over to the jewelry section with a 60% off sign on the counter. Deb chose a plain, thin, gold necklace with a tiny, cream-colored pearl and the same matching pearl earrings.

We then headed for the shoe department, and Debbie picked out a cream pair with no backing. Lori normally took a 7 1/2 shoe but we bought a size 9 to fit her swollen feet.

"Oh, Mom, we need to buy underwear and a bra for her. You check out, and I'll meet you at the front door."

I squeezed into one of two thick lines with shoppers eager to pay for their purchases. I saw Debbie hurry around the corner to the lingerie department. People were arguing at the registers over the wrong prices on the discounted sale items. I waited in line for twenty minutes without any progress toward the register. The 60% sale was supposed to end at noon, which was only ten minutes away, but the store extended the time because so many people were still rummaging through the displays.

I felt faint from the heat because I was wearing too many layers of clothing. I started to feel nauseous, and standing took every ounce of strength I had. I wondered how many in the crowd would be shocked to learn that I was buying clothing for my daughter's wake and funeral.

Two women behind me were talking excitedly about what they were buying to give as gifts. One of them held up a gorgeous, light pink, angora sweater to show her friend. "I'm sure Betty will love this for Christmas. What do you think?"

Christmas! Lori won't be with us! Oh, God, I can't stand this. Please, get me out of this store!

Her remark had instantly depressed me and waiting in line was now unbearable.

These are going to be the last items I'll ever buy for Lori, I thought, as I held them close to my chest.

My swollen feet felt glued to the floor as I tried to control my emotions. The line wasn't moving fast enough for me. I wasn't able to remove any of the heavy clothing I was wearing because my hands were full. I could feel the sweat beading on my forehead and under my sweater. I was getting weak from nervous tension and felt light headed. I was hyperventilating from the strain of shopping, and I couldn't see Debbie anywhere.

There wasn't any counter space on which to place some of my items. If there had been, the out-of-control bargain hunters would have scooped up my pieces of clothing thinking they were available. They were acting like a mad mob, grabbing anything with a red sticker on the price tag.

I could feel the wetness on my shirt, and my clothes were sticking to me, something that never happens to me. My heart raced, and I felt stressed out, the lines were at a stand still. If the items weren't for Lori, I would have dropped them on the floor and walked out. My eyes started to fill with tears. I wanted to scream.

Lord, how do people live through this? Of all days to shop!

Finally, after what seemed like hours, my turn came to pay. I handed the clerk my credit card; I couldn't wait to leave. Once the items were rung up, and the credit slip was signed, I grabbed the bags and headed toward the entrance to the mall. I looked for Debbie, but she was nowhere in sight.

I decided to call my brother, Joe, on my cell phone while I waited for her. I wanted to see how my mother was doing; he was supposed to tell her about Lori's death. Lori's passing was going to hit her hard. She was ninety-two and a resident of the Liberty Commons Nursing Home in Chatham. I was almost tempted to keep the tragedy from her.

"Hi, Joe, it's Alberta."

"Hi."

"Did you talk to Mom?"

"We took her into the library at the nursing home and told her. She was so upset that she cried for over a half hour. I asked if she wanted to attend the wake or funeral, but she said that she wants to remember Lori the way she was. How do you feel about that?"

"Thrilled—I don't want her there. Lori doesn't look like herself. Mom's too old to go through this pain, and she doesn't need all this commotion. The stress could kill her."

We talked a short time and hung up. I continued looking for Debbie while the mob rushed in and out the mall door. The store had no chairs on which to sit. The waiting seemed like forever, I couldn't believe it took that long just to get underwear, and I started to question myself on where we had agreed to meet. My mind wasn't clear because of all the turmoil.

Debbie arrived, looking exhausted. "I was trying to decide what kind of material to get with the underwear pants. I felt that the cotton ones would be the most comfortable on her. Imagine, Mom, she's dead—and I'm thinking this way."

Her eyes filled up with tears that she had held back while shopping all morning. I wrapped my arm around her as we walked out of the mall toward my car.

We went directly to the funeral home to drop off the items. Jay looked at them assuring us that they would fit Lori. I had a weird, uneasy feeling, knowing Lori was downstairs in the funeral home. I wanted to ask to see her, but the words wouldn't come out of me.

The next morning, The Standard Times newspaper arrived, and Al pointed out Lori's obituary. It took me a while to get the courage to look at the notice. It was on the second page.

Her picture doesn't belong here. She's another statistic of this killer called alcoholism. This can't be. It's not real. My precious, precious daughter! She was supposed to live. Her life's history was in one short obituary. *How will people ever know how wonderful she had been?*

The write up stated that she had passed after a short illness. It had been cirrhosis of the liver! I was disappointed her disease wasn't listed as the actual cause of death. Other alcoholics needed to see the reason for her death. I wanted them to look at this beautiful, young woman and see how she had died from a crippling demon.

That night the family met for a Mass at St. Joseph's Church in North Dighton. Father Jim wanted to go over the service arrangements for the funeral the next day. He needed to know who would be saying the readings. My sister, Leona and her husband, Bob, had arrived from Pennsylvania and met us at the church. Once we finished talking to the priest, we went to Debbie's.

Brian and Debbie planned a night for friends to come over and talk about the special moments with Lori and share in food and drinks. Everyone had brought pictures of Lori so we could pick out the ones we wanted to display at the funeral home. Debbie walked around refilling drinks and the empty trays of food. I watched as she went from one to another to make sure that everyone was comfortable while battling her own loss.

The Final Goodbye

After an hour looking at pictures of Lori, Al and I returned home. I took a shower and went straight to bed. The gathering at Debbie's had been an emotional rollercoaster that had my nerves on edge. I had gone along with everyone's joking about Lori's crazy moments, but the evening had drained me. I had heard things about Lori that I never knew; what her favorite flower was, and how she loved the sunsets, things kids don't think to share with their parents.

I couldn't relax lying in bed, knowing that tomorrow we'd be going to the funeral home where I'd see Lori in a coffin. Because she didn't look like herself, I wanted it closed, Debbie preferred it open. How was I going to handle this reality? I took a tranquilizer to stay calm; I wasn't going to fight sleep. Within a half hour, I drifted off.

Morning arrived, and my body was shaking even before I got out of bed. Not wanting to face the wake, I stayed under the covers longer than normal. Al was still sleeping, so I slipped out of bed quietly. I got dressed and went downstairs to the kitchen. I forced half of a raisin bagel into me so that I'd have some nourishment before we left for the funeral home. Within minutes, my stomach felt like a piece of lead settled in it, making me feel queasy.

What would I have done without Al? The past three weeks, everyday, he had driven us back and forth to the hospital. Al and I walked around talking about everything but Lori's death. I was ignoring the reality of the last couple of days. If I faced the truth, the hurt would have been too much. I would have gone to pieces and not been able to walk into the funeral home.

We pulled into the parking lot at Crapo-Hathaway Funeral Home in Taunton. My stomach turned upside down; Lori was in there, waiting for her family and friends to say their goodbyes. We waited for all of the family to arrive so we could all go in together. Within five minutes Joseph and Jackie Cahill arrived. My brother, Albert, arrived in a car he had rented after landing at Logan Airport in Boston. He had flown up from Boynton Beach in Florida. Bob and Leona pulled in, and right after them Lori's son, Joey, arrived with his father. Five minutes later Brian and Debbie came with Kerri, Michael, and Meagan. The kids carried the boards on which the family had all worked the night before, arranging the pictures of Lori.

Jay greeted us at the back door. Claudette Petit, a close friend of ours, came over and hugged me. She worked for the Hathaway Funeral Homes and requested to be the coordinator for the wake and funeral. I broke down in her arms. She knew the pain I was in; she and her husband, Ray, had lost two sons.

My dearest friend, Rita Vasconcellos, came out of a side room to console me. We talked for awhile. I was stalling, trying to avoid having to make that dreadful walk to Lori.

Jay took me by the arm. "Are you ready?"

He knew that I couldn't go into the room. He led me over to the casket, and I knelt in front of my daughter.

Facing me was a stranger. There was no resemblance to her beautiful face. If I had walked in alone, I would have been looking in another room, searching for my daughter. Her swollen lips had pink lipstick applied to them, a shade unfamiliar; she always wore a copper tone. I studied her face, neck, and body, all of which were swollen far beyond her normal size.

"It doesn't look like Lori, Jay." I didn't feel like her body was in front of me.

"We couldn't remove all the fluid from her. It had settled in her body cells, I'm sorry. With her kidneys not working, it had nowhere to go."

I studied her to find something recognizable. Her gorgeous, thick, curly hair had been blown straight; there wasn't one curl, and it seemed thin. Her eyebrows were perfectly shaped above her closed eyes. I knew she would have wanted a closed casket so no one would see her in this condition. I didn't think of requesting to see her before the public viewing. By now, people were coming through the doors and standing in line. I saw them gathering around the pictures on the boards.

I broke down and touched her. I laid my warm hands on hers, which were stone cold. I looked at the gifts that were next to her; the rosaries that had been placed between her fingers, a Medjugorje picture of Our Blessed Mother that I had left, and a cross in her casket. Debbie had placed a straw angel next to her sister that Lori had given her. It was a private secret just between the two of them. My book, *A Healing Heart*, which had been published sixteen days before her death; the one I had given her, was laid by her side. Tom had been kind enough to read a few pages to her in the hospital before she went into a coma. Personal items and letters from my grandkids were placed with her.

I got into the family line and fought constantly to keep myself together. I'd be fine until I saw a close friend, and then my emotions overflowed. My eyes felt swollen from my contacts that burned from the constant tears. I wore a white blouse, with black slacks and a black jacket, and low shoes to keep me comfortable while I stood from 3 pm-7 pm. I wondered why families stood when they were so weak from the heartache of loss.

The funeral home had a non-stop flow of mourners for an hour. Jay warned us that it would thin out at four o'clock because there was a Patriot's football game on at that time. He was right. We managed to smile for the people trying to console us.

It was a relief when the wake ended and the family gathered to go out for something to eat. Brian and Debbie took the kids for pizza while Leona, her husband Bob, my brother Albert, Al, and I went to the 99 Restaurant in Raynham. We laughed and talked for a few hours, and our conversation about what everyone had been doing the past few years erased the pain of the day—at least for a short time. It was nice to catch up on my sister and brother's lives. We hadn't spent time with one another in years. We said our goodbyes around 9:00 pm. My siblings went back to the hotel where they were staying, and Al and I departed in a different direction for our forty minute ride home.

I crawled into bed and felt restless. Al dozed right off as he always did. I got up and went downstairs to watch television for a while. It was there, in the darkness, that I cried my heart out alone. The depression and feeling of emptiness was overwhelming. Al and I still hadn't spoken at length about Lori's death.

I awoke the next morning and felt numb as I went through the motions of getting dressed for the funeral. My insides were a mess. This would be the last time that I'd see Lori or be able to touch her. I wanted Al to hold me and stay away at the same time. I was fighting to keep my sorrow deep within me. I didn't tell Al what I needed. I guess that's something I had done all my life without realizing my actions. We had to be at the funeral home by 8:30 am.

Al and I arrived ten minutes early. Claudette and Rita came over to hug me one more time. The compassion they showed started my tears flowing. This moment seemed worse than yesterday. I fell apart walking up to Lori. I touched her hands and kissed her cheeks and forehead.

Lori returned to God. I had tried to bring her faith back to her. She knew now the mystery of death more than I did. Jesus calls so many of His children home too early. It's a moment when we have to trust that He has His own reasons to take them. He is too merciful and loving to make us suffer purposely.

Yes, she was in a better place without fear or pain anymore. I had to stand there and try to mend my heart as a mother while feeling the tremendous, excruciating void.

It was difficult to tear myself away from her when the other family members came. I went to my seat and watched as others who loved her fell apart. While each one consoled me, I tried to console them. Cries echoed through the room as everyone said their last goodbye.

At 9:30 am, Jay walked over and asked me to join him at the kneeler in front of Lori to say some prayers before leaving for the ten o'clock Mass. The rest of the family joined us. My eyes tried to absorb all I could of my daughter for the last time. If only the woman in the casket, looked like Lori! I placed my last kiss on her before leaving.

Totally empty of any feeling, I sat in the family car. *I don't belong here*, I thought. The hearse with her casket joined the procession. My eyes focused on the hearse as it passed in front of our vehicle. The rest of the mourners' cars followed in order.

When we arrived at the church, the reality of what was happening began to sink in. As I walked down the aisle, I spotted my friends, Sue Schuster and Trisha Igoe, from Perkins Paper, my former job site. I almost fell apart looking at them.

Father Jim waited at the altar until the family was seated in the front pews. He gave a beautiful sermon, but his words didn't help me find peace. He mentioned the souls who return to God.

I was extremely upset when I learned that the organist and singers hadn't shown up. The Mass seemed cold with no music to send Lori home to the angels. If I had known the day before, I would have called and complained. No one should leave this world without singing in the church.

Debbie's son, Michael, and his aunt, Cheryl, gave the readings. Lori's son, Joey, and his cousin, Kerri, brought the gifts of the bread and the wine, symbolizing the Body and Blood of Christ, to the priest. Joey had told me that he wasn't very religious, but I hoped deep down that he still had some faith.

After the service, Brian walked to the lectern to give the eulogy. The night before, he'd wondered if he was going to be able to do it. He so loved and enjoyed Lori. He spoke about her life being filled with laughter, love, and compassion. He touched on her laidback clothes, their camping trips and the laughs they'd had. He mentioned Lori's love for animals and how her home was called "Fatal Farm" due to the abnormally high mortality rate of the animals that took up residence there. I had never heard anyone mention her deep love for stray animals before.

He said, "It wasn't love or laughter that was the true essence of Lori or what made her special. It was her passion when she looked you in the eyes with love or touched you. There was electricity that she emitted and you could truly feel it. Now that Lori is no longer here on earth with us, we need to carry her spirit on in our lives as we move forward without her."

He continued, "I want to read a line to one of Kerri's favorite songs by Leeanne Womack, *I Hope You Dance*. The song is about the choices we make in life, and there's a line in the song that says, 'When you get a choice to sit it out or dance, I hope you dance.' Well, let me tell you—Lori never sat it out. She danced and she danced with passion. Life is short, and we never know when the Lord will take us or one of our family members home. So, the next time you get the choice, think of Lori, and dance with a passion for life!"

Brian almost made it without tears, until he said the last word. The ending of someone's life doesn't make us strong. He felt the passion that Lori had for life and family. There are no words to explain the jabbing pain I felt when I looked at Joey and Meagan, so young, at eighteen and seventeen, to go through life without their mother's love or to feel her arms around them when they needed her.

The service ended, and we all stood up to leave the church. I followed behind Lori's casket. The deep, heart wrenching sobs that were buried in me, were beyond description. I almost lost my control when I spotted Lori's dearest friend, Wendy, sitting all alone in the last pew near the front door. Tears were running down her face.

The procession of cars lined up, and fifteen minutes later, we reached St. Patrick's Cemetery in Somerset. The casket was placed inside a small, low- structured building with seats setup inside. It was November, but the day was sunny, with temperatures in the high forties. All the people who attended could not fit inside the building so some stood outside the door. A priest from Somerset came to administer the last blessing.

After the short ceremony, family members and friends started walking to the location where Lori was to be buried. It was next to Richie. The earth had been turned-up, and the plot was covered with boards. Richie's tombstone had been moved so that Lori could be buried next to him. Her name was to be placed on the same stone.

I had lost them both to a terrible disease. It gave me comfort knowing she was going to be with her father, although any kind of solace was beyond my reach at that time. She never got over losing Richie. Now our loving daughter was going to be put to rest next to him. The plot had been a precious gift to Lori from Sonny and Anita; it was one of their family plots. Seeing the ground turned over made Lori's death final.

I wanted to fall to the ground and just let all the emotion come pouring out of me, but couldn't. I probably seemed fine to those around me, but I knew if one sob came out of me, I'd be uncontrollable; I would have become hysterical. The pain of keeping my grief bottled up was tearing me apart.

I wanted every person at the grave site to disappear and leave me alone with Lori and Richie. They had been my life. Two innocent souls were taken by this devastating disease. It was such a waste. Debbie and I were the only ones left with the memory of our once happy family. I never would have thought all those years ago that as a young bride, I'd be standing on this site trying to deal with the loss of my husband and daughter.

The cars started to fill up with friends leaving the cemetery. The funeral car with the family followed, and I sat in silence. My mind didn't want to handle her death at the moment. When we had reached the funeral home's parking lot, we switched to our own cars to go to Benjamin's Restaurant in Taunton for brunch.

We arrived at the restaurant and people were already in the Library Lounge with a banquet table full to capacity with a large assortment of food. Benjamin's is one of the finest and most elegant restaurants in the Greater Taunton area. The walls were lined with hundreds of books squeezed together on bookshelves. The brick fireplace was lit, and the whole restaurant had already been decorated for Christmas. On any weekend night the room would echo with live entertainment.

Our tragedy had been replaced with a few hours of conversation, laughter, and a beautiful banquet. I watched coldly with the strange feeling that no one was showing any sign of deep sadness that Lori wasn't part of the crowd. Deep down, I knew that this event was meant to help the family in the healing process and that the funny stories and amusement helped to ease the tragedy. Still, I felt resentment, knowing my daughter wasn't with us and would never be again.

It's amazing how we seemed to go on as though nothing had happened. We buried the heartbreak by acting normal while interacting with people just to survive. I tried to block my mind as to the actual reason we were all together. Couples started to leave after eating, offering condolences to the family as they left. The remaining close friends and family stayed longer. We lingered to talk about our memories of Lori.

Debbie made a toast to her sister. "No more tears," she said.

With the glasses raised, we heard the clinking sounds as they touched each one. It wasn't long before my sister-in-law, Marge, came back in to give Debbie and me something that she and my brother, Joe, had in their car.

"We almost forgot to give this to you two," she said.

A few months before Lori died; she had given Joe her favorite picture of her and Debbie to repair. It had some tears in the photo. He loved photography and had a program in his computer at home that could repair the damage. The snapshot showed Debbie at six years old with her arm around Lori who was two.

I remembered Lori's words when she had handed me the picture, "Don't forget to get my picture back from Uncle Joe, Mom. It's my favorite."

Joe had mended and framed the treasured picture. Debbie and I held the picture and cried, breaking our promise of *no more tears*. My heart broke. It was such a special picture, and she never got to see her photo finished.

Lori's Favorite Picture with Debbie

A Vision of Lori

Soon after receiving the picture from Marge, Al and I decided to leave Benjamin's. I suddenly felt all my energy leave me and wondered if my legs were going to get me out of my chair and the restaurant, I was worn out. Before leaving the group, I noticed Paula sitting at the other end of the table holding a drink. She was blind to the path she was taking. Richie and Lori's deaths hadn't instilled any fear in her, or a need not to drink. I could only shake my head. Finally, we hugged and said our goodbyes to everyone and headed home.

After I was upstairs in our bedroom, the only desire I had was to take a hot shower. The force of the spray against my body comforted me; I felt mentally relaxed for the first time that day. I let the steam fill the enclosed area and the hot water flow over every part of my body to soothe my tense muscles.

A few minutes later, I stepped out of the shower and toweled off. I put on winter pajamas and crawled into bed under the heated electric blanket. I couldn't picture a winter without one. I felt like someone had put their warm arms around me.

Al fell asleep right away, but I was wide awake. Although I was totally exhausted physically, my eyes were wide open. My mind raced back to the day I had turned the electric blanket on for Lori when she came home with us. Now, she was buried beneath the cold, hard, winter ground, covered with dirt, a horrible thought, but a fact of reality. I pictured the plot in the night with her next to her father. My daughter was no longer breathing the air that I did. I now thought of alcohol as not just a sickness—but a killer.

If only the shock of the event would leave me. Whenever I thought of the finality of her being gone, a panic sensation rushed inside me and left a tingling feeling in my chest. The emotion was something I had never experienced before. It was like a cold chill traveling through my body; it took my breath away. The tears ran down my cheeks onto my pillow. I looked over at Al and wondered how he could put all that had happened in the past few days out of his mind.

It seemed like hours had passed before I fell asleep.

At 8 o'clock, I woke up with daylight just starting to fill the room. It was a beautiful, clear morning, a day I would have welcomed for November, but today was different. There was no excitement as I lay in bed, unable to move. My nightmare was real and not a bad dream.

Al was missing from our bed. I could hear him walking around downstairs as the aroma of coffee reached our bedroom. He was giving me private time. I wanted to see his compassion for me, and at the same time, I cherished being alone. I didn't know what I needed.

I started to think back to my special moments with Lori. My life would no longer be filled with her beautiful smile and energetic attitude toward living. She wouldn't be attending any family events; no more phone calls. I would have given anything to have them back, even the disturbing ones. No longer would she bounce into a room to hug and kiss everyone.

I smiled with my own private recollections, thinking back to how her ritual of arriving late at family functions was accepted as normal. She'd enter Debbie's kitchen and grab a spoon and sample whatever was cooking on the stove. Each of us had special talents to contribute to preparing the meals. Lori made the best mashed potatoes and was always counted on to bring her string bean casserole.

After dinner, she'd be the first to lie on the couch with a pillow to have a "cat nap" only to wake up, faking shock that the dishes were done and the dining room and kitchen were spotless. She'd awake at the time that the desserts were being served. After filling ourselves with the pastries, Lori would lie on the living room rug and play with Brandy; Brian and

Debbie's family's chocolate Lab. Lori and the kids always brought their black, mongrel pup, Angelica, on their visits. Lori also loved to cuddle with her children to watch a movie. Back then, Joey and Meg filled her life.

Those special moments from now on would be an empty hole in our hearts. That gap will remain for the rest of my life as I watch Debbie accomplishing so much as a mother, wife, and professional woman. She would no longer share the events of her day with Lori. No more sister talks or sitting together laughing their heads off about the crazy things that happened in the family, with friends, or about something special between the two of them. For Al and me, we'd be watching Debbie and Brian raising Lori's children.

I struggled to shake the immobilizing feeling. I got up and put on my heavy, white terry robe, not really wanting to be in anyone's company. I just wanted to vegetate somewhere alone and spend the whole day in remembrance of my daughter, without any conversation, not even with my wonderful husband. At the time, I wanted him to sense my hurt inside and walk over and tell me that he understood what I was feeling. I don't think even deep love from someone else can convey the feeling of this kind of agony. I couldn't say what I wanted or needed from Al. Why couldn't I?

How did Debbie ever go to work today? I wondered. She's the most wonderful, compassionate daughter, and she's full of strength and always able to mask her emotions. She has the added responsibility of providing for Joe and Meagan, along with the substantial duties of her position at the Lopes Company. When does her alone time come? Maybe the hectic pace keeps her going. I only prayed she had time to think, feel, and act on her personal loss.

God gave me two beautiful daughters and took one home with Him. Now more than ever, I wanted to fill Debbie's life and heart with my love and support when she needed it. How could I not be proud of her warm personality, being a wonderful mother who supports her children, having a desire to help anyone in need and who loves so freely? I didn't want to take her life with me for granted. Losing Lori woke me up to how fast we can lose a child, and the fact that they may not be with us forever.

Debbie has a heart of gold. On holidays she'd remark, "If you know someone who is alone, bring them along for dinner." Brian and Debbie always welcomed anyone into their home.

The phone rang; it was Debbie calling from work. "Mom, Jill told me that she had a vision of Lori the day before the funeral."

Jill had been so strong in faith when she and her husband, John, came to the hospital to pray for Lori's soul with Debbie and me.

"What kind of vision?"

"She saw Lori."

"Are you serious? I'd like to talk to her."

Debbie gave me Jill's email address at work, and I asked her if she could tell me about her vision.

She replied to my e-mail.

"John and I are not anybody special or in any special ministry. Like you, we are just true believers in Jesus. We go to a non-denominational charismatic church which was founded by Catholic individuals out of the charismatic movement in the Catholic Church.

"John and I are born again Christians. All that means is that we believe that Jesus Christ is our Lord and Savior and have confessed our belief with our lips. You must be born again of water and the Spirit of God. I have asked the Holy Spirit to come into my heart and control my life. John has done the same.

"It's hard for me to explain how God talks with people. He talks with all that have a relationship with Him. He says things in different ways to different people. Some will feel it in their hearts. Others hear an audible word. To some, He uses words or pictures. I'm in that last category.

"Sometimes, He will show me something. How He speaks to me is backed up in His Word. The Holy Spirit gives us gifts, and one is the gift of prophesying. I believe that is the gift God has given me, not because I am special, but because He is. John also talks with God in the same way. When God talks with us, we try with all our heart to be obedient.

"To answer your question about Lori; when we were on our way to the hospital to pray for her, we knew that God wanted us to do something special. We prayed almost the entire way there. When we walked into the room, John saw either one or two angels behind Lori's head—I think he said sitting on the top of the bed.

"When we prayed, we relied on the Holy Spirit to tell us what to pray for. He wanted us to pray for her belief in Jesus, so she could be given another opportunity to truly believe that Jesus was her Lord and Savior. Only God knew what she believed or didn't. I think He knew at that moment she was going to truly believe in Him and be entitled to inherit the Kingdom of God. All I know is, after we were done praying, you said that you had peace for the first time about her dying.

"I attend a non-denominational church. Everything is done through prayer. I find that I can physically feel His presence more during corporate worship. The day before Lori's funeral, I went to my church and was at the altar praying during worship. I was on my knees bent over with my face to the floor praying. Remember, the Holy Spirit sometimes talks with me by showing me things by vision. He told me that he wanted to show me someone.

"Suddenly, I was shown a vision of Lori. She was dressed in a white gown, and she was smiling and looked so happy and beautiful. She waved to me, turned and walked into the whiteness and disappeared. He told me that she had made it into heaven, and it was in part because I had gone and prayed with her. Jesus thanked me. Can you imagine? God actually thanked me for helping Him! I sat on the floor and just cried because I was so overwhelmed by the entire thing.

"I hope this helps you. What I want to stress is that I'm not anyone special. These things happen because God is awesome. God will speak with anyone, but the question is, will they listen? God bless, and I'll be praying for you. If you would like to talk more, I would be happy to." Jill

Angels were seen around my daughter! I couldn't fathom being blessed to see such a miraculous sight. The Holy Spirit wanted them to pray for her belief in Jesus to become stronger. It overwhelmed me because a year before, Lori had admitted to me that she questioned if there was really a God. Jill didn't know anything about that.

In May of 2005, I had prayed a Novena of the Divine Mercy five times a day for forty-five days for Lori's healing and asked the Holy Spirit to pull her back to Him. The Miracle Prayer which, if said faithfully, no matter how you feel and when you reach the point where you sincerely mean every word with all your heart, will bring about spiritual depth, growth, and an understanding of the Love and Mercy of Jesus. You will experience Jesus, and He will change your whole life in a very special way. Daily rosaries were said for her during the last two years of her illness. I asked the Blessed Mother to bring Lori's faith back to her Son.

Were Jill and John's prayers stronger than mine? Would Lori have made it to heaven without theirs? Were they finalizing mine? I'm ashamed to say that I was envious and confused about how I hadn't been blessed with knowing my prayers were answered, yet in my daily prayers, I asked Our Lady to give signs to others instead of me, because I already believed.

God gave me my answer through Jill and John. Hearing her say that Lori was wearing a white dress brought me back to her being buried in a cream colored dress. What a gift from God; He was trying to bring me peace.

Facing Reality

I was still battling my cold, but the virus wasn't leaving me. I felt the congestion deep in my chest, so I decided to go and get checked at Tobey Hospital in Wareham. I had been sick since Lori's hospital stay, and the antibiotics weren't helping me.

As I entered the emergency room to undress for my examination, an overpowering fear hit me with the remembrance of Lori's treatment in her ward. It had only been a few days since the funeral, and I choked up from the same hospital smells, sounds, voices on the intercom paging the staff, seeing the IV stands, beds without sheets against the walls, doctors and nurses walking in the corridors, the blue latex gloves, the lined baskets, and outlets behind the hospital beds; they all made my knees weak and brought visible tears to my eyes.

The doctor pushed the white curtain aside, came into my room, and stood in front of me. He studied my chart, which I had filled out with the nurse before being taken to the assigned bed to wait to be seen.

"With all the antibiotics that you've had in the last few weeks, I can't give you anything. You're allergic to almost everything. We'll take a chest x-ray and blood work to see if you have whooping cough. If you do, you won't be contagious because you've been on two antibiotics, but the treatment takes around 100 days to end it."

A technician came in within ten minutes and led me down the hall to the x-ray room. She stopped in front of closed, swinging doors and pushed a large button on the wall to open them. My heart sank; memories of the same button at Charlton Memorial Hospital that had to be pushed to get into the ICU unit to Lori's room flashed in my heart. The hospital atmosphere had me desperately wanting to run out and go home.

The x-ray took minutes, and the girl walked me back to my room. The waiting seemed like forever before the doctor came back to see me.

"Doctor, I lost my daughter less than a week ago." It was hard to say it out loud.

"I'm sorry to hear that. You're run-down, have you been sleeping?"

"No, I'm up for hours or fall asleep for a half hour and wake up." I fought to stay composed.

"It's normal to be under a great amount of stress from a loss, especially losing a child. This can cause your immune system to be weak. I'll give you a prescription for the cough. This is just going to have to take its own course."

I took the written prescription and stopped at the drugstore before going home. Another waiting period for the order to be filled took all my strength. I drove home, parked the car in our garage, and walked down our long driveway to get our mail from the mailbox across the street.

Our neighbors, Lou and Janet, were working in their front yard when I opened the mailbox. After spotting me, they came over to talk.

Lou spoke, "We're so sorry about your daughter."

Janet hugged me.

I filled up and started to cry. "I'm fine until someone hugs me."

"You have the right to cry. Was she sick a long time?" Lou asked.

I told them about Lori's drinking and how her father had died from the same disease. Sharing my loss felt like a healing process trying to kick in. The family had no reason to be ashamed because she had been an alcoholic; it's an illness like cancer or tuberculosis.

"My brother died from the same thing," Lou told me. "We'd find him roaming the streets, and no matter what any of us did to help him, the support didn't work."

It's odd how neighbors can talk for years and not really know each other's past pain and losses until a tragedy happens.

During our conversation, I thought of how many people had lost a loved one to alcoholism or drug abuse. The three of us talked a few minutes, and then I walked back to the house. I felt stronger for having spoken about Lori, even though her death was tearing my heart out.

I sat on the couch in the living room and put my head down into my hands. I let the pain out and sobbed. Al came in from the kitchen and asked what was wrong.

I cried, "This is too painful without Lori."

He came over to me. "Why don't you go upstairs and get under the covers and take a nap. I know you're not sleeping."

Nap? I needed his arms around me—not a nap. He hadn't held me since Lori had been admitted to the hospital. He went off into the computer room, and I sat there by myself. Ten minutes later, I walked into the kitchen, and he was sitting at the table, staring outside.

"What's the matter, Al?"

"I'm thinking about going to the AA meeting on our church grounds tonight and talking to the group."

"Honey, you can't just show up and talk. They have scheduled speakers. We're not ready for that yet. Why don't you put a small speech together and maybe in a month we can contact the group. If you go, I'll feel guilty not going with you, and I can't handle that right now."

Suddenly, his lips started to quiver and his eyes flooded with tears. "I should have done what I wanted to do with her when she got out of The Emerson House. I knew it was wrong to let her go to that halfway house in Fall River; we should have insisted that she stay here with us. She couldn't have gone if we didn't give her the money. I would have gone with her to AA meetings, and anywhere else she had to go. She wouldn't have been able to drink so easily. I could have gone everywhere with her until she got on her feet."

"Al, there's no way we could have done that, even I know that. You can't hold a thirty-nine-year-old in the house. Lori would have sneaked out the first chance she got, and she would have resented us."

At that moment, I understood why he had been avoiding me. He was hurting inside trying to keep himself together. His love for Lori burst out of him.

I went over and put my arms around him. "Al, she could make her own decisions and, not being a child, she could leave and do whatever she wanted. We had no control over her, even if she made bad choices."

"I know that." Al said. "It's just so damn frustrating not being able to do a thing to keep them from destroying themselves."

I held his hand, and he grabbed onto it. He stood up to take the turkey that he had been cooking out of the oven. Seeing it was heavy and clumsy, I helped him put it on the counter. He always cooked one for us after Thanksgiving, if we didn't celebrate the holiday at our house.

He smiled, placed it down, and said, "Team work!" His hands free, he put his arms around me.

That's all it took. I held onto him crying, "I don't want this to be real."

We clung to each other for a long time as we released our pent-up pain. His tight grip was what I had been waiting for the last three weeks.

I looked up at him. "That's what's been missing."

No wonder they say a child's death can separate a couple. I didn't feel connected to Al with his daily distance from me. His actions of going on as if nothing had happened made me begin to resent him. At the same time, I couldn't reach out to him or open up to what I needed. I had those same faults in my first marriage.

I took Al's advice and went upstairs to rest awhile. I noticed two cards on the dresser from Lori that I had been bypassing for months. She hadn't been one for sending any kind of cards, whether it was a birthday or a holiday. Sometimes she'd shock us, but this custom was just her way. She'd joked about Debbie being so good at remembering every occasion.

She always remarked to Debbie, "Thanks for showing me up, Deb!"

God has a way of planting love letters for us to place in our hearts. The last time Lori lived with us, she had given both of us cards.

February 28, 2006, had been Al's birthday, and she had given him a card. It wasn't so much the card itself, but the private, loving note to him was priceless. She had written how much it had meant to her when we came to get her from Judy's house.

It read: "I had a card before this one, but this said it all. I don't know how to put it in 'perfect' words—but all I know is the night you came to Judy's was when I needed a dad—not a father. You gave me that, and I will never forget it. Through all the years, you have been there for me, and I didn't see it. I saw exactly what I needed without anything being said. I'm thankful we shared the ride home alone together. I don't know why, but I will never forget that moment, or take it for granted. I love you. I saw your true side." Love, Lori

Her last gift to me was a birthday card in September 2005.

It read: "As children, we don't realize our mother's sacrifice. The time she gives to teach us things or the love behind her advice. But now when I look back on all the things you've done for me, my heart is filled with gratitude for every memory." Love, Lori.

How odd to have these two cards given to us when Lori rarely gave any, and especially since she died. These are the treasures that I hold onto, they are her unexpected gifts. They're the last things of Lori that we have, not only the wording in the cards but also her neat, clear penmanship. I can feel and see her because the note was a part of her. I still haven't erased her notes on the pad of paper on the refrigerator; they've been there for three years. She had written down the dates of her doctor appointments. She's with me in those scribbled notes.

After the funeral, Debbie had been rummaging through boxes in her cellar with some of Lori's belongings that she had missed before. She came upon one that had pictures taken out of the photo holders and scattered loosely in a box. Lori had written on the back of each picture. Little notes to her children on their baby pictures. It was as if she knew that she wouldn't be here much longer. Debbie had shared them with me, and we cried together. How lonely Lori had to be feeling then. And yet, she still couldn't reach out and call a family member.

I had no pictures left of my daughter, Lori. Four years before, I had collected all the loose pictures we had of our six children, which were stored in boxes in the attic. I decided to make albums for each one of them for Christmas. I titled them "This is Your Life!" They had contained pictures from when they were babies, through their teenage years, marriage, and their own families. How could I have ever known? I know that I'll soon be digging into Debbie's overstuffed boxes of photos that were saved through the years.

We're Not Alone with Grief

After a half hour of tossing and turning and not achieving any resemblance of a nap, I went downstairs to make supper for us. Al told me to sit in the living room and went into the kitchen. In about a half hour, he came in with a plate of sliced turkey, a baked potato and peas, as well as cranberry sauce and butter. While I ate, he went to get a plate for himself. When he returned for a second time, we settled in the living room, ate our meal off of the TV trays, and turned on the television. There wasn't much conversation as we watched the shows that were on. After finishing, I collected the dirty dishes and washed them.

I came back to the couch, and we continued to be engaged with the shows for the next four hours. Al switched channels when each commercial came on, and I didn't have the energy to complain. My eyes were on the television screen, but my mind drifted to Lori. I had no idea what was on, and I really didn't care; the sound of the programs just filled the gap. Nothing was important to me, except concentrating on my loss.

A year ago, Lori had lived with us. I rubbed my hand on the cushion remembering her sitting on this couch. My mind drifted to her loud laughter as she watched the comedy sitcoms with me. I also had held her in my arms on this same couch. I knew she'd never be with me like that again in my lifetime. I never realized, at the time, that it would be the last time in my life that I would ever hold her.

Ten o'clock came and we did our usual routine of turning down the heat, shutting off the lights, and getting a glass of water to take up to our bedroom. We settled in bed to watch "Frazier." The television set always stayed on until the late news was over.

Al reached over and put his arms around me and for the first time in over a month, I tried to connect emotionally. I was torn with wanting to make love, yet, I didn't want anything physical. I had no energy or mental desire for closeness. I felt like someone had cut my whole insides out, and I was just a shell. My mind raced—Lori will never have a man make love to her again.

I fell asleep in Al's arms and woke up three times from horrible dreams, but after I awoke, I couldn't remember them. Every morning, I'd have no strength to get out of bed. It was an effort to sit up and put my feet on the floor. There was no excitement in facing the day.

One afternoon the phone rang; it was Debbie. "Mom, Aunt Anita was taking Paula to Charlton Memorial Hospital because the doctor thought she had a kidney problem. She picked Paula up at home and on the way to the hospital, Anita had to stop at home to pick something up, and Paula went into convulsions. They had to call 911. By the time the ambulance got there, she was okay, but they took her to the hospital for a checkup."

"Oh, how terrible!" I gasped.

She continued, "Eileen and I went to meet them at the hospital. Mom, going through the same corridors as we had to visit Lori a few weeks ago, was so painful." (Eileen is Gilly's wife).

"I know how you feel, honey. The same thing happened to me at Tobey Hospital; it had to be worse for you being at the same hospital Lori was in. How's Paula doing? Is she going to be all right?"

"This is about the fourth time she's gone into convulsions. She tries giving up alcohol on her own, but she can't do this treatment alone. They told her she had to be hospitalized to get weaned off her addiction. I had to go back to work, but Eileen stayed. She's going to call me when they find out Paula's condition."

"Give me a call no matter what time it is."

"Okay, I will."

At five o'clock, Debbie reported, "Paula's at Aunt Anita's now, she has a bladder infection. The doctor wants her to get help with her drinking and to go to an alcoholic rehabilitation center. Paula told him that she has done that before and feels she doesn't need to be admitted and can do this on her own. They gave her a list of AA meetings to attend."

"What a shame. Even after being treated in Florida, at one of the best alcoholic rehabilitation centers in the country, and also at Butler Hospital, she still can't give up drinking. She's following the same path that her uncle and Lori took. There's no way she can rehabilitate herself. I wish someone could stop the drinking in this family. We only have tragedy from losing family members. The fact is sad, but we can't force her to get help, she has to want it."

"Paula wanted to go home, but Aunt Anita said she wanted her to stay at her home overnight."

"Well, I'll give Anita a call sometime tomorrow. Thanks for calling."

"I'll call you if I hear anything more."

"Okay. Have a good night. I love you."

"Love you, too."

Since Lori's death, Debbie and I never hang up without saying, 'I love you.' We didn't know what tomorrow may bring.

The next morning, I went shopping, and bumped into my friend, Stacy.

"I heard about your daughter, Alberta. I'm so sorry," she said.

"We never knew she was an alcoholic, she hid her illness so well. My stomach turns when I think of how weak she had to be the last weeks before she went to the hospital. She couldn't have had the strength to even put meals together. Where was I? I'm constantly feeling guilty. I get nauseous thinking about her condition back then. I can't eat."

"Don't do that, Alberta. I went to counseling after my husband died, and I was told never to feel guilty when someone dies because it's the work of the devil. He keeps us from believing that our loved ones are with God. We have to believe in His promises. His death gave us life."

"I truly believe that, but my heart's aching."

We both talked about dreading Christmas with our loved ones missing from our lives.

Months went by, and I couldn't control the feeling of needing to see or hold Lori. I wanted to be able to kiss her one more time.

This isn't fair. I didn't get to say goodbye to her. Oh, God, when does this pain go away?

Each morning was the same. I'd feel the emptiness, praying it wasn't real. I placed Lori's prayer card from the funeral home, with her picture and a piece of her hair, at my prayer table. It's placed between the Blessed Mother's statue and a picture of the Sacred Heart of Jesus. I'd kneel in prayer and bring her hair to my nose, hoping the last locket of curls will still contain some of the scent from her body. A clipping of her beautiful, black, curly hair was all I have left. I crunched the strands up to my mouth, kissing them as my tears overflowed.

I felt the shock. It all happened too fast. We weren't prepared to adjust to her death. We went from hope to a dreadful sadness.

Debbie called me Monday morning. "I talked to Paula. She said she's feeling better, but she doesn't sound good."

"She probably isn't."

"I told her to go to a doctor to make sure everything is okay, and she blows the seriousness of her condition off. She still has a fever and feels dizzy. She stopped taking the Librium for the seizures. She says that's what's causing the unsteadiness. You're supposed to wean yourself off the medicine. I told her the symptoms should be checked out."

I feared another family member was going to pass away from this disease. How could Paula not see the danger?

Richie and Lori hadn't either. Everyone in the family was now begging Paula to seek help, but nothing seemed to motivate her to get counseling. Were the demons coming for her too?

Christmas Shopping

The bright sun shone through our sliding bedroom window, and I stared out at the clear, blue sky filled with passing white, puffy clouds with their light grayish tints blending together. I was mesmerized by their slow movements.

I had survived another day. I take my living, one day at a time, just as Alcoholics Anonymous teaches the alcoholics. I cry a lot, and when I don't, I feel guilty. I try to control the strong desire to pickup the phone to call Lori and hear her voice. *Why didn't I tape a conversation with her on the telephone so that I could hear her talking?* I think to myself, while lying quietly in bed.

I have to manage the sick longing to get into my car and drive to Charlton Memorial Hospital's parking lot to just sit in my car and stare up at the bedroom window where Lori once stayed. I want to imagine that I can go up to the third floor to her room and visit. I close my eyes and picture her lying in bed waiting for me to come and see her. It's unhealthy thinking and I don't dare tell Al. These thoughts are like being on a drug; I needed to get a fix by seeing her. Too much time had passed without a call from her or a knock on the door. I wanted her to enter our home, see her smile and hear her happy, "Hi, Ma."

How will I go on missing her for a lifetime?

I looked forward to driving anywhere alone. It gave me private time to scream and cry out loud with no one to hear me. The bathroom upstairs is another place where I can have my alone time to sob my heart out.

As I leaned against the shower wall, I said Lori's name over and over again out loud to hear the sound of that blessed name that had been picked for her. The first time I had been introduced to Anita's sister, Loree, her name seemed like music to me. That's who I had named Lori after. Loree is as wonderful as her name.

I cling to Jill and John's vision and try to picture Lori in eternal happiness and peace. God had given me a year to lead Lori back to her faith before He called her home.

We survived Thanksgiving, but Christmas was around the corner. How would I mentally make it through another holiday? None of us would hear Lori coming through Debbie's front door yelling, "Hello—I 'm here," while Joey and Meagan smiled with excitement in helping their mother carry the many Christmas gifts into the family room; gifts she couldn't afford, but somehow managed to buy. They were placed with the large stack of presents already under the seven foot tall pine tree. Holidays were the best times in our families. They were a joyful period with a house full of laughter and a home filled with aromas from the festive meal that had been cooking for hours.

Lori and Brian usually fought over the large living room couch, but neither lost because Lori thought nothing of placing a pillow on his lap and falling asleep. Those treasured moments, which we had taken for granted, would be no more for any of us.

I'm so blessed having Debbie; I try not to ignore her. What a sweetheart. There's so much good in her. She was there for Lori in every way. I thank God that I had hugged Lori many times, telling her what a wonderful mother she was to Joey and Meagan before she got swallowed up by alcoholism.

I took the dreaded ride alone to the Taunton Galleria Mall to do some of my Christmas shopping. The holiday was three weeks away. By August, I'd usually have ninety percent of my shopping done. I had ten family members left to buy for, but my mind was in a fog trying to decide what each person would be happy to receive this year. I strolled through JC Penny, and my stomach twisted; this was where

Debbie and I had searched for Lori's clothes for the wake. My body started to shake.

The mall was dazzling with huge Christmas trees that sparkled with the usual red, green, and gold lights that went as far as your eye could see and every assortment of decorations in the stores. It's a shame a holiday that used to be so exciting, that sent a warm, tingling feeling through me with the hustle and bustle, meant nothing this year. I wondered if it ever would again.

My heart wasn't into the shopping at all. I pushed myself knowing there were other people in my life whom I had to think about for the holiday. Maybe that's what keeps us going—others needing and loving us. How do people do it when they have no one? I had to count my blessings more than the losses. Al's children loved me and that was a gift in itself. Debbie loved Al like a father, so we were lucky.

I came home mentally exhausted. I lugged all the packages upstairs to the guest room and threw them on the bed. Some things fell out onto the floor. My patience was gone after fighting the crowd of bargain hunters all afternoon. I started to swear at anything that aggravated me.

I always wrapped the gifts, so I started choosing the Christmas paper that seemed perfect for each person. It had been a delight doing these chores each year, but a month after Lori's death, there was no joy in me. I never believed in waiting until the last minute, but having waited until it was so close to the holiday to do the wrapping, made me feel rushed to finish everything. The time limit became too much and I sat on the edge of the bed and broke down. Presents were everywhere, but none for Lori. Her name wasn't going to be on any tag. I put the rest of the gifts aside and decided to wait another day.

A Visit to Liberty Commons Nursing Home

I hadn't seen my mother since Lori died. I knew I had to take a ride to the Liberty Commons Nursing Home in Chatham. Mom was ninety-two and still had an alert mind, but her body was breaking down; she was losing her sight and hearing. She gave up using her walker and surrendered to using a wheelchair; her legs had become too painful to walk any longer.

I wasn't looking forward to this visit. My mother had lost my brother, Walter, and I felt now what my parents had gone through. No one knows the true, dreadful sense of loss until this ungodly heartbreak happens to you. You hear about other people losing a child on the radio, through friends, read it in newspapers, or see it on television, but it's not supposed to happen to you. Those tragedies happened to other families. Somehow, I thought I was protected from such disaster. I needed my mother's strength; she'd be the one person to talk to that would understand all that I was going through. Mom would hold me in her arms like I held Lori that night on the couch. Al didn't come with me; I wanted time alone with her.

Mom was informed of my coming and was sitting in the lobby area of the nursing home, next to the fireplace, which heated the room on this cold day. She lit up when she saw the Christmas gifts in my hands. I had collected them from the family members who had bought her presents. It would have been wonderful if everyone could have surprised her, but if they had, I wouldn't have the private time with her.

She was like a child at this time of the year. Buying for her had become difficult for my siblings and me because she didn't require much in material things anymore. With poor eyesight, a good book or crafts were out of the question.

One year, Al and I had bought her audio books and a headphone set, but she couldn't hear them. Even hearing aids didn't help.

I walked up and kissed her with a warm squeeze.

"Where's Al?"

"He had to go somewhere so I took a ride to spend time with you."

My brother, Joe, came in a few minutes later and was happy to see me. It wasn't unusual for my brother Billy to show up on the same day for a visit, but this wasn't one of them. After an hour, we slowly worked our way down to Mom's bedroom. Joe left early to give us mother and daughter time. He left with a smile on his face, seeing Mom and me together. I treated her by creaming her hands and painting her fingernails.

We both acted as if nothing devastating had happened to me. Neither of us brought up Lori's death. We talked about everything and everyone—but not Lori. She hadn't been strong when she had lost Walter; she had a breakdown. I think she purposely avoided the topic, and I couldn't bring the painful subject to the surface. I was afraid of falling apart.

The point was I didn't share my feelings with her so that she might have given me the comfort that I needed. I hated this path that I continuously traveled down, not connecting to my loved ones about my emotions and wishes. I think Lori had experienced the same thing without realizing that I, too, was caught in the same trap. It was an odd visit with neither of us mentioning the horrible tragedy of me losing a child, and Mom a granddaughter. I didn't want to handle the emotional turmoil that would surely have come had we discussed Lori, maybe she felt the same, but we would have at least *shared* our hurt. It seems that all I do after a painful event is realize the things I could have said or done only after the moment is gone.

I pushed mom's wheelchair into the dining room, and we had a cup of tea together. We continued with small talk, not really touching on any meaningful subjects. It was close to 4 in the afternoon, and being winter, dark came early. I had an hour's drive and wanted to go while there was still daylight.

I took my mother back to her room and hugged her goodbye. She was eager to open her Christmas gifts. I told her she had to save them until Joe, Marge, Billy and Sharon came with their kids for Christmas. I'm not sure if she did. She never could wait to open presents.

She disliked the changes in her life. Since she had entered the nursing home seven months earlier, Christmas couldn't have been the same for her, since this would be her first Christmas without being home with her family.

I tried blocking the emptiness of her being away from family out of my heart. I usually cried going home after my visits. Aging is so lonely!

During the drive home, I tried analyzing my relationship with my mother. Why couldn't I start the conversation with her about Lori? I should have been comfortable to open up to my own mother about my loss. Instead, I avoided the discussion.

I blamed her, but the problem was with both of us. I never tried to achieve closure or find peace with a situation. I drove, realizing how it wasn't my nature to open up to my parents; my mother had the same trait, never talking about any emotional or personal problems in her life. She didn't share her hurts or disappointments, either.

I started to wonder if Lori went through the same stuck feelings with me when she craved to open up but held back from fear of crying and not being in control of her emotions. Was she just as scared as I was to start a conversation? Was she afraid of hurting me with something she had to say?

This visit made me face the fact that I couldn't talk to my parents, but I could chew the ears off a close and dear friend. I felt comfortable being myself, right or wrong, with my friends; they loved me for who I was. I wouldn't feel threatened by being analyzed about my way of thinking or hurt if they questioned my actions. With my parents, I was always looking for approval; the same way Lori was searching for approval from me.

This quirk had been passed from my mother to me and from me to Lori, who was petrified to stand up for herself and feared voicing her own opinion. Like me, she desperately needed to be a people pleaser. I was just like her, and she never came to see or realize this trait before dying because we never discussed this problem or any others.

Mom and Alberta

Al, Mom, and Alberta enjoying clams

Christmas Day

Christmas morning came and Al and I arrived early at Debbie's to help prepare the holiday dinner. We had spent the night before with Al's kids and our grandchildren. The four kids were going through the house in different directions. Kerri was setting the dining room table with the familiar fiesta Christmas-themed china plates. The room was decorated with the gala table cover, holly napkins, red candles and an enormous, colorful, flower arrangement as the center-piece.

Debbie's famous, homemade chocolate chip cookies, along with brownies and gifts of pastry, that were given to her at work, were placed on the bottom shelf of the hutch. I wondered how she could have done all this only a month after her sister's death. It was another holiday that others had offered to take over for Debbie this year, but she refused; she continued with the tradition of having the event at her home. Meagan had just finished showering and came down the front stairs in her new outfit of casual slacks and a top that she received as a Christmas gift, opened earlier that morning when the family exchanged their gifts. Joey was alone in his bedroom, which he continued to do quite often, while Michael was emptying wastebaskets and helping his dad.

The house started to fill with Brian's family. His parents, Merlyn and Larry, were the first to arrive after us. Tom, Lori's fiancé, came over for a few minutes. He had lost twenty-five pounds from the stress of losing Lori. I felt so bad for him and knew the feeling of loss he had to be experiencing.

I walked into Joey's bedroom and talked to him while he was at his computer. We started to discuss a few family issues. Somehow marriage came into it.

"I'm never going to get married and have children, Grammy."

"Joey, don't say that. You had a special way of caring and showing your love for Carl, which showed me you'd make a wonderful father. Don't cheat yourself of that happiness. You feel this way because of all the hurt and pain your mother had from losing the men in her life. You and Meagan were lost along the way, too. Mark was a father figure who came and went out of your life. You loved him. Your own father hasn't been steady about seeing you since you were a child. You've had no one to hold onto, except your mother, and now she's gone. If the right girl comes your way, you'll feel differently."

"I feel guilty, Grammy, because my mother kept asking me to visit her at Tom's. I never did."

I put my arm around him. "When we lose someone, we all feel guilty over something that we could have said or done, but didn't. You avoided going to Tom's because you didn't know him, and you weren't comfortable going to his home and meeting his teenage daughters. You were also envious, and maybe angry, that your mom was with his girls every day and not with you. Was it right? Maybe not, but we can't turn the clocks back."

I continued, "Why didn't I go to Tiverton and visit her? Why did I let five months go by without driving out there to see her? I think about how she must have needed an arm around her."

"You didn't know, Grammy."

"Neither did you. If we had gone to see her, do you think that would have eased our pain? Probably not. It's so easy for someone not emotionally involved to tell us not to feel guilty. Tell that to our hearts. We can't be so consumed by the guilt that it causes us to stop living or to make bad choices in our lives. Don't get depressed and blame yourself to the point that you start to go down the wrong path. Don't hang out with the wrong crowd, make bad decisions or turn to drinking.

"I'd never do that."

"We don't know what depression will do to us. I want you to always remember, Joey, that your mother watches you every day, so do what will make her proud of you."

"You think she does?'

"When I was in Medjugorje, I was told that the visionary, Ivanka, had lost her mother three months after the apparitions started back in 1981. On the six visionaries' birthdays, Our Lady appears to them and asks what they would like. Ivanka was asked if she had any special requests. Because it was her birthday, she asked to see her mother. Within seconds, her mother not only appeared but physically hugged and kissed her. She told Ivanka, 'I watch you each and every day, and I'm proud of you.' Then she disappeared. What more proof do we need to believe that our loved ones who have passed on see us? So talk to your mother when you're lonely or have the need to connect with her. And most of all, pray for her soul, because the departed souls can't get out of purgatory without our prayers from earth. They can't pray for themselves. When we die, they'll pray for us."

I embraced him thinking how hard it had to be for any teen to lose a parent. Joey and Meagan needed a parent in their lives. I knew that, no matter how wonderful Debbie and Brian were to them, they'd be left with a void in their hearts, just like the rest of us.

I walked back into the kitchen and mixed in with the laughs and conversations. It wasn't long before the prime rib was placed on the table. Every year, we waited for Brian's delicious meal. As everyone gathered around the tables, I felt the emptiness without Lori sitting at one of the places.

"Mom, do you think you can say the blessing?" Debbie asked.

My lip shook as I replied, "I can't." Just the thought of mentioning the absence of Lori did me in. "I'm sorry."

Merlyn stood up. "Lord, we always ask for the same blessing, but this year, Lori isn't with us."

She lost control and couldn't say anything else. I leaned over and held her hand. It took a while for me to get in control of my emotions so I could speak to anyone. I smiled through the tears but couldn't talk.

Joey and Meagan had plans to go to their grandparents for dinner with their father. They were starting to go once a week to visit them. What a shame Lori had to die for the families to pull together. Divorced people with children spend more time trying to get back at each other, rather than spending their energy on being loving parents and having a healthy relationship with their kids.

After dinner, the customary time we reserved for opening gifts arrived. Lori wouldn't be sitting in the sunroom with us to open any. I tried to appear normal and happy as the grandkids started to open their presents. There was none of the laughter or joking that had filled the room every year.

The grandkids were all teenagers now. Joey was nineteen-years old and working at Lopes Construction. Meagan was eighteen and had graduated from Dighton-Rehoboth High School and was about to start her first year at Massasoit Community College in Brockton to study nursing. She worked part-time at Lopes Construction. Kerri was nineteen and in her first year at Amherst College in Amherst, MA; she also worked at Lopes Construction during the summer and holidays. Michael was sixteen with one more year at Somerset High School.

I watched as they tried to look happy opening their presents. Deep down, I knew no one in the room was really excited. It had been only a month since Lori died, but we did well. I watched Debbie open her gifts without her sister sitting next to her on the couch as she always did.

My heart ached not seeing Lori with her children. I'm sure they were devastated, not having her with them. We all got through the moment, but no one mentioned Lori's empty seat. That's what kept us together emotionally; pushing our grief deep down inside us. If we didn't talk about the vacant feeling, then maybe we could hide the loss of Lori for a few hours.

Debbie and Lori

Joey, Lori, and Meagan

Mom's Passing

On February 2, 2007, while I was having breakfast, our phone rang. I had been falling asleep late every night and waking early. I couldn't stop thinking about Lori once the lights were off and the house was quiet.

It was 6:45 am.

"*Who would be calling this early?*" I thought, as I reached for the phone.

"Alberta, it's Joe." My brother was calling, and that wasn't a good sign. "The ambulance is taking Mom to the Cape Cod Hospital in Hyannis. They think she had a stroke. They walked by her room and heard her having trouble breathing and found her semi-conscious."

"I'll get ready and meet you there."

I ran to our bedroom to tell Al.

"Honey, wake up. My mother is being rushed to Cape Cod Hospital." I said, out of breath from running up the stairs and from the fright of the situation.

I grabbed my clothes and got dressed. I hopped on one foot as I tried to put my sneaker on standing up.

"That doesn't sound good," Al said as he jumped into his jeans.

"Al, I think we'd better leave now," I stated, grabbing my coat from the back of the kitchen chair.

"Honey, I have to stay here. Remember the men are coming to start the renovations upstairs. Someone has to be here to make decisions if they run into a problem."

"I completely forgot about them coming. I'll keep in touch and let you know what's going on when I get there."

I didn't want to waste precious time, so I rushed out to the car.

Oh God, don't let her die. I won't be able to handle it.
Lori had died two months earlier.

I was thankful there was no snow or ice on the roads to deal with as I drove the hour to the hospital located on Cape Cod. Upon arriving, I discovered the parking lot near the emergency room entrance was full. The other parking area on the side of the hospital was just as bad. My eye caught a woman leaving two rows from the emergency area as I drove by. I put my blinker on and waited to take her spot.

My brother Bill and his wife, Sharon, arrived as I walked through the automatic doors.

"Oh, I'm so glad to see you two," I said, hugging them.

Joe and Marge were with Mom in the emergency room, but the three of us had to sit in the waiting room. Ten minutes passed before a nurse came out and said that we could go in together.

I wasn't prepared for what faced me. I slid the curtains back and saw Joe sitting at Mom's bedside. She was holding her right hand up in the air. Her eyes were closed, and she was fighting for a breath. Her stomach was rising and falling forcefully, trying to get air into her lungs. Her facial expression showed fright and confusion, though she couldn't talk or open her eyes.

Bill tried calming her, "Its okay, Mom. We're not going to leave you, breathe slowly." He grabbed her hand. "Rest your elbow on the bed, I won't let go." He rubbed her head softly and kissed her on the cheek.

Joe was standing at the foot of the bed and came over to me. I backed out of the room so she wouldn't hear me when I completely broke down, sobbing deeply.

"Oh, Joe, she looks awful," I tried to whisper.

I composed myself and walked back in and went over to kiss her on the forehead and whispered, "Mom, it's Alberta."

I felt sick watching her struggling to breathe. The nurse had put the oxygen tube into her nose. I knew this situation was really grim. The time that we had talked about so many times, but hoped would never arrive, was here. In six weeks she would be ninety-three years old.

The nurse made her comfortable. "If you need me, my name is Lori," she stated as she walked out of the room.

Lori—of all names to hear! There'd be no problem remembering.

I rubbed my fingers through Mom's hair. How she loved that through the years. Her hand tightened like a vise around mine. She had to be terrified, locked in her body, unable to open her eyes or talk to us.

It was an ordeal of waiting five hours in the Emergency Room. The nurse returned and said they had a room upstairs for her. Another hour passed before they finally came to take her up. We all squeezed into the elevator to go to the third floor with Mom. Other nurses were waiting in the room to move her onto the bed. They were so gentle and talked to her, though she couldn't answer them.

"It's ok, Sophie. We're going to get you comfortable in a nice, big bed."

Bill and Sharon had to leave, but I sat with Joe another four hours as I held Mom's hand. By 7:00 pm, I had to start home. I was so frightened that she would die after I left.

"Alberta, go home. I'll call if something changes," Joe said. He lived only ten minutes away.

I hugged Mom and said, "I'll be back in the morning." I felt like I was deserting her.

Joe and Marge were at the hospital when I had arrived the next morning. They had their daughter, Molly, with them. They had adopted her three years before from Guatemala. Mom had the chance to enjoy her for those years. Molly loved to sit on her grandmother's lap in the wheelchair and be wheeled around the rooms at the house when she lived there and also at the nursing home.

For the next two days, Mom struggled nonstop with the heavy, labored breaths. I didn't know how her heart was holding out. I had taken some clothes with me, packed in a small suitcase; I had decided to stay overnight. The patient's rooms had a couch that opened into a bed. That day Bill decided to stay with me, and we took turns sleeping while the other one held Mom's hand, or we'd fall asleep in a chair with our head on the side of her bed.

Her condition didn't change, and her breathing still wasn't normal. She couldn't converse with anyone, but by the way she squeezed our hand when we asked her a question, we believed she could hear us. My heart broke for her. A priest came to say the last rites over her. The words from the priest touched my brother deeply, and he cried.

Joe had been holding off calling our brother, Albert, and my sister, Leona.

"Joe, I don't think you should wait any longer. They have a long way to travel, and they have to make travel arrangements."

"You're right." He left the room to call them.

Bob and Leona were coming by car from Pennsylvania, a twelve hour ride. Albert had scheduled a flight from Boynton Beach, Florida to Boston and then arranged for a rental car. I prayed they'd get there in time. I couldn't help but wonder if Mom was holding on to hear their voices.

On the third morning, the doctor came in to talk to us about taking Mom back to the nursing home. We heard Mom give a groan, as if she was trying to say no. Within minutes, I noticed Mom's breathing change; it was calmer, as though she was giving up her fight. Joe and I held her hand as we watched her fade from our lives. There had been no gasping. Her eyes opened halfway for a few seconds, she took a short breath, and then stopped.

The nurse came over and listened to her heart. She put her hand on my shoulder. "I'm sorry, honey, she's gone."

I held my mother's hand to my face and sobbed. First Lori, and now my mother! Two precious people were gone from me forever. No more calls, hugs or hellos. Holidays would include their empty chairs facing me. Only six weeks had passed since Lori died; now I faced another funeral.

I thought back to my last visit to the nursing home to see her. I had let a precious moment go by without sharing my pain, and the loss of Lori, with my mother. The talk could have been something to remember all my life, instead I was agonizing over not having shared my feelings.

Joey remarked, "Does anyone see the change in her skin? It looks tighter." No one else saw it.

Albert reached Hyannis an hour after Mom had passed away. It would be another three hours before Bob and Leona arrived. They missed their goodbyes, and so did Mom.

I stayed over at Joe's and helped him with the funeral arrangements. My knees went weak walking into the funeral home and smelling the flowers in the familiar atmosphere. My brother had done most of the planning. We were faced with choosing the casket, flowers, prayer cards and clothes.

I don't know how God gave me the strength to walk this dark path again, but He did. I truly believe that we're put in a state of numbness while we go through the process.

I instructed the funeral director to put no makeup or lipstick on her; she never wore any. I told them not to style her hair, just brush it forward; giving her bangs, her everyday style.

We had the wake and funeral in one day because her two sisters and brother were from the Boston area and in their middle and late eighties. Mom looked like she was sixty. Joe was right about her skin tightening up. Family members couldn't get over how young she looked.

My siblings were too nervous or shy to give a eulogy, so I put one together. I wasn't sure how I was going to hold up, but I didn't want her to leave this world without us talking about the love she had given us, and our wonderful memories. I made it through the ten minute talk. I held up until I told Mom to take everyone's love with her. Then I broke down and walked to my seat, crying for both her and Lori and also for myself, knowing I'd have more sadness in my life because of the loss of their presence in it.

Mom was laid to rest at the Massachusetts National Cemetery in Bourne at Otis Airbase next to our father. Sixteen years before, we had buried Dad. Now they were together again.

Feeling a Presence

The new renovations upstairs had the bedrooms in disarray. It was an effort to get to our bed, and the one in the guestroom. I was under too much stress to lift things off either bed to get to one. Al could reach our bed on one side, but I decided to sleep downstairs. With Mom's passing, I couldn't sleep, so I turned on the television set in the living room, hoping to relax. I placed my soft pillow on the couch and wrapped the afghan around me.

Although, I started to doze off around 1:00 am, I felt restless. I couldn't sleep; it was too soon after another death. Sleeping seemed impossible for me. I'd be up until 3:00 am, sleep an hour, or be up all night quietly watching television in the dark. I wanted to be alone. My world had collapsed, and I desperately wanted sleep to erase my pain.

The only light that glowed in the living room came from the television set. An odd sensation came over me, and I had a strong awareness of someone near me; it didn't feel like Lori. I tried to brush the perception off and went to sleep. Not long afterwards, I woke up startled.

I opened my eyes, and my heart was beating fast. I expected to see Al standing over me. I felt a presence only inches from my face. I actually sensed breathing on me. I had no fear, but I was confused with this aura around me. I felt my mother. I was on the verge of saying out loud, "Are you here, Mom?" I held back because I was frightened that if I did, she would appear.

I tried to push the consciousness away and pulled the afghan up to my neck. I lay there with my eyes open, not daring to move. Somehow, I fell asleep again.

At 4:15 am, I awoke again, noting it wasn't quite light out. When I opened my eyes, I saw streams of smoke floating through the room. In fact, some went directly by my face. I sat up fast, thinking something was burning in the house. I was wide awake, and definitely not dreaming. I studied the smoke and realized that the haze didn't fill the room. This *presence* had a shape that traveled like cigarette smoke after being blown from someone's mouth.

I jumped up and switched the light on. When I did, the presence disappeared. I sat there wishing I hadn't moved. Whatever this strange smoke was, it wasn't natural. I sat still, wondering what I had witnessed. I was upset that I had sent this unknown presence away.

I passed through the kitchen to go into the bathroom. The smell of oxygen engulfed me. It smelled exactly like the oxygen mask Mom had worn the whole four days that I had been with her. When I came out of the bathroom, it was gone.

I had never felt anyone's presence after his or her death, but I had no doubt that I had an experience with a spirit being around me. It felt like my mother trying to connect with me. Maybe she came to make sure I was okay. No one will ever convince me that it wasn't a spiritual phenomenon.

The next day I emailed my brother, Joe, to tell him about what had happened. He replied back, "I had something similar happen to me Tuesday, the day after Mom died. I had an urge to go into Mom's bedroom and look out her large, bay window for a few minutes. I got to the window and right away, a very thick energy filled the air and encompassed me. I sat on the bed and just started thanking Mom for all she had done for me. The energy felt like it was moving and not singular. It felt like two because I had a sense of it holding hands. I asked if she was with Dad, and the phone rang. When I got up off the bed to make my way to the phone, I could feel all the thickness just peel away as if they were saying, 'We've got to go.' There was a tremendous sense of freedom and whimsy behind it. All in all, the whole experience lasted about a minute."

His experience confirmed mine. I have never doubted, to this day, that Mom came to Joe and me.

A Visit to the Gravesite

Joey's grandparents, Joseph and Jackie Cahill, offered to pay for him to go back to night school in order to get his high school diploma. He accepted and went twice a week. We were all so proud of him, and within three months, Joey had his diploma. It was a wonderful gift to him.

While Al and I were visiting Debbie on a Saturday morning, Tom brought Lori's car back and parked the vehicle in Debbie's front yard.

"I can't stand coming home after work and seeing her car in my driveway, the sight is too painful," he explained. "I put all her clothes and belongings that I found at the house in the trunk and the back seat."

After he left, I went to the front door and looked out at the white Pontiac that she had bought from us. I put my head against the window pane and cried. The reality of her death kept haunting us as we removed her last possessions, one by one.

Debbie and I went through five large, green, plastic containers full of Lori's remaining clothes. Meagan was in a size 0, so she couldn't wear her mother's outfits. She and Joey took other items their mother had, which wasn't much. One storage bin held Lori's winter jackets and coats, and I could picture her in each outfit as we held them up. We divided what we each wanted, and I placed those I could use in the trunk of my car.

The next day, Al went to the gym at the Holiday Inn in Taunton, and I sat on the floor in the sunroom going through Lori's items again. I crunched each outfit up against my chest and cried; I couldn't stop the flow of tears. I was alone to let my emotions free.

This is the last of her physical belongings—mismatched clothing. This is all I have left of her. Why? Why couldn't I have saved her? Why was my love not enough?

I got up to do a few hours of house cleaning that had been neglected for months and came back to spend the rest of the morning sifting through both Mom and Lori's belongings. Mentally exhausted, I sat in Dad's big, oversized rocker in the sunroom, which I had taken when he died.

Like a child, I rocked slowly, sitting in the spot where the sun radiated through the glass panels warming my body. Before long, I drifted off, still sitting up in the chair. I awoke a half hour later, but I was too drained to do anything else and left the room. It felt like all my energy had left me and had been replaced with total weakness. I plopped on the couch in the living room and lay there in a daze. I didn't care about anything or anyone at the moment; I felt nothing. I fell into a deep sleep for over an hour.

The next day, I had my semi-annual appointment with Dr. Norris, my cardiologist. I had to have my pacemaker read. I sat on the examining table and waited for the doctor.

Soon she walked in with a happy stride, as always. I had been lucky in finding this wonderful woman. She was such a compassionate person.

"Hi, Alberta, how are you?" she asked.

I could feel the lump in my throat building, but I fought to hold it back.

"I'm doing okay."

"Everything looks good from your tests," she said sitting down in a chair in front of me. She looked down at my chart. "Blood pressure is perfect and the pacemaker is fine."

I sat up straight and tried to look composed.

"So, tell me what's been going on with you personally. How's your daughter doing with her drinking? Last time you said that she was in the hospital."

Wrong question...I lost control.

"I'm not doing so well," I answered trying not to sound sorry for myself. I couldn't control the flood of tears.

She came over and took my hand, "Alberta, come and sit in this chair next to me."

"I'll be okay. Just give me a minute."

"No, you're not okay. Get comfortable and talk to me."

I tried settling into the chair calmly, but I couldn't control my shaking hands.

"My daughter passed away on November 22nd, and my mother died February 5th."

"Oh, I'm so sorry. You're under a lot of stress."

"I shouldn't bother you with this. You're my cardiologist, not a counselor."

"You should share this with me. These issues affect your heart. Stress is the number one killer. Do you have someone to talk to about your deep feelings going through your pain?"

"A dear friend, but she's in Florida. I have other friends but I haven't been getting out much lately. I don't talk about it often because I can't keep myself together."

"You should talk about this to someone. Don't hold this in, Alberta. If you want to cry, do it. If you feel too tired to do housework, lie down and read a book, take a nap or watch television. Don't push yourself. It's only been four months; don't put on an act about how strong you are. You've had two tragedies back to back."

Dr. Noris went to a desk and got a notepad. "I'm giving you this doctor's name and telephone number. Call him and schedule an appointment to talk."

I took the information, but I knew I wouldn't call. I just needed for time to pass for me to heal. I acted like Lori; I had all the information for help and ignored it. "I can do it on my own," we all say.

She walked up to me when I stood up. "Now let me give you a hug."

Smiling through tears, I relied, "If you touch me, I'll lose it."

"You need to be held. Take care of yourself, and if you don't have anyone to talk to, call me. We'll set up an appointment to just chat for awhile." Looking straight in my eyes she gently grabbed my two shoulders, "I mean it, you call me."

"I will, and thank you for taking the time to listen to me."

I went to the office to schedule my next appointment and headed straight to the elevator. I could feel the dam ready to burst again. I got into the car and collapsed in deep sobs that came from the depths of my soul. My shoulders shook as I put my head into my hands to let all the bottled up sorrow flow from me. I was constantly trying to hold my hurt deep inside me. Dr. Noris was right; I try to show how strong I am, when I'm not.

May 31, 2007, Memorial Day, Al, Debbie, Joey, Meagan, Kerri, Michael and I went to St. Patrick's Cemetery, in Somerset to visit Richie and Lori's gravesite. A few weeks earlier her name had been engraved on the stone. We had been waiting for that to be completed; it was six months after her death. As we pulled in front of the row in which their plot was located, the tears automatically kicked in and my heart pounded hard and fast in my chest. Knowing that her name had been inscribed into Richie's stone was going to make the reality harder to face. I didn't want to walk over to the site.

The family strolled slowly toward the gravesite. There were baskets of flowers on both sides of the stone.

My God! There it is—Beloved Daughter, "Lori" Laura Cahill, July 29, 1967—November 22, 2006.

My heart felt like it would break open. I turned, holding back the tears that wanted to burst out of me. Instead, I swallowed painfully because I didn't want to upset Joey and Meagan. I desperately needed to be *alone*.

Then the truth hit me head on; she was really gone. Lori's name had been officially written on Richie's tombstone. I stood there and thought back to May 5, 2003, when Lori had telephoned me one afternoon.

Alberta H. Sequeira

"Mom, I want to take you to Dad's gravesite. You've never been."

"I don't know if I can handle going."

"This would mean so much to me if we went together. I don't want anyone else to come with us. Please, Mom, this would heal me and you."

I didn't have the heart to say no to her. She needed to heal from so many hurts, and this was one I could help her with. She actually asked for my assistance in her emotional mending. I had no knowledge to what else bothered her.

"Ok. I'll come down tomorrow."

The next day, I arrived early in the morning. Before driving to the cemetery, we stopped at a flower stand on route 138 in Somerset for a beautiful flower arrangement to take with us.

We pulled into St. Patrick's Cemetery, but I had to sit a moment before getting out of the car. We started our walk through two rows, and there it was: Lopes, Richard— January 2, 1945 - February 10, 1985. I couldn't believe that it had been eighteen years since my husband's death, and I was finally visiting his grave.

"Mom, last night, I wrote this letter to Dad. It's time for you two to say goodbye. I know he'll understand my reasons for bringing you. I don't really believe he wanted to hurt you. I'm going to walk around to leave you alone." She placed the letter in my hand. I opened her private note and started to read.

Dear Dad,

'First, I love and miss you more than you will ever know. I took a big step tonight that has been bothering me since you were taken from us. I hope I didn't go against your wishes, but if I didn't feel so strongly, I wouldn't have done it. Mom has never visited your resting place because she thought that's what you wanted. I've always believed that was your defense. She respected your wish, but I saw it tear her apart. I think it did the same to you. I know it did me. I asked her to come with me and say her goodbye. Please, understand it'll help close a painful void in my life. I know that you two had shared a lot of love. Debbie and I are proof of that. You have four beautiful grandchildren (2boys/2girls). My son Joey looks *exactly* like you, Dad. Swallow your pride and smile down on Mom. She loves you. I wouldn't do this if I didn't love you more than words can say. I miss you in a way I cannot express. This can help the emptiness I feel. Please give me a sign of peace, love, and a lifetime of memories that I will never forget.' Love, Lori

I knelt and placed my hands on the top of his stone. I let my years of built up tears flow freely. What foolish, stupid things that we do in life. They were meaningless and left such painful impacts on our lives forever. They kept Lori from moving on or ever fully feeling loved. The decision by Richie's family, to ban me from the funeral, had left me devastated.

After a few minutes, Lori came over and put her arms around me. She smiled and said, "Mom, look where Dad has been buried."

I looked up and saw a huge, white statue of the Blessed Mother in front of him.

"It gives me so much comfort knowing that she's watching over him," she said.

Her remark made me realize that Lori did have a religious belief in life after death.

Our Lady's arms were opened and stretched wide. There was only one other large statue in the cemetery; it was the Crucifix of Jesus at the other end of the graveyard.

"I'm sure he's in her loving arms, Lori." I kissed her softly on the cheek and hugged her. "Thank you for bringing me. I wouldn't have come on my own."

Three years later, I was standing on the same spot where Lori and I had our conversation, such a special daughter and mother moment. It had been one rare time that we had reached out and cried together. That day, however, didn't help Lori open up about her past life that disturbed her so much. It could have been the right time once we got back to her house to talk about her demons. Little did Lori and I know then that within three years, she would be buried beside her father.

It was so agonizing not being able to let my torment out alone. Debbie came over and put her arms around me. I'm sure she had sensed my emotions.

"She's at peace, Mom, and she's no longer suffering like she was on earth. I'm sure she feels the love that's here with all of us."

"I know," I replied, trying to get a hold on myself. I was the one who was not at total peace. I never had closure with either of them.

Joey came over and put his arm around me. I looked up at him with red eyes, "I'm supposed to be strong for you kids."

"Its okay, Grammy."

I passed out beautiful, red roses for everyone to leave at the grave. They were artificial, but someone would have to touch them to realize it. I knew that they would last a long time, even if we had bad weather. The hard wire stems slipped easily into the spring ground. Each of us placed them close to the stone.

"Is everyone ready to go?" Debbie asked.

The five of us started toward the car. I resisted the desire deep within me to sit there by myself. I wanted to talk to Richie and Lori privately. It would have to be another time. I left, knowing one day I'd have to fill this need for healing.

As we pulled out, I thought of what a precious gift Anita and Sonny had bestowed on us, arranging for my husband and our daughter be buried together. They had been the truest friends to me. They promised Richie that they'd take care of his daughters, and they continued to do so for over two decades.

St. Patrick's Cemetery in Somerset, MA

Our Lady watching over Richie and Lori

My beloved family

Searching for Answers

Because Lori had lived with Debbie and Brian for over a year, Al and I met with them in the fall of 2007 to talk about Lori's past. I was searching for answers, just as Lori had been. I needed to know if Debbie knew more than I did about Lori's emotional state and the problems she kept hidden.

I had been in the planning stage of writing this sequel about Lori's battle with alcoholism. I had decided on the title of the memoir some time ago, *Please, God, Not Two*; This Killer Called Alcoholism.

We went to Debbie's home on a Sunday afternoon. All the kids had plans so we were free to have adult talk without them hearing any of our conversation.

"You know, Debbie, I was wrong keeping your father in our home when he was drinking. I was in my early twenties and feared being on my own without a job. Once I began work at the Dighton Police Department, I still had to count pennies. That's why I had to get three jobs. I had difficult times, but one special moment sticks in my memory the most.

"What was that?" Debbie asked.

"Lori's twelfth birthday was coming up, and I had no extra money that week to buy her a cake or even a present. You were working part-time at Almacs Grocery Store and came home that night with a cake, soda, ice cream, and a small gift from the two of us. I can't find the words to explain the love I felt for you that day. You thought nothing of spending your whole check on your sister.

"I don't remember that, Mom."

"Well, I do, and I was proud of you."

"Debbie, can you remember how far back it was that you felt the confusion in our lives caused by your father's drinking? When did you realize that there was a problem? Did you live in fear as a child as Lori did?"

Debbie was now forty-three years old, and there was so much about the past that we had never talked about, but maybe talking would help us find peace or reason for our years of confusion. I didn't take the time to sit and share the past with Lori. Now, I had to stop this cycle that I had been stuck in all my life and go forward through my fears to get the answers. I only wish Lori had lived to read my memoir *Someone Stop This Merry-Go-Round*; An Alcoholic Family in Crisis. The story was about our whole life with the confusion and fear from the past. It might have helped Lori to open up about being so scared.

"I think it was as far back as elementary school. When it was time for school, I didn't want to leave you. We were living in Cindy Atwood's apartment. When I was in middle school, you and Dad got divorced. I was embarrassed and didn't want to tell my friends that my parents were divorced, but they started asking me questions like, 'Why did you move?' When I mentioned the divorce, someone would say, 'Oh, my parents are divorced, too.' Then I didn't feel so alone."

"During that time, Debbie, I felt the same way as a mother and a wife. It seemed that everyone had a happy marriage and mine was the only one crumbling. When we left our house to go to the apartment, our life was better. I was relieved that I didn't have to worry about when or in what condition your father was in coming home."

I took the time to tell Debbie about the day Lori refused to leave the apartment to go to school. I explained how the principal helped me get her out of the car. I talked about our counseling. Debbie wasn't aware of all these episodes; I never shared them with her. How wrong I had been.

Now I realize that I should have talked to the girls when these things were happening. Lori would have understood more, rather than living a life of searching and wondering what was real and what wasn't. Everything was hushed up back in those days, but our fears and confusion should have been talked out within our family. I truly believe that if we had conversations about matters while they were happening, and especially Lori's uncertainties, that our discussions would have helped keep her from being so emotionally upset and scared all of her life.

I went back to a moment in my life. "I remember one day, when I was about seven years old; that my mother was at the top of the stairs in our house in West Springfield. She was pulling me by one of my arms trying to get me up the stairway. At the same time, my father was pulling my other arm trying to drag me down toward him. It frightened me for years. Later, I came to learn that my mother had had a breakdown and wanted me home while Dad was trying to take me with him. At least someone explained that frightening moment to me. Lori needed her horrible circumstances explained to her."

I returned to our previous topic. "Most of my guilt came from trying to keep your father in your life and Lori's. I realize now that by making that decision, I messed you kids up, both mentally and physically. Alcoholism wasn't something that people talked about back then. I knew you witnessed our fights. I tried to keep Dad calm, but I couldn't. He always wanted to fight. He wasn't a fun loving drunk. Near the end of our time together, he was mean and abusive in blackouts."

Debbie started to think deeper. "I remember that if he wasn't home before we went to bed, I'd lie awake waiting to hear the ladders rattle on his truck when he came into the driveway. There were times when he fought with you that Lori would come into my room, and we'd stay together. If the arguments got really bad, I'd go into your room, and he stopped."

"I read a book titled *It Will Never Happen to Me* by Claudia Black. It talks about the oldest child becoming the parent in situations within the alcoholic family. I guess you did that, Debbie. Your father never wanted to upset you. That's why I couldn't understand why he kept going into Lori's bedroom. He'd sit on the edge of her bed and wake her up saying, 'Hi Lori, Daddy's home.' I didn't know if it was because he knew that it would upset me or because he thought, in his drunken state, that he had to say goodnight to her. I always took him back into our bedroom."

It was hard listening to the scared moments our daughters had gone through in their younger years. I should have protected them from that life.

"Lori had hang ups with Dad," Debbie said.

"What were they? Did she share them with you?"

"We did our own things, Mom. Lori had her own friends because she was four years younger. We weren't even in the same school. I met Brian when I was seventeen, and I spent all my time with him. I had Donna Ferreira, across the street, and all the kids would group over there. Lori had Diane and Wendy for her friends.

"Were you aware of the wild parties that she was having at the house?"

"No. I went to Aunt Anita's on weekends when you went to Al's."

"That's why I stopped staying at his place. It left Lori free to have her parties."

"She'd be invited to go with me. I'd get there and Aunt Anita would say, 'Where's your sister?' I'd have to say that she didn't want to come. After awhile, I got tired of explaining why she wasn't with me."

"Was your father living at Aunt Anita's then?"

"I never saw Dad there. I didn't know what he did. I only found out after he got sick that he had been living with Sara. That was the first time I heard about her."

"Writing this sequel has made me realize how I should have sat down with you and Lori to talk about the events that happened to us, just as we're doing now. How different Lori would have felt being able to face her demons with us, instead of trying to cope with them alone. It's my fault."

"Mom, I didn't want to bring those things up. I just wanted the bad times to be gone."

Al jumped in. "Anita hit it on the head. It wasn't that anyone treated Lori differently. Lori treated everyone else differently. She was a loner."

"Lori would withdraw herself from everyone and family events. She wouldn't show up, and I'd always be questioned about where she was," Debbie said.

"She had deep rooted problems that should have been talked about, rather than living her life not knowing what was real in her past and what was not. I couldn't help her, because she never told me she had problems. Did you know that your sister was bulimic when she was living on Somerset Avenue?"

"No!"

"I can't believe she kept that from you. Obviously, she didn't open up about her life at all. I assumed you two were close enough that she'd tell you everything. I feel better because I thought she only felt distanced from me."

"We were close, but she never opened up. She had a way of hiding a lot of things, or she'd lie. Brian and I wanted to help her because she feared that she'd die like Dad. She had so many hang ups with him. If she had a night of drinking, she'd start talking about him. I'd say, 'Lori that was so long ago. You have to get over this. It was twenty years ago."

"Deb, I want to tell you about a conversation that I had with Lori about a year before she died."

"Lori called me, and I could tell she had been drinking because she slurred her words. She said, 'You know, Mom, a lot of things happened to me.'

"I said, 'What things?'

'Well—with Dad.'

"What do you mean—with Dad?"

"She got angry and said, 'Mom—I know you know.'"

"Lori, I don't know what you're talking about. Are you telling me that your father did something to you?"

'Why do you think I left the house?'

"You told me that when you were eighteen, you were going to live with Jimmy, and that I couldn't stop you. Why would I think there was any other reason?"

'Don't you remember all the times that I waited up for Dad?'

"I don't ever remember you waiting up for him, Lori. Why would I go to bed and allow you to wait up for him, when I knew that he might walk through the door drunk? She dropped the topic and wouldn't go any further.

"I don't know if it was her drinking, or if she was just confused. Your father hadn't been with us for years before she left the house; I can't understand why she would expect me to think that she left because of any issues with him. She would hint at things when we talked, but she'd never fully explain them, which left me wondering what she meant."

Debbie replied, "The day before Lori went to Gosnold, she told me that she had a lot of issues with Dad. I told her that I didn't understand what they were because she never talked to me about them. I said that maybe it would be good for her to get these things off her chest with her counselor. She looked at me and said, 'Don't you remember that stuff?' I replied, "What stuff? Again, she wouldn't tell me."

I felt my heart break. "God, Debbie, why didn't anyone ever tell me this poor kid had things eating at her? I honestly didn't know. She was young, and things might not have happened the way she thought, but if they had, I could have talked to her about them. If only she had shared them with me. All her growing years, I never knew she had issues with her father. I'm not saying she made them up, but when she told me, I was a mess. She needed to hear that if something did happen with him that the incidents weren't her fault. They would have been her father's. I wondered if something had happened to *you*. I asked her to go to counseling with me, just the two of us, but she wouldn't go. She couldn't talk about what happened to her, and the counselors at the clinics never allowed me in the room with her. They couldn't tell me anything. Yet, they'd say how serious Lori's condition was with her emotional state. Can you imagine how I felt? My daughter needed my help to survive the confusion and abuse that had happened in our family, and she refused it."

Debbie interjected, "She was closed mouthed with everyone. I felt bad for her at Christmas. It's a time to be happy, and she was always depressed. It was like a black cloud was over her."

"Debbie, I never knew any of this. She always seemed happy. God, I could have helped her."

"Alberta, you wouldn't have reached her." Al said. "She never let on if anything was bothering her, especially around you. Even if she did, if you asked her about her issues, she'd either lie or avoid the subject altogether. There was no way she'd open up about her past. Stop beating yourself up; you're carrying guilt about things you had no control over."

"But I could have tried. It's painful to know that she had suffered so much inside. Debbie, when did you realize that she had a drinking problem?"

"I never knew she had a drinking problem, never mind being an alcoholic. Everyone in her group was drinking. She never got really drunk or caused a scene. There was never a time that she got out-of-control with alcohol abuse."

Debbie stopped for a minute and continued. "You'd think that with me working with her all those years at the construction company, that I'd see my sister's problems. She came to work, did whatever it took to get by, and went right out the door at five.

"One Sunday night, she called me, and asked if she could take a vacation day Monday because she wanted to go somewhere. The payroll had been her responsibility, and her position was an important one. Being her manager, I had to cover up for her.

"There'd be days that she wouldn't come to work, and Gilly was getting upset about her absenteeism. After all, cousin or not, he's the owner, and we depended on her. Her job had a lot of tasks, but she couldn't understand why Gilly would be mad at her. She lost her job because she was never there, or she came in an hour and a half late without an explanation or an apology."

Talking to Debbie gave me some relief that Lori's problem wasn't just with me. Her problem stemmed from not wanting to open up to anyone about her bad memories of the past. Drinking only added confusion to her state of mind. Her decisions must have seemed rational to her when she was drinking.

Lori died leaving me with no answers. I think only her closest girlfriends or Paula might have known the problems that she kept hidden deep within her. The counselors, who wouldn't give me permission to sit with my daughter in meetings because Lori didn't want me to attend them, probably knew, too. Her family will have to wonder why she couldn't open up to any of us. We'll never know; she took all her secrets with her.

"Did you know that Lori had hepatitis?" Debbie asked.

"No. When?"

"When she got back from a trip to Key West with Mark, Paula, and Scott, she had blood work done. I'm not sure why, but I remember she was so upset because they told her she had a form of hepatitis. That was probably between the years of 2001-2003. She told me she asked them if it was from drinking, and I think they said no, you can get if from other things. She seemed to be concerned and scared that it could be from drinking.

"The only other time I heard anything about her liver was after she went to Gosnold the first time, and she told Brian that there was something wrong with her liver."

"She told me, Debbie, that the doctors said she had no problems with her liver."

"I think she found out again when she was in Morton to get new blood, but she didn't tell anyone. I remember the Easter at your house her eyes were all yellow, and I asked her what was wrong with her eyes."

"She just said it was from allergies. That's when I made her go to Morton the next day or so to be checked and they ended up admitting her.

"When she was in Charlton and her stomach was so swollen from her liver, the doctor said she would probably stay like that the rest of her life. I remember thinking that would kill her to be like that."

"I feel so guilty over her death," I said.

"Don't feel guilty, Mom. I could feel the same way. If people don't reach out, you can't help them. She lived with me for quite a while; I couldn't help her either, and I was right there. There were also quite a few times you had made plans with her to get together and go out to talk and she kept canceling.

"I know the instinct is to feel guilty, but please don't. I'm sure I would probably feel like you too if it was Kerri; but Mom like you said, 'Lori never opened up to anyone.' She even went to rehabs and counseling and it still didn't help. She knew in her heart that we all loved her."

After our talk, I left disappointed. It was amazing to think Lori couldn't even open up with her own sister. I wondered if she would have, if she had been in a deep conversation with us that day.

The Secret of Recovery

My cousin, Gail Brazil, had sent me an angel card after she heard that Lori had died. Many years before, her daughter, Justine, had been struck and killed by a truck in front of her house when she was just five years old. Gail understood my suffering.

After receiving her card, we became more than email friends. It was the first time in over thirty years that we had contacted each other. Her sisters, Linda and Marie, were closer to my age. Gail was younger so we didn't play together through the years when our families met at our grandparents' home in Revere, Massachusetts. Having each lost a child caused us to remain in touch. It took losing our daughters to renew our relationship.

One day Gail told me that her son, Patrick, who was in his early twenties, had been in and out of rehabs because of drug abuse. The news led me to begin writing to him.

I enjoyed corresponding with Patrick, hoping my letters gave him strength to fight his illness. I told him about Lori and sent him a picture of her. He seemed to enjoy getting my letters, more so because we were family. I felt the same way about his letters, which allowed us to share his private hardships with substance abuse.

Months went by, and I followed his ups and downs while he was in halfway homes. I wrote continuously to him, trying to give him all the encouragement I could. Patrick finally got a job, rebuilt his relationship with his parents, and took his substance abuse more seriously. He began getting help and staying with the recovery program. It was through my constant connection with Patrick that I began to realize the importance of keeping a daily, tight bond with an abuser, whether the problem was abuse of alcohol or drugs.

I felt sad wishing that I had done the same with Lori. We had allowed too many situations in her life to pass when we had numerous opportunities to help her through them, especially by talking. So many times, I had no idea where she was or what she was doing. I just sat back and waited for her to reach out to me, without realizing that she might have been too sick to do so.

I asked Gail, "What does it take for an abuser to see that they're killing themselves?"

She answered, "I often think the same; what does it take when it comes to addiction, bad situations, or unhappiness for someone to reach out for help? I don't know what it took for Pat... but he did it. Maybe you just get so tired of living a certain way that you just make up your mind to change. Most people, when they're down, look for someone or something to rescue them. That's the problem; you have to rescue yourself, and I don't think most people understand that they actually have the power to do it. Maybe it's the ones who come to the realization that no one is going to rescue them, and that they have to pull themselves out? Maybe it's those people who succeed?

"That kind of power isn't reserved for a few lucky people... everyone has it, and they just need someone to tell them, whether it's in a story, a book, or a talk....so they can believe it. Once they believe it, they can do it. Not that it's easy, but it's do-able. They have to do the work, and Alberta, you're one of those catalysts.... I hope you keep up your talks and writings and all that you do... the more catalysts in the world... the more hope!"

Reaching Out to Other Alcoholics

At the end of October 2007, I felt a strong desire to contact Gosnold Rehabilitation Center in Falmouth, Massachusetts, where Lori had twice been a patient. With great anxiety and many doubts, I picked up the phone and called.

"Hello, Gosnold Rehabilitation Center. This is Cathy speaking."

"Hi, my name is Alberta Sequeira, and my daughter, Lori Nadeau, was a patient of yours in 2005 and 2006. She died on November 22, 2006 at thirty-nine years old."

"I'm sorry to hear that."

"Thank you." My voice started to break, and I had to stop.

"It's okay. I understand how emotional this is for you to call," Cathy replied with true compassion in her voice.

"I was wondering if you ever had families talk at your group meetings. I'd like to talk to the girls about my experience as a mother of an alcoholic."

"We did a long time ago. I think it would be a great idea. I'll have a counselor contact you."

I gave her all my information and hung up. Those few moments talking about Lori, and trying to get the courage to take this new step, left me so emotionally drained, that my body shook.

Just thinking about driving to Gosnold, where I had gone so many times to visit Lori, made my head spin in confusion. *How would I hold up?* I could never talk in front of people. I'd freeze, stumble on my words and sweat from fear.

Two days later, a call came from a counselor. "Hi, this is Denise from Gosnold. Is this Alberta?"

"Yes, it is. Thank you for calling me back."

"Cathy told me about your conversation. We had a woman come in five years ago to speak, but since then we haven't had anyone offer to talk. I think your story would be good for the girls. Can you come in Tuesday of next week?"

"I'm free at that time, I'd be happy to come."

"It's at The Emerson House. Do you know where that is?"

"Yes, Lori stayed there."

"Come to the building next door first. That's where the counselors work. We can go over to the house together."

I penciled in the date and time, November 1 at 1:00 pm, on the calendar. I sat at the computer and began to write my speech. It included the good, the bad, and the ugly. I wrote about the horrible way that an alcoholic dies from liver disease. They needed to hear the cold, hard fact that alcoholism does kill.

The following week, I went to the Emerson House, which was a facility of the Gosnold Rehabilitation Center, for my first private speaking engagement. Al came to give me support. It was the most emotional thing that I'd ever done in my life.

We pulled into their driveway, and I started to fill up with tears, remembering having been at the same location a year ago, visiting Lori and taking her home. I could picture her walking the grounds with the other women and having a cigarette. They'd all be laughing and joking. The scene was all too familiar.

We went into the counselors' building first. Two women greeted us. I was holding up well, until one of them came over and put her hand on my shoulder. I lost it. Tears rolled down my check.

"How am I going to talk to the girls?" I asked. By then, I was a wreck.

"It's all right to cry. This is very hard. I give you credit for coming." The counselor was very understanding. By acknowledging my pain and saying it was okay to cry, she broke down my shield, and I cried harder.

We waited for Denise to come to take us to The Emerson House. It wasn't long before she came in and introduced herself. Al and I walked over with her and went up the front stairs to the house.

Al pulled the heavy front door open. We walked into the hallway, and I spotted the winding stairway on my left going up to the second floor to the girls' bedrooms. They were the same stairs that Lori had come down when we went to visit her. I could picture her bouncing down those steps with her beautiful smile and usual greeting, 'Hi, Ma…Hi, Al.' I wanted to feel the hugs and kisses that she gave so freely. I tried desperately to hide my emotions and concentrate on my reason for being there. I was on the verge of not only crying uncontrollably, but collapsing. I couldn't speak.

My God, I had to be insane to think I could do this!

I saw mounds of black, trash bags on the hall floor. They belonged to the girls signing in at The Emerson House. I remembered them when we had visited Lori.

I could see the women in the living room sitting in chairs and on a couch, and some actually sitting on the rug, waiting for me. I felt my legs turn to jelly, my heart pounded in my chest, and my throat ached with the lump that I was forcing to stay down. Tears blurred my eyes, and my body started to shake; I wanted to run back out the door. The old feeling of being too frightened to talk at an Al-Anon meeting years ago was trying to take over.

"The girls are ready for you," Denise said, leading us through the doorway of the living room. The room was packed with girls of all ages, from teens to women in their late sixties or early seventies. Three young teenage girls sat on the same couch that Lori had sat on several times. They looked to be as young as fourteen years old.

Al and I sat on folding chairs at the front of the room facing them. The room was packed with girls sitting on the rug next to Al and on the other side of me. Because they were so near, I couldn't hide my shaking hands; I felt faint. The dam was ready to burst.

God, keep me together.

"Girls, this is Al and Alberta. They came to share their story with you."

"...Hi Al...Hi Alberta." The same warm, routine greeting that alcoholic's give every speaker, using just the first names, echoed through the room.

It brought me back to the years going to the AA meetings with Richie and then with Lori. If folks had told me years ago that I'd be talking about losing two loved ones at an alcoholic rehabilitation center, I would not have believed them.

"Hi, everyone, my name is Alberta Sequeira." I wanted them to hear my full name. My heart was full of love for Lori and Richie as I started my talk. "My husband and daughter were alcoholics, and they died from this demon."

I could see a woman in her middle thirties shake her head and start to cry. Maybe she couldn't believe what she heard about me losing two family members from this disease. Perhaps reality hit her.

"I wanted to come here and tell my story about the effects of alcoholism on the whole family. I watched my husband and daughter's lives and personalities go from happy, fun-loving individuals, who had everything to live for, to people I didn't recognize. This story is about their addiction and the sad consequences that their drinking caused them and their family."

I talked to thirty women for forty-five minutes about the reality of being an alcoholic, the suffering, mentally and physically, and the way an alcoholic can die from cirrhosis of the liver.

Not one woman moved or left the room. When I spoke, I turned to face every person so that I could talk directly to them and make eye contact. I stressed the disease itself.

"There is nothing wrong with any of you sitting here, except for the fact that you have a *disease*. It's the *disease* that's making you say and do the things that you normally wouldn't be doing. It's the *disease* that's making you lose your jobs, families, friends, relationships, and most importantly, yourselves."

I had moments of having to stop in order to get a grip on my feelings. I held the tears at bay. I could talk about the disease, but saying Lori's name turned me inside out.

"I want you to look in the mirror every morning and tell yourself that you're a good person. That's what Lori couldn't do. She thought that she was such a bad person, that she had caused all these terrible things that had happened to her. She hated the fact that she kept disappointing her family, her kids, her friends, and herself."

I saw that a few women had tears rolling down their cheeks after a half hour of listening to me.

"I need to stress the importance of bringing God back into your life. Give it all up to a power greater than yours. He's the one who gives you strength. He's there everyday, but you have to talk to Him. You need something to hold onto, and He's there, waiting for you. Allow Him to help you. I've brought some rosaries that have been blessed by a priest, which I'm going to give to any of you who want them. I also brought some booklets on how to pray the rosary. If you don't want to say them, that's okay. When you need Him, hold the rosary beads in your hands. Keep them in your pocketbook or your jeans. Keep them with you. You don't have to say the *Our Father, Hail Mary* or other prayers. Remember, prayer is just talking to God, like I'm doing with you. Ask Him to get you through the day. Thank Him at the end of the day for all that you have. Each day is a lesson and a chance to get your lives back."

I continued, "Be thankful that you're here, whether it's because you were pushed by family, a court order, or your own desire for help. There are many girls roaming the streets or living day in and day out with no one to turn to. You have the counselors here, doctors and other girls to lean on for help. You can reach out and learn a new way to live life, or you can leave and go down the same path again. I will tell you this—if you continue drinking, you will die. I'm not saying, you might, you could, or maybe—you will die. I'm living proof of that fact, after losing a husband and daughter because they wouldn't seek the help available to them. I'm trying to save you. Hold your heads up high because you have nothing to be ashamed of. You have a disease. You didn't ask for this illness. Get well for yourselves, not for anyone else. You can't take care of another person when you're in this condition."

I stressed the importance of bringing family into their counseling. I explained what Lori had lost with her recovery because she didn't get rid of the garbage she held from her past. To move on and heal, they had to talk about the pain.

By the time I ended, many tears had been shed, along with mine. I handed the counselor my poem "The Demon" in a clear double frame. I had autographed it in memory of Richie and Lori. The girls lined up to get copies of the poem on postcards that I had had printed up. They were also eager to accept the rosaries and the pamphlet, along with the prayer card, "Come Holy Spirit," which Lori loved. I placed a 4x6 framed picture of Lori and Richie on a table to donate to the center. I came to learn later, at another halfway home from a young girl, that The Emerson House had their pictures blown up and put on the wall in the living room.

The girls came up to hug me. "Thank you so much for coming," one said as I hugged her back. I closed my eyes and tried to picture holding Lori. Embracing girls, who were close to Lori's age and were struggling to combat the same disease she had, brought more tears, tears that I should have shed in front of Lori when she needed to see and feel my love while she was suffering. Now I was sharing them with strangers.

Denise walked up to me. "That had to be the most powerful talk that I've ever heard at this house. I've never seen the girls sit still for an hour. You couldn't have picked a better topic. We are discussing "Family" this week."

My talk was the most gratifying experience that I ever had. Recovery for the women was left in God's hands with the hope that I had reached a few of the girls. I heard one say to another, 'I never knew that we hurt our family like this.'

If, by talking about the loss of Richie and Lori to this dreadful disease, someone else could be saved, then maybe their deaths were not in vain. Hopefully, other substance abuse locations will come to know who I am and of my desire to talk to their patients. I'm not really brave; standing up in front of people frightens me, but my desire to help someone is more important than my fear. After all, it's not about me, it's about them.

I walked out the front door and down the steps sobbing uncontrollably all the way to our car. *Why didn't I say those things to Lori? Why did I have to lose her before I could get the knowledge of this horrible, suffocating disease?*

After talking to the women, I learned what I believed God had planned for me all along. I wouldn't be retired sitting on some warm tropical island soaking up the sun and enjoying the beautiful green-blue waters. I believe my mission will be talking to other substance abusers and their families. I don't know where this journey will lead me, but I trust Him to guide me.

My talk at the Providence Marriott Hotel in Rhode Island

Coping With Grief

Two years had gone by since we lost Lori, but going to certain locations where Lori had been would never be the same for me; they will always bring sadness. The pain engulfs me each time I have to go to Charlton Memorial Hospital in Fall River, where she spent her last days.

In the fall of 2008, Al and I had to go to this same hospital to visit Anita Lopes, who had been hospitalized because of a blood clot in her leg. We parked in the same back parking lot, traveled the same route in the hospital that we had taken to visit Lori; and took the same familiar elevator to the same third floor.

To add to my throbbing memory, Anita was only one room away from where Lori had stayed. As odd as it may sound, I wanted to walk to the next room and look in so I could picture Lori sitting in bed and smiling at me. The pain was so excruciating that I had to let Al go in first to see Anita while I got control of the crushing feeling in my chest.

Tears—the tears, they're always there! How do I stop them? How do I talk about Lori without them starting to flow? How do I think about her without choking up? God had given me a gift through Jill saying that Lori was with Jesus, I knew that Lori was at peace. How do I find my peace with her out of my life? Please, tell me that it gets better.

I hugged Anita when I entered her room and was relieved to see that she was in good spirits and that she would be all right. She had been given medication to break up the clot. Her sister, Loree, came in to see her, and after an hour of small talk, Al and I left for home. I didn't feel that I was much company, but I put up what I thought was a good front.

I spent the following week in deep depression, privately crying every day. The visit to the hospital had reopened the wound. Everything I saw reminded me of Lori. I hid my tears from Al, and I pushed myself to the point of being sick. I needed to see, hold or talk to Lori. My body and mind craved it.

I went upstairs, and while cleaning out my nightstand, I came across my book, *Life After Life* by Raymond A. Moody, Jr., MD., which I had read about fifteen years before. Now it had resurfaced; why?

This book describes the feelings of immense peace and contentment which the dying person experiences. Mr. Moody speaks about two reasons for writing his book. The first was to help the dying person keep in mind the nature of each new wondrous phenomenon as he experiences it. The second reason was to help those still living to think positive thoughts without emotional concerns, so that our loved ones, who have passed, could enter into the afterlife in a proper frame of mind, released from all earthly concerns.

I remembered back to my mother having had an experience with Jesus after the death of my brother. (The story is told in *A Healing Heart; A Spiritual Renewal*). They were in bed, when Mom's face lit up as if someone had put a flashlight under her skin. Dad saw her look up at the ceiling and her lips moved, but he heard nothing from her.

When the moment passed, Dad asked her, "Are you okay?" He was shocked by what he had witnessed.

"I heard Jesus speak to me." She said.

"Did you see Him?"

"No, He was a light in the corner of the ceiling, I was very aware that the brightness was Jesus. He told us to stop mourning so that Walter could enter into heaven. He said our tears were holding him from passing over to the other side. Walter was torn between comforting us and wanting to go with Jesus."

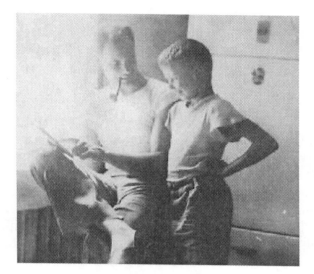

Dad and Walter

Walter

A week after that incident, after some twenty years of crying and mourning, my parents and my sister, Leona, went to the cemetery in Worcester where Walter was buried. Leona watched them dig a small hole in the ground near the stone and place something in it. They covered it, patted the earth smooth, and Mom said, "Now he's not alone." We never knew what item they had buried at the gravesite.

I sat there motionless on my bed. Were my tears holding Lori back? My actions were the same as my parents' had been. Their experience had slipped from my memory. I had been crying for myself, not for Lori. She was with God. What other gift could possibly beat that? My guilt from thinking of all the wrong decisions I had made with Lori was causing me to hold on instead of letting go and putting my trust in God. I knew this in my mind, but couldn't, as a mother, feel the peace in my heart. We all have to return to Our Savior, and He wanted her at a young age for a reason. Parents will never understand this judgment, but perhaps His decision will be revealed to us when we too, are with Him.

If some weeks went by without sadness in my heart, I'd fight the feeling of guilt. Maybe a healing process was trying to kick in. With love of God in my heart, I still had moments of being lost. I feared forgetting what she looked like. She will always be thirty-nine years old, no matter how many years pass with her no longer in our lives.

I'd have days when I would go to pieces when I sensed a familiar smell or certain sight, have a thought, see Joe and Meagan, hear a certain word or a hearty laugh, watch as someone hugged their child, attend a wedding or see a newborn baby; almost anything.

One day, I watched a young mother sitting on the floor at a doctor's office playing with her two little girls with building blocks. One looked to be around four and the baby was about two years old. My mind raced back to Debbie and Lori. Those were special moments with them. How I wished I could relive those treasured moments I had with them.

Conversations about Lori, when I was in the company of her friends, brought back the emptiness that I tried to fight. Dealing with the pain was my own burden, and I always kept my emotions hidden in public.

I would have moments of questioning myself. Why didn't I use the knowledge that I had, from dealing with Richie's drinking, to help Lori? It wasn't until her last two years when we found out she had any problems from her past or with alcohol abuse. It's so easy for professionals to say alcoholics have to want the help and have to deal with their problems in order to be saved. Thinking back to how sick he and Lori had to have been, tore at my insides. They wanted to live and these damn demons wouldn't let go.

One night, while trying to find something interesting to watch on television, I came upon a program called "Intervention." It was on the A&E network and airs every Monday night at 8 o'clock. I never took notice of this program while Lori was alive, I don't know if it was even airing at that time. Now I tune in often to try to understand fully the disease from the drinker's standpoint. If only I could have discovered this program two years before.

As I sat and listened to the abusers' stories and the families' struggles to help their loved ones, I had mixed feelings. I knew in my heart that I couldn't control any of Lori's actions with her illness, yet I still felt that I could have done something more.

The alcoholic abuser's story was like watching our own lives in the past with the battle to control Lori's drinking and trying to force her to stay in a recovery program for three months. I remembered back to when Lori told me that the doctor at Butler Hospital in Providence, Rhode Island, wanted to send her to a long term alcoholic rehabilitation center in Florida. Why couldn't we, as a family, have had the authority to send her, even if she refused? If she had gone, the treatment and counseling might have saved her.

The alcoholics on the program had the same resentments Lori had toward anyone trying to tell them what to do, and they showed the same anger when they were accused of being an alcoholic. They all felt smothered by any person trying to suggest that they had a problem and needed help. Not one of them believed they had a problem. They thought they could give up drinking anytime they chose to. Excuses flowed about what *caused* their drinking and *who* made them drink. Not one realized or admitted that they had a disease.

It was sad; when even after agreeing to go into the rehab program, some would leave after only a few weeks or be thrown out because they would break the rules. The results of some of the cases would be shown in writing at the end of the program; some were clean after so many months, some would relapse and start over, and some would continue the abuse and die as a result. It was especially heartbreaking to me when I'd see that one died from cirrhosis of the liver, as Lori and Richie had.

I wanted desperately to understand what Lori had been going through, but watching the abuser's loneliness and the sickness that overwhelms the alcoholic brought me to heartbreaking tears of guilt. I'd sit on the couch sobbing. It was my private time to let the pain and hurt out, while Al was upstairs watching another program on the television set in our bedroom.

Loving your children and seeing this demon taking over their lives, knowing this illness was going to kill them, is beyond expression. Even the reality of being educated to the fact that, until Lori wanted the help, she was going to keep going deeper into this life of hell, didn't help. A lot of pain came when I thought of the years she must have suffered mentally and physically, without my ever being aware of what she was going through. Why do our loved ones turn from the people who love them the most? I couldn't understand it.

Grief is indeed excruciating, and seems like it'll never stop. Death will touch every family at one time or another. There's no hiding from the reality. I had to go on living even if there was an empty, black hole that had swallowed me up like Lori had been.

Knowing that others were also going through this same sorrow didn't comfort me by any means. There should have been a time for me to cry without apologizing to anyone, but I always held the emotion inside me; I still do. If I let the tears flow, I'd feel weak or be worried that I might make someone uncomfortable because they didn't know how to console me. I'll always have memories, and I'll ache, knowing my eyes will never see her again. The truth of it is sometimes too much to tolerate.

I brought Lori into this world, loved her beyond words, and hoped to see her live a full, productive life. She gave us two beautiful grandchildren. I wanted her to be happy with the life that she was meant to have. When she hurt; I hurt. That was because she had been physically a part of me. Mothers are supposed to protect and nurture their children.

I felt separated when I watched other parents at functions interact with their adult children. Thank God I have Debbie. How do parents survive the loss of multiple children? I can't fathom losing Debbie.

Lori had been unique; each individual child has their own personality. With all her hurts and disappointments, she loved freely and wasn't afraid to show us her affection; she looked forward to, and enjoyed every family gathering. She had spent her life searching for that one special man to love her after her father died. She never found him.

I suppose I could discern that Lori had chosen the road to alcohol dependency and self-destruction that ultimately killed her, but I'll never believe that she or any other alcoholic wants to die. She had too many reasons to live—the most important of which were Joey and Meagan. I feel in my heart that she had crossed over the line and was unable to stop. She had become another victim of this killer we call alcoholism.

I believe that Lori had turned away from her family because she saw no way out of her painful situation. She hated her weaknesses: she had always apologized to me when she did something wrong. It must have embarrassed her to realize that her life was so out-of-control.

A close relative had once said to me, "I can't comprehend how Lori could have turned away from her children."

I knew they made the remark because they had no alcoholism in their family and had no understanding of what the disease can do to people. Lori had lost herself and could no longer make good decisions. Alcoholism affects the brain cells, thereby making the alcoholic unable to think rationally.

Some may ask, "What are the signs of substance abuse and when is it a problem?" The answer is—when it causes unrest and distress in our lives. Excessive drinking disrupts family life, our jobs, relationships, and everything associated with being happy and living a normal life. Watch for any changes in your children's daily behavior with the family, especially if they start to hide their activities and friends from you.

I heard Dr. Phil say, "We need to cause discomfort for the abuser by handling the situation differently, take a different path or action."

We need to get off the merry-go-round, which consists of family members protecting the abuser and defending their actions. Make demands. Our changes make them face their addiction and take responsibility for their declining health.

We should never give up on our loved ones and leave them feeling abandoned, to handle this disease alone. Lori had always held me at a distance. I should have kept banging on that wall of resistance until it collapsed. I should have given her the confidence to know that she could open up to me without being hurt and that she could trust me. This would have made her feel more loved. I tried to do the best that I could with the little knowledge that I had at the time, obviously my support wasn't enough for Lori. She didn't even come to realize that my love and help was available to her.

Lori feared sharing her secrets and pain, not only with me but also with her family. What she did, without meaning to, was to keep us from being aware and understanding all the horrible events that had happened in her life; not only with her father but also her relationships with the men in her life. She had kept her feelings to herself.

My daughter must have suffered with more afflictions than just her drinking, and I'll never know what they were. I'm going to wonder all my life if she suffered at the hands of her father, who, at one time, was a loving, caring man.

I had stayed in an alcoholic marriage too long, and I believe that's why Lori grew up scared and having no confidence. She couldn't stand up for herself. My daughters saw too much fighting and abuse in their young lives, which wasn't healthy for them. There is a time to pack up and leave to keep our children from witnessing adult arguments and physical abuse; they shouldn't be subjected to adult conflicts. We should always endeavor to protect our children from such horrible scenes.

Before Lori died, she had told Paula that she wished she could talk to me about her problems. That wish will lie heavy on my heart forever. Children think parents know what they're thinking and feeling without ever communicating their troubles, or if they even have problems.

By holding her feelings in, Lori had imprisoned herself; keeping her from moving to recovery. She was stuck in the past and could see no future.

I would advise parents and family members to talk to your loved one about their drinking, even if they keep ignoring the problem. *Never let up!* Talk calmly, patiently and with love. I'm not saying it's easy, but one day they may surprise you. If not, you can say that you did all that you could for them.

Abuse of alcohol or drugs has to be confronted. The abusers need to be in detoxification and rehabilitation centers, and families should do everything possible to meet with counselors and doctors and try for *long term* recovery programs. Don't omit your own mental state; attend Al-Anon and Alateen meetings. Get help for the whole family; we all become sick from this frightening, worldwide disease. It's killing too many people.

Erma Bombeck had many quotes about life. The one that resonated most to me while writing my story is, 'When I stand before God at the end of my life, I would hope that I would not have a single list of talents left, and could say, 'I used everything You gave me.'

Well—I had a lot left that could have been used differently with Richie and Lori, and my daughter, Debbie. Hopefully, some of the signs of addiction, or ways to handle this disease, which I was blind to, will open the eyes of other family members, and the abusers fighting substance abuse, *to what is* happening. There is always help and hope, through love.

Paula Lopes, Judy Brown, Lori

Lori and Debbie at Lori's Wedding Shower

Lori's Wedding Day with Her Friends

Front Left: Debbie Dutra, Paula Lopes, Karin Brady
Back Left: Donna Perry, Eileen Lopes, Lori Cahill,
Lucy Nadeau, Jeannie Coelho, Judy Brown, Margie Rogers

I'M FREE

Don't grieve for me, for now I'm free. I'm following the path God laid for me.

I took God's hand when I heard the call; I turned my back and left it all.

I could not stay another day to laugh, to love, to work or play. Tasks left undone must stay that way; I found that place at the close of day.

If my parting has left a void, then fill it with remembered joy. A friendship shared, a laugh, a kiss. Ah yes, these things, I too, will miss.

Be not burdened with times of sorrow, I wish you the sunshine of tomorrow. My life's been full; I savored much, good friends, good times; a loved one's touch.

Perhaps my time seemed all too brief; don't lengthen it now with undue grief. Lift up your heart and share with me; God wanted me now, God set me free.

"OUR GOODBYES TO LORI"

Meagan Cahill

Mom,

After all this time, it still doesn't seem real. Some days I'm fine and others, I realize that you are really gone forever. I wish I had known more about the disease so that I could have spent less time being mad at you, and more time trying to help you. Although we grew apart toward the last couple of months we had together, I think about you every day and miss you more than anyone knows. I know you are looking down on me, and I hope I am making you proud.

I love you always, Meagan

Meagan graduated from Massasoit College in Bridgewater, MA and entered into their CNA Program and got certified in May 2009 to be a Certified Nursing Assistant and became CPR certified. She is now attending the Bristol Community College in Fall River, MA, and is studying Human Growth and Development, Anatomy & Physiology 1 & 2, and Child Development. Meagan's main goal is to do something in the medical field; in nursing, physical therapy and Psychology. She will graduate in the summer of 2010 after receiving her Liberal Arts: Professional Option Degree.

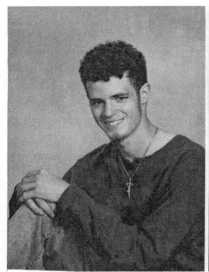

Joey Cahill

Mom,

There's not a day that goes by in which I don't think of you. I can still hear your voice and your laughter so clearly. Even though you've been gone for so long it feels like you're always by my side, walking right next to me. During Boot Camp, through all of the pain and exhaustion that I was experiencing, it felt like you were right there with me, pushing me forward. Once I had finished Boot Camp, when I got my Eagle Globe and Anchor, also when I graduated, all I could think about was how much I wanted you to be there and how I would never be able to physically show you my accomplishment. All I can hope for is that you could see it and that you are proud of me.

Words can not describe how much I love you and miss you. I'm looking forward to the day that I can pass through the gates and see you standing there, on the other side, waiting to greet me. Until then, I know that you are looking down on me and the rest of the family. I can only pray that what I'm doing with my life is making you proud to call me your son. Every time I read this verse it makes me think of you so, I thought it would be fitting to add it at the end.

Psalm 23:4,"Yea, though I walk through the valley of the shadow of death, I will fear no evil; for You are with me;" You are always missed and never forgotten. I love you more than you know.

Love, Joey

Joey was trained at Parris Island, South Carolina from September 21, 2009 to Dec. 18, 2009. He became a Marine on Dec.12, 2009. His next training was from January 18, 2010 to February 16, 2010 at the Marine Combat Training (MCT) at Camp Geiger, North Carolina at the Marine Corps detachment inside Redstone Arsenal, located at the Army Base in Huntsville Alabama. As of April 2010, he is now in the 1st Bn., 12th Marines, 3rd MARDIV (Marine Division), Kaneohe Bay, Hawaii. He is a Lance Corporal (Lcpl). The family plans on making a trip to Hawaii in 2011 to visit him.

Brian Dutra

Lori,

Thanks for all of the love and laughter you brought into my life and for all of the great memories I have of our time together. We always had a special bond, and you were always my number one fan. You lived life with a passion and you shared that so willingly with others. Whenever you were around, you brightened up the room with your presence.

Your virtues far outweighed your flaws and that is the sign of a good caring person. Because of that, I know you are in heaven with your friends and family who have also passed through the gates. I look forward to the day that we can meet again if I am fortunate enough to get there with you.

Love, Brian

Brian is the Senior Manager, in Level 2 Network Support in the data communications field for the CompuCom Company located in Foxboro, Massachusetts for the past eleven years. The company's home base is in Dallas, Texas.

He is the husband of Debbie Dutra of Berkley, Massachusetts. They enjoy their activities with their two children, Kerri, twenty-two years old and Michael, nineteen years. For the past four years, since Lori's death in 2006, their niece, Meagan, twenty-one, and nephew, Joey, twenty-two have lived with them.

Brian enjoys sports and spending time with his family and friends.

Debbie Dutra

To Lori, my sister & best friend,

We shared so much through the years. There are so many good memories.

At the end, the disease changed the life we had together, we grew apart. Real love never dies, and you will always be in my heart. I'm at peace knowing that you have no more worries, and you're now in heaven looking down at all of us. Joe and Meagan are a special gift from you to both Brian and me. They are a constant memory of you, and they are now a permanent part of our family, whom we love as our own.

I know one day we will be together again, and I look forward to all our "forever" moments.

Love, Debbie

Debbie is forty-six years old and has lived in Berkley, Massachusetts for the last 20 years with her husband, Brian, and their two children Kerri and Michael. They have been married twenty-four years. Lori's children, Joe, and Meagan, along with their family dog, Angelica, are now part of their family.

She has worked at G. Lopes Construction in Taunton, MA for the last twenty-eight years and is currently the treasurer and office manager. It's a family owned business since 1964 and employs over 200 employees. Debbie enjoys traveling and being with family and friends.

Lori and Debbie were very close and spent a lot of time together, especially once their kids were born. The four children were only three years apart. Debbie's worst moments missing her sister, Lori, is especially at holidays and family events, but Lori will *always* be in our hearts.

Kerri Dutra

Auntie Lori,

You brought out the best in others and your smile and laughter were contagious. You left us with wonderful memories. You gave me a best friend and the sister I never had and a second brother.

I love you more than I ever found a way to tell you. I miss you all the time, but carry you with me wherever I go. I know you're watching over all of us in heaven, and I hope that I will be with you again someday.

Love, Kerri

Kerri graduated from UMASS Amherst on May 15, 2010 with a Bachelor's degree in Business, where her major was Accounting. After graduating, Kerri will be attending grad school at UMASS to get her MSA. While she's studying at grad school, she'll be working at Lopes Construction Company in Taunton, Massachusetts for a year until she gets her Masters and takes the CPA exam. Kerri will be starting at Pricewaterhouse Coopers in Boston in September 2011 as an auditor.

Michael Dutra

Aunt Lori,

You were always there for me and everything I could have asked for in an aunt. I felt that we had a special relationship, and I enjoyed every moment that we spent together. I always looked forward to the times that Kerri and I would stay at your house when Mom and Dad went away and the days that you, Joey, and Meg would come over to our house.

You always had the ability to brighten up a room, or pick somebody up when they were down. Even when you first entered the hospital you were still joking and laughing and were able to make everybody feel comfortable. I feel that you lived life to the fullest and made the absolute most of your time with us. We have so many great memories together that will never fade, and I won't forget the passion that you lived with. Thank you for it all and for bringing Joey, Meg, and even your dog, Angelica, closer to all of us.

Love, Michael

Michael is in his second semester at Northeastern University in Boston and will graduate in 2014. He's majoring in Industrial Engineering and in Communications. After college, he'll apply for a job at an engineering firm in Boston. Michael had been a quarterback of the Somerset High School and hopes to coach football or basketball in the near future.

Alberta Sequeira

Dear Lori,

Days, months and years may go by, but your love can never be erased from my heart. God had blessed me with a child who loved freely and compassionately. Your smile and laughter will forever be deep within my soul. You walk and breathe through your children; Joey and Meagan, your gift to me, and all of us.

You're by my side each day, and when I talk to you, I feel your spirit. Take my love and wrap it around you until I can hold you once again.

Love, Mom

Alberta is an author, speaker and instructor. Her memoirs are *A Healing Heart;* A Spiritual Renewal by PublishedAmerica (2006). The memoir received the **Reviewers Choice Award 2008 Semi-Finalist by Reader Views from Austin, Texas.**

Her second book is *Someone Stop This Merry-Go-Round;* An Alcoholic Family in Crisis by Infinity Publishing (2009). In January of 2010, her memoir was nominated for the **Editor's Choice Award by Allbooks Review of Canada.**

Alberta and four other authors from "Authors Without Borders" have published *Loose Ends,* a book of short stories.

She teaches workshops titled **Bring Your Manuscript to Publication.** Ms. Sequeira offers speaking engagements on her "Spiritual Renewal" and "The Effects of Alcoholism on the Whole Family."

Visit her website www.albertasequeira.com
Blog: http://albertasequeira.wordpress.com

Lori, Alberta, and Debbie

Al Sequeira

Lori,

We never dreamed that we'd lose you so soon, and regret not telling you more often how much we loved and cherished you. Whenever you walked into the house, usually late, your mere presence lifted everyone's spirits. I know you're at peace now and probably in a better place, but, selfishly wish you were still here with us. We miss you every day and carry you in our hearts always.

With love forever, Al

Al was a sales manager and general manager for car dealerships throughout eastern Massachusetts for over thirty-five years. He is now retired and living in Rochester, Massachusetts with his wife, Alberta. He is slowly becoming her editor.

Al and Lori

Al, Lori, and Al's sister, Evelyn Ciociolo

Gary Lopes

On February 5, 2010, while completing this story, our beloved nephew, Gary Lopes, and son of Gilbert (Sonny) and Anita Lopes, Sr., of North Dighton, Massachusetts, died at the age of forty-six years old in a snowmobile accident in Pittsbury, New Hampshire. He was the loving husband of Maria (Mota) and the caring father of two sons—Gary Lopes, Jr. and John Lopes. He is survived by his brother Gilbert (Gilly) and his wife, Eileen, and his sister Paula Lopes and her husband, Scott Eagelson. Among his extended family are his loving cousin Debbie Dutra and her husband Brian, his mother-in-law, Connie Melo, and his brothers-in-law, David Mota and his wife Toni, and Joseph Mota, along with several nieces, nephews, aunts and uncles.

Gary's favorite pastimes included racing Pro-Stocks for Lopes Motor Sports, camping, and snowmobiling, cooking and fishing.

Along with his brother, Gil, he was a supporter of philanthropic causes within his community and throughout southern Massachusetts. Among them are: The Lopes complex in Dighton which is used for baseball and Lewis Field at the Taunton Boys & Girls Club. Gary was an ardent supporter of the Dighton-Rehoboth High School Marching Band.

Gary Lopes Remembered at Ceremonies

From left Dighton-Rehoboth band director Doug Kelly, Gary Lopes Jr., Sonny Lopes and Gil Lopes take a moment to reflect on all Gary Lopes did for the community during the opening ceremonies.

Left: Gary Lopes, Jr., Sonny Lopes, Gil Lopes

By Kendra Leigh Miller
Staff writer
Posted May 01, 2010 @ 09:41 PM

DIGHTON —

It was time to play ball Saturday at opening day of the Dighton baseball/softball league.

Hundreds of kids from dozens of teams welcomed the new season with Wally the Green Monster along with the Dighton-Rehoboth High School Marching Band and Dighton Elementary School chorus.

Peter Roach, league president, has been involved for a decade. He said kids come from all over the area to the event. "It's a great community event and they pay tribute to someone each year, which is nice too, said Heather Cooke. This year it's Gary Lopes. It's just a great sense of community. The kids see their friends. The Lopes family has

341

done a great job with the field and we like just seeing the kids have fun."

The organization dedicated this years' opening day to Gary Lopes, who was tragically killed earlier this year in a snow mobile accident.

"Lopes was very humble," Roach said. "He always said the complex was named after him and that was enough, he didn't need anything else."

Roach said something Lopes was working to do was change the bylaw so the marching band had a place to practice on the Babe Ruth field if they ever needed it. "Gary was extremely close to the band, so we've been asked to perform in his memory," said Doug Kelly, director of the band.

Gil Lopes, Gary's brother, threw out the first pitch for baseball. "Gary loved the field and the band," Lopes said. "He spearheaded creating the complex. It's great to see what this does for the community." Lopes said his brother was a very humble guy who never wanted to be recognized for anything. "He'd be very embarrassed by all this attention," Lopes said.

Gil Lopes Jr., currently 50 years old, has been married to Eileen for almost 30 years, and has 3 daughters, Erica, Kayla & Jenna. He has worked at the family business for over 33 years. He is President of New England Recycling and Vice President of G. Lopes Construction. He enjoys farming and restoring antique tractors.

Recommended Books

Rewriting Life Scripts: Transformational Recovery for Families of Addicts by Desjardins, Oelklaus & Watson. ISBN# 978-1-932690-97-2. Published by Life Scripts Press.

Love First: Intervention for Alcoholism and Drug Addiction/ **Jeff and Debra Jay's** with a forward by George McGovern. Published by Hazelden Foundation 2000. ISBN# 978-1-56838-521 (pbk).

It Will Never Happen to Me by Cluadia Black, Ph.D. Published by Hazelden, Center City, Minnesota 1981, 2001. ISBN 13: 978-56838-798-7.

Adult Children Of Alcoholics by Janet Geringer Woititz, Ed.D. Published by Health Communications, Inc., Dearfield Beach, Florida. (1983); ISBN 13: 978-1-55874-112-6, ISBN 10:1-445874-112-7.

7 Ways to Protect Your Teen from Alcohol & Other Drugs: Source: Published by Bureau of Substance Abuse Services, Mass. Dept. of Public Health

- Be a role model for your teen
- Be clear about your expectations
- Set rules, limits and follow through
- Be involved in your teen's life
- Help your teen become well-rounded
- Encourage your teen to try hard in school
- Reach out and support your teen

Contact Alberta at memoirs@albertasequeira.com